THE SECOND ADAM,

AND THE NEW BIRTH;

OR,

THE DOCTRINE OF BAPTISM AS CONTAINED IN HOLY SCRIPTURE.

BY THE

REV. M. F. SADLER, M.A.

PREBENDARY OF WELLS; VICAR OF ST. PAUL'S, BEDFORD;
AUTHOR OF "THE SACRAMENT OF RESPONSIBILITY;" "EMMANUEL;"
"CHURCH DOCTRINE—BIBLE TRUTH," ETC.

" Adam, who is the figure of Him that was to come."
"The Word was made flesh, and dwelt among us."
"The second man is the Lord from heaven."
"The last Adam was made a quickening spirit."
"We are members of His body, of His flesh, and of His bones."
"Know ye not that your bodies are the members of Christ?"

FIFTH EDITION, ENLARGED.

LONDON:
BELL & DALDY, YORK STREET, COVENT GARDEN.

1869.

PREFACE.

THE object of this short treatise is to give, in as plain terms as possible, the Scripture testimony to the doctrine of the Initial Sacrament.

To this end, the reader's attention is called to the position assigned to Baptism by Christ and His Apostles.

The more prominent places of Scripture which teach us any truth respecting it are examined, and their plain meaning vindicated from interpretations falsely called spiritual.

The analogy between the two Adams, as implying the transmission of the nature of each respectively, is considered with 'reference to its bearing on Sacramental doctrine.

The terms used by the inspired writers, in addressing the whole body of the Church, are also carefully examined, with the view of ascertaining in what state, whether of grace or otherwise, the persons they speak to are presumed to be.

As the limits which the writer has prescribed to himself preclude his noticing a number of minor objections to the doctrine contained in the following pages, he desires to refer to a former publication on the same subject, entitled "The Sacrament of Responsibility; or, the Testimony of Scripture to the Teaching of the Church on Holy Baptism;" where the reader will find a multitude of misconceptions met and answered.

The writer has endeavoured to make his work a handbook of Scripture reference on the subject of Baptismal Doctrine.

To this end he has reviewed at some length the teaching of the Apostolical Epistles, especially those of St. Paul to the Romans, Corinthians, Galatians, Ephesians, and Hebrews, and also that of our Lord's parables, and has shown how, both by express statement and general coincidence of thought and expression, they uphold the doctrine of the Church.

He has devoted a chapter to showing the harmony of the Church's doctrine of Regeneration with the most unreserved preaching of Conversion or Renewal; and another to the Scripture statements respecting Election and Final Perseverance, and their bearing on the question of Baptismal grace.

Three Appendices complete the work: the first (A) bringing before the reader how full the Old Testament Prophets are of a mode of addressing the visible Church of their day, anticipatory of, and answering to, that adopted by the Apostles and by the Church in her formularies; the second (B) giving the testimony of the great leaders of the Reformation, as well as that of such divines as Mede, Jeremy

Taylor, Pearson, and Beveridge ; the third (C) exhibiting, side by side, the opinions of St. Augustine on Election and on Baptismal Regeneration, and their influence on our Reformers.

He must beg the critical reader to remember that he has attempted to adapt his treatise to the wants and the habits of thought of those who are only acquainted with our English translation of the Bible, and that it has been written under the manifold interruptions and distractions attending the ministry of a large parish in a populous town.

The more he thinks of the present state of the controversy, the more he is convinced that it must be treated as a Bible rather than a Church question.

It involves no less than the one principle on which the hortatory teaching of God's word can be applied, in its entirety, to the present visible Church.

We are asked for a revision of the Prayer-book, with the view of modifying or omitting those statements in the Baptismal Service and Catechism which assert that the present Kingdom of God's grace is designed by its Divine Founder for all infants, and that at Baptism they are in very deed born into it, and made partakers of its distinguishing grace.[1]

---

[1] In a pamphlet published by the writer of this work, entitled "Doctrinal Revision of the Liturgy " (Bell and Daldy), he has shown at some length that the Doctrine of Baptismal Regeneration so pervades our formularies, that no "slight modification," or "alteration, or omission of a few words," or "bracketing of a sentence or two," would satisfy the scruples of those who desire alteration on Puritan grounds. It would not be honest to erase some few words, and yet, virtually, to retain the obnoxious doctrine in every part of the service.

The writer has abundantly shown in the following pages, that this language of the Prayer-book, taken in its most literal sense, is the mere echo of the language of God's word. The expressions which include the whole Church in the net of Divine grace, are more absolute in the New Testament than in the Prayer-book.

May God in His infinite mercy grant that this appeal to His word may be to His glory, the sanctification of His people, and the peace of His Church, for Jesus Christ's sake!

PREFACE TO THE FOURTH EDITION.

SINCE the publication of the former editions of
this work, questions have been raised respecting the
origin of man, and the period of his existence upon
the earth, which affect the historical character of
the account of the creation and fall of man given
to us in the Book of Genesis, and so are supposed
to render more uncertain the truth of the parallel
drawn by the Apostle between the two federal heads
of the race, and, by consequence, the validity of the
premises assumed in the following pages.

Even those who, like the Duke of Argyle, in his
" Reign of Law," seem to reject the theory of natural
selection, appear also to reject that usually received
interpretation of the Scripture account which implies
the sudden and independent creation of man. They
would have us believe, that God acted according to,
or that He made use of, some slow process of law in
creating man, though the law of creation itself, and
the conditions under which it brought about the
existence of man, they confess to be utterly above
our comprehension.

Now, the argument of the following work seems

to me to be totally unaffected by any theory respecting the origin of man, or the date of the commencement of his existence upon the earth.

Supposing, for instance, that the Darwinian theory, or some modification of it, should ever obtain acceptance amongst scientific men as affording a probable account of the origin of mankind, still it would not affect the parallel between the two Adams drawn out by the Apostle in Romans v., for there must have been a time when some member of the series of creatures began to have a mind and conscience which enabled him to recognise God and his obligations to Him, and to pray to God. Man's sense of responsibility to God, and consciousness of immortality, must be accounted for. That a creature, in any such a series as those with which we are acquainted, should begin to have desires beyond the satisfaction of his natural wants, and to recognise God and his own moral nature, is surely as astonishing a fact as any in natural science, and ought to be beyond measure interesting to us, who have the power of reflecting upon our relations to the Moral Governor of all.

The Bible gives us some solution of this in that it tells us that God made man in His image, after His likeness: and, of course, if man was made in God's image, it must have been in God's moral and spiritual image and likeness.

The Bible also gives us a solution of the equally astonishing fact that man has lost this image and likeness. It is as great a mystery as any in the natural world, that a being, possessed of a conscience and the capability of recognising and holding converse with God, should fall so miserably below His type or ideal.

How is such a fall to be accounted for? The Scriptures also give us the solution of this mystery; for they teach us that all mankind had one human father; that he fell, and involved his posterity in his ruin.

Hard as many things are connected with this, it is, after all, the only solution of the problem of human nature. Here is a creature, with the highest moral capacities, utterly depraved; a being endowed with a conscience as his moral instinct to direct him in his moral conduct, going contrary to that conscience in an infinitely greater degree than any unreasoning creature goes contrary to its natural instinct. "The stork in the heavens knoweth her appointed times, and the turtle and the crane and the swallow observe the time of their coming, but God's people know not His judgment." This problem surely requires solution, and the Scriptures give us the only solution worthy of notice.

We are taught by the Scriptures that this likeness of man to God was not a development of man's natural powers, but a creation of God.

It affects not at all the argument of these pages whether this first man be a new creation out of inorganic matter, or whether he be the last of a series of forms leading gradually up to him as their perfection and culminating point.

The Scripture doctrine of the two Adams does not

so much depend upon the means employed by God in bringing man into being, as upon the fact that the *one* man in whose loins were the whole race, was tempted and fell. It is only multiplying indefinitely what, in the nature of things, is a most extravagant improbability, to suppose that many anthropoid apes, incapable of knowing God, generated men with souls capable of knowing Him. One such astounding development of the animal into the man, seems to answer all purposes. The true brotherhood of mankind is not to be set aside by such absurdities; much less can any truth of religion be affected by them.

The principal additions in this fourth edition consist of a note of some length (p. 66), on the nature of the Patristic testimony to infant Baptism; of another note (p. 170), on the right translation and interpretation of 2 Corinthians v. 17; and a concluding chapter, containing a review or recapitulation of the whole argument, with some remarks on the bearing of the controversy on Christianity, considered as at one and the same time an educational and a supernatural system.

CONTENTS.

CHAPTER VII.

CHAPTER VIII.

CHAPTER IX.

CHAPTER X

CHAPTER XI.

CHAPTER XII.

CHAPTER XIII.

CHAPTER XIV.

CHAPTER XV.

CHAPTER XVI.

CHAPTER XVII.

CHAPTER XVIII.

CHAPTER XIX.

CHAPTER XX.

THE SECOND ADAM,
AND THE NEW BIRTH.

CHAPTER I.

POSITION ASSIGNED TO BAPTISM BY CHRIST AND HIS APOSTLES.

THE SON of the MOST HIGH GOD, the Eternal WORD, was made flesh, and came among us, to be our Second Adam.

To this end He was born without sin, and having lived without sin, He died for sinful man, as his atonement.

To this end the fulness of the Spirit was committed to Him, for the sanctification of His brethren.

The religion which He taught is, as might have been expected, a spiritual religion.

He had said of God, "God is a Spirit, and they that worship Him must worship Him in spirit and in truth;" and so the religion which He brought in requires a faith of the heart, an obedience of love, a reasonable service.

But, lo! in the very first demand of this spiritual religion, on its very front, the Incarnate Wisdom ordains an act or rite not purely spiritual, for it touches our bodies as well as our souls.

He, the Son of God, and Wisdom of God, in laying down the terms of admission into His kingdom, not only says, "He that believeth," but adds, "and is baptized."

B

" He that believeth and is baptized shall be saved."
(St. Mark xvi. 16.)

And under what circumstances did He say this ?

Under the most solemn possible,—on the eve of His
Ascension, just before He left this scene of His humiliation.

Reader, have you ever thought it incumbent upon you
to realize why the Incarnate Word should, in His last
words on earth, thus join together two things so diverse,
as " believing" and " being baptized ? "

One, the conscious act of the immortal spirit recognising
its Saviour, and embracing His promises ; the other, to all
outward appearance, but a paltry washing of the perishable
body.

He came to set aside a religion of types and figures, and
to bring in a religion of realities. Why should He ordain
a type, if a type it be, on the front of a spiritual system ?

Some time before this, a ruler of His nation had come
to inquire of Him the nature of His religion; and to this
man the Saviour vouchsafed to make known the first
mystery of His kingdom,—the new birth.

And in what terms does He set forth this first truth ?
Does He so declare it as to leave no room for misconception about *such* a thing, so that every child of the kingdom
should know that the new birth is a purely spiritual thing,
i.e. an act of God's Spirit on our spirit, independent of,
and unconnected with, any form, any rite, any element of
this outward creation ; identical in fact with that conversion unto life by which the ungodly becomes the godly, and
the nominal Christian the true ?

Marvellous to relate, He connects this new birth with
water,—" Verily, verily, I say unto you, Except a man be
born of water and of the Spirit, he cannot enter into the
kingdom of God." (John iii. 5.)

Again, we find the rite of Baptism expressly included in

the few words of that parting commission, whereby the
Apostles were empowered to set up His kingdom : " Go ye,
and make disciples of ($\mu\alpha\theta\eta\tau\epsilon\acute{\upsilon}\sigma\alpha\tau\epsilon$) all nations, baptizing
them in the name of the Father, and of the Son, and of
the Holy Ghost ; teaching them to observe all things whatsoever I have commanded you." (Matthew xxviii. 19.)

Then He ascended into heaven, and sent down the Holy
Ghost to gather His Church out of the world, and to guide
it into all truth.

His coming was seen in the cloven tongues of fire, and
His power manifested in the gift of languages, and in the
conviction with which the testimony of Jesus came home
to the hearts of an immense multitude. " Men and
brethren," asked three thousand anxious inquirers, " what
shall we do ? "

Marvellous to relate, again Baptism, again " *the water*,"
in the answer of the Holy Ghost, directing them what
to do to be saved. " Repent, and be baptized every one
of you in the name of Jesus Christ for the remission of
sins." (Acts ii. 38.)

But further, a new era in God's dealings was about to
commence. The salvation of God was not to be confined
to one race, but was to be preached to all nations for the
obedience of faith.

To this end, it pleased God to raise up a new instrument—Saul of Tarsus. He was converted by the vision of
Christ in glory, and sent by Him to Damascus, there to be
told what he must do.

And again we have the " water," again Baptism, in the
message sent to the man raised up to contend for the fulness of Christian liberty, as opposed to a ceremonial way
of access to God. " Arise, and be baptized, and wash away
thy sins, calling on the name of the Lord." (Acts
xxii. 16.)

Again, it pleased God to make this man the instrument
of conveying to His Church the only outlines which we
find in His Word, of a *system* of Divine truth.   In his
epistolary writings alone have we anything like a *scheme*
of Christian doctrine.

In the Epistle to the Romans, for instance, we have the
great outlines of the work of salvation.   First (in the first
five chapters), it is looked upon as all of God's free grace ;
then (chaps. viii. ix. x. xi.), as of God's eternal purpose ;
then (chaps. xii. xiii. xiv.), as working by love : but, in the
very midst of this Divine scheme, we have Baptism and
the grace God has annexed to it.   We have it introduced
for a most important practical purpose,—to prevent a
man from abusing to his own destruction the doctrine of
God's free grace.

" What shall we say then ?   Shall we continue in sin,
that grace may abound ? God forbid.   How shall we, that
are dead to sin, live any longer therein ?   Know ye not,
that so many of us as were baptized into Jesus Christ were
baptized into His death ?   Therefore we are buried with
Him by baptism into death : that like as Christ was raised
up from the dead by the glory of the Father, even so we
also should walk in newness of life."   (Rom. vi. 1—4.)

But more, as if to mark with greater emphasis the importance of this aspect of the grace of Baptism, we have the
same view of it in almost the same words in another Epistle.
" Buried with Him in Baptism, wherein also ye are risen
with Him through the faith of the operation of God, who
hath raised Him from the dead." (Coloss. ii. 12.)

The exposition and practical bearing of these texts, I
shall give more fully further on.   I only now advert to
them, as indicating the high place which Baptismal doctrine
occupied in the mind of the Apostle.

Again, the same Apostle is inspired to write another

Epistle—that to the Ephesians—also containing, though in fewer words than in that to the Romans, a systematic sketch of Divine truth.

In this Epistle we have the initial sacrament twice alluded to.

The first mention of it occurs in an exhortation to unity (Ephes. iv. 1): "I therefore, the prisoner of the Lord, beseech you that ye walk worthy of the vocation wherewith ye are called, with all lowliness and meekness, with long-suffering, forbearing one another in love; endeavouring to keep the unity of the Spirit in the bond of peace. There is one body, and one Spirit, even as ye are called in one hope of your calling; one Lord, one faith, one Baptism, one God and Father of all, who is above all, and through all, and in you all."

The Apostle, in these words, beseeches the members of an (apparently) most advanced and spiritual Church to abide in unity.

He adjures them by their oneness in the Divine Persons in Whom they believed, and the greatness of the divine and spiritual bonds which united them.

One Father from Whom all grace flowed, One Lord their Redeemer, One Sanctifying Spirit, one body the Church, one animating hope, one faith professed throughout the world; and in the midst of such as these, "one Baptism," as a reason why they should be "one."

Surely he must have thought that God worked some great thing by that (mean though it be in the eyes of some) which he thus joins with the one faith, the one hope, the one elect body!

In another place in this Epistle he mentions it as the means whereby God cleanses His Church,—"that He might sanctify and cleanse it with the washing of water by the word." (Ephes. v. 26.)

Again, in another Epistle, that to Titus, he speaks of
God having " by His mercy saved us by the washing (or
as it is literally, bath) of regeneration ; " evidently referring to Baptism and its attendant spiritual grace.[1]

No wonder then that in another Epistle,—that to the
Hebrews,—the doctrine of Baptism is included among the
first principles of the doctrine of Christ, the foundations
of divine truth :—

"The foundation of repentance from dead works, and of
faith towards God, of the doctrine of baptisms,[2] and of
laying on of hands, and of resurrection of the dead, and of
eternal judgment." (Heb. vi.)

But again, the Apostle Paul was inspired to write another
Epistle,—that to the Galatians,—to assert Christian liberty
against the claims of a ceremonial system ; and in this

---

[1] This place has been ignorantly and unfairly tortured with the
view of eliminating from it any reference to the outward rite—so as
to make St. Paul say, " He saved us by spiritual regeneration
independent of any outward washing." The use by the Apostle of
the word λουτρὸν fixes the meaning as referring to Baptism. As
Dean Alford explains it, " By means of the laver (not 'washing,'
as English version : see the Lexx.: but always a vessel or pool in
which washing takes place). Here the Baptismal font." So also
Bp. Ellicott. That the Church's meaning is the true one is also evident from internal considerations—for on the principle of those who
deny Baptismal Regeneration (in order, as they wrongly think, to
exalt spiritual religion) Regeneration is not a washing, but a change
of heart wrought by the Spirit. Now it does seem a most forced
and violent figure to express a change of heart by such a term as the
bath of new birth. This passage is understood as alluding to the
grace of Baptism by every early Christian writer who cites it ; and
among the moderns by Luther, Melancthon, Calvin, Jewel, Hooker,
Mede, Taylor, Barrow, Bp. Hall, Beveridge, Wesley ; and amongst
living writers by Alford, Wordsworth, and Ellicott.

[2] Augustine understands this of Baptism. See *De Fide et Operibus*, page 52, Oxford Translation.

also we have another testimony to the important position of Baptism. " As many of you as have been baptized into Christ have put on Christ." (Gal. iii. 27.)

From these places but one inference can be drawn,—that no matter how spiritual the Christian system be, that spirituality is coincident with the most wondrous grace being attached, in God's infinite wisdom, to a rite not purely spiritual, in which not only the *soul* but the *body* has its part.

We must reverently search and see whether God has given any clue to the understanding of this mystery.

But, before doing so, let us turn for a moment from the words to the life and example of Christ.

When the fulness of time arrived for Christ to enter upon His public ministry, a remarkable person, miraculously born, and full of God's Holy Spirit, was sent before Him to prepare His way.

This he did by exercising a ministry, the leading feature of which was a Baptism in water. Christ submitted to receive this Baptism at the hands of His servant, and God honoured His submission by accompanying it with His first testimony to Christ's Eternal Sonship. Then, too, He was anointed with the fulness of the Spirit for the work of His Messiahship.

Now, consider the prominence given in the word of God to this submission of our Lord.

It is recorded in full by two out of the four Evangelists; another (St. Mark) begins his Gospel with the notice of it; and the remaining one (St. John), in the first chapter of his Gospel, makes the first testimony to Christ's Messiahship to be that of John the Baptist witnessing to the descent of the Holy Ghost on Jesus at His Baptism. By each of the four it is implied to be the gate by which our Lord entered on His Ministry.

And why was all this written? Why was such honour
put upon the Baptism of John— the Baptism of water
only, the imperfect Baptism which had to be repeated?
(Acts i. 5 ; xix. 4, 5.) Why, but for our sakes ; that if
such was the honour put upon the Baptism of the servant,
how should we regard our Baptism—the Baptism of the
Master ! [1] How should we reverently acknowledge the
One Baptism ! How should we believe in, confess, uphold
its place in Christ's kingdom, its divine reality !

From these considerations, then, one thing is abundantly
plain, that the deeper the spirituality of the Christian
scheme, the more reason for us to consider why Christ
should have exalted to such a place in it an ordinance not
purely spiritual.

No truly spiritual man can ignore the place which Christ
has assigned to Baptism ; for the first element of Christian
spirituality must be a submission of the whole inner man
to all that God reveals,—and this because *He* reveals it
whose weakness is stronger and whose foolishness is wiser
than men.

Let us remember that St. Paul would have the Corinthians test their spirituality by their submission to God's
revealed will : "If any man think himself to be a prophet,
or spiritual, let him acknowledge that the things that
I write unto you are the commandments of the Lord."
(1 Cor. xiv. 37.)

---

[1] Not for any other purpose was the office of Baptizing given to
John, than that our Lord who gave it to him might, in not dis-
daining to accept the Baptism of a servant, commend the path
of humility, and declare how much His own Baptism was to be
valued. (Augustine, De Bapt. cont. Don. lib. iv. ch. 23.)

CHAPTER II.

ANALOGY OF THE TWO ADAMS.

ARE we then permitted to discern any reason why Christ has placed, as the gate into His kingdom, an ordinance not purely spiritual, touching the body through an element (water) of God's outer creation?

I think that we are so permitted.

I think that God, by having introduced into Christianity not only an evangelical and a moral, but also a *sacramental* element, has looked to the "supply of all our need, according to the riches of His glory in Christ Jesus."

We are not merely spiritual beings, nor shall we be through eternity.

As Christ our Head is, so shall we be. He, the Son of God, is now in His glorified *humanity* at God's right hand, not a mere spirit, but clothed in that BODY in which there dwells the fulness of the Godhead.

And in our perfect state of bliss, we also shall be *body* and spirit ; our bodies spiritualized and glorified, but yet *bodies.*

The sacramental doctrine of Scripture has to do with the fact, that Christ in His glorified *human nature* is our Second Adam, and that we are saved in Him, not in soul only, but in *body, soul, and spirit.*

Reader, I ask your patient and prayerful attention to the exposition of this which I am now going to offer you.

God, in His all-wise purposes, ordained that the race of mankind should spring from one parent. Adam was the fountain from which the whole river of human being was to flow. He was the root from which the whole tree of human life was to spring.

God ordained that he should transmit his human nature, whatever that nature might be, to his posterity; so that if he continued holy, he should transmit to them a holy nature, but that, if he became sinful, he must, of necessity, transmit to them a sinful nature. Through his own free-will he ate of the forbidden fruit, and became sinful, and this before any children had been born to him; so that when he begat children, he transmitted to them, not the sinless nature which he possessed originally, but the sinful nature he received the moment he transgressed. Hence the fountain of human nature became poisoned at its source; the root of human nature became evil before a single branch or bud had sprung out of it. Hence when Adam begat children, they were in his likeness. Hence all mankind are sinners from the womb.

There are three ways in which sin may be engendered in a person,—by nature, by temptation, and by example. Now, we find that evil tempers and dispositions show themselves in children spontaneously, as it were, when no temptation presents itself; so it cannot be by temptation that all mankind are sinful. And we find that the children of godly parents, who have seen in their parents a holy example, show the same seeds of evil as the children of the ungodly. It is through natural generation then, and that alone, that each one of the human race exhibits so early the traces of moral evil in his nature and disposition.

This doctrine of the transmission by natural generation of an evil nature, from the first Adam to all his posterity, is the doctrine of *original* or *birth sin.*

Though an infinitely mysterious truth, it is a truth which no one, not even an unbeliever, can gainsay; for its proof lies not only in the pages of inspiration,—not only in such texts as, " I was shapen in iniquity, and in sin did my mother conceive me," " We were by nature children of wrath," " As in Adam all die," but its proof lies in the history of every family, and of every individual of the human race, in the experience of every parent, and in the memory of each one of us as to what we were when little children.

Here, then, is the mystery of *moral* evil *naturally* engendered ; of moral evil transmitted to those who receive it whilst they are in a state of unconsciousness,— with the very seeds of their being.

Along with the flesh and blood of our parents, we receive their spiritual corruption, as they received theirs from their parents, and they from theirs.

Our first parent, in whose loins were all his posterity, sinned, and so received into his nature the seeds of corruption, both moral and physical ; and he begat children in his own likeness, not only with outward frames like his, but with souls like his in their taint of evil.   And he transmitted to each one that was engendered of him and of his offspring the corruption which he had received.   To each unconscious babe he transmitted the corruption which he himself had received in a state of the highest moral consciousness.

In the words of Inspiration, "By one man sin entered into the world, and death by sin ; and so death passed upon all men ;" " Death reigned even over them that had not sinned after the similitude of Adam's transgression, who is the figure of Him that was to come ;" " By one man's disobedience many were made sinners." (Rom. v. 12, 14, 19.)

At last God, in fulfilment of His ancient promise, provided the remedy.   He interposed by an act of love surpassing all conception,—"The Word was made flesh and dwelt amongst us." In the fulness of time One was conceived and born, not in the way of nature, but by miracle ;—not in sin, as every other human being had been born, but sinless : One was born, of Whom alone it could not be said that " He was shapen in iniquity, and in sin did His mother conceive Him."

He—the One Sinless Man—was marked out by God to be the Saviour of His sinful brethren.

To be their full and complete Deliverer, He must procure them two things—pardon and a new nature ; pardon for past transgressions, and a new nature to enable them to live to God ; for what would be the use of pardon to such creatures as we are, if we were pardoned and then left to continue under the bondage of sin ?

He, if He is to be in very deed the Second Adam, must be not only our Atonement for the guilt of actual transgressions, but He must also be to us a source of life and spiritual health, to counteract the moral and physical corruption or poisoned nature transfused through the race from its very fountain.

But how could He be these things to us ? How could He be Atonement, seeing He was *One*, but One—alone in His holiness, and we, His sinful brethren, as the sand upon the sea-shore ?

How could One make reconciliation for all ?

We know that when God thus interposed to insert into the line of our sinful race this sinless One, He caused His Only-Begotten Son to become one of us. " The Word was made flesh ; " " God was manifest in the flesh ; " " God sent His own Son in the likeness of sinful flesh." Such is the union of the Godhead and the manhood in Jesus, that " God and man is one Christ, who suffered for our salvation."

This *one Man* was able to make Atonement for all.
because the Godhead which was inseparably united to the
manhood in Him, made everything which Jesus suffered,
of infinite account. His Eternal Godhead imparted such
dignity to the human nature which He had taken into Himself, that the sufferings of that nature were a world's ransom.

In this way Christ's undefiled human nature was able
to fulfil the first condition of our salvation,—to make
Atonement.

But the Second Adam must not only atone for the
guilt, He must also be a fountain of healing to His brethren, as His prototype was a fountain of corruption.

How was this to be? for the Second Adam was born
when the earth was peopled with myriads of a sinful race.

It could not be in the way of nature, seeing that mankind, by the very condition of their being, could have
but one origin : they could only spring from one man,
because God originally created but one ; and having
derived their being from him, they could not be born, by
way of nature, from another.

If in this respect Jesus Christ, the Second Adam, is
to answer to the first (*i.e.* if He is to be an ADAM at all),
—if His undefiled human nature is to be to mankind, or
any part of them, a principle of life counteracting the
death received from the human nature of the first Adam,
it cannot be in the way of nature ; it must be effected
supernaturally.

If this is to be, the nature of the Lord Jesus must be
made so that it could be imparted to, and diffused
amongst, His brethren, and means also must be taken
to diffuse it.

That Christ's nature was so constituted (after His resurrection) that it could be imparted, is expressly asserted in
1 Cor. xv. 45 : "The first Adam was made a living soul,

the last Adam was made a quickening" (*i.e.* life-imparting)
"spirit."

Now, what is meant by this? Certainly not *merely* that
Christ's Spirit imparts religious knowledge; for if that be
all, in no sense would He be an Adam. Adam imparted
not instruction, but a nature, to those sprung from him.

What is meant, then? for Christ had a body in all
respects like unto ours.

Before His Resurrection, they nailed His body to the
cross; after His Resurrection, He had a real body, because
He invited His disciples to handle Him, and said to
them, "A spirit hath not flesh and bones, as ye see me
have." How is it, then, that as the Second Adam He
was made a Spirit; and not only so, but a life-imparting
spirit (πνεῦμα ζωοποιοῦν)? This must mean that His
body received, by God's almighty power, not only the
properties of a spirit, but that His entire nature became
life-diffusing. That such is the meaning is also evident
from this, that this text closely follows upon the
assertion, "There is a natural body, and there is a
spiritual body."

St. Paul had just been speaking of the marvellous
change to be wrought in our bodies at the resurrection.
In answer to the objector's question, "How are the dead
raised up, and with what body do they come?" he directs
men to consider the wondrous difference between the little
insignificant seed sown, "the bare grain," and the plant
which springs from it. Then he speaks of the different
sorts of bodies, celestial and terrestrial, and the different
glories belonging to each; "So," he says, "is the resurrection of the dead; it is sown in corruption, it is raised
in incorruption; it is sown in dishonour, it is raised in
glory; it is sown in weakness, it is raised in power; it is
sown a natural body, it is raised a spiritual body;" and

then he concludes, " There is a natural body, and there is a spiritual body."

We cannot understand what this spiritual body is. We are only told some of its properties,—that it will be incorruptible, glorious, powerful. We gather from the Apostle's comparison, that it will as far surpass our present bodies as the plant clothed with leaves and flowers surpasses the, to all appearance, lifeless seed. What St. Paul really means by a spiritual body we cannot tell ; for we know absolutely nothing of the mode in which a spirit exists, much less do we know what a *spiritual body* is.

If, then, our sin-defiled bodies are to be raised so glorious, with such new and transcendent qualities, because they are to be raised spiritual bodies, what must have been the glory and power in which That Body was raised which is in union with the Eternal Word, in which the Only-Begotten Son of God is to be manifested throughout eternity ? If *our* bodies are to be raised " in power," in what " power " must God have raised up the body of His Only-begotten ?

I believe, then, from all these overwhelming considerations, that these words of the Holy Ghost must be taken in their fullest meaning, viz. that Christ's body, because the body of the Second Adam, was raised up a spiritual body, capable of infinitely diffusing its life—life-giving, quickening, and spiritual.

Three questions here present themselves :

How can this be ?

Why should it be ?

Has the analogy between the two Adams ever been drawn out in this way ? Is this a new interpretation, or has it ever been held in the Church ?

First, How can it be ?

How can it be that the whole nature of Christ should

be imparted to His brethren, and be in them eternal life
of body, soul, and spirit?

To which we answer,—By the power of the Holy
Ghost.

The especial work of the Holy Ghost, in the economy
of grace, is to make Christ present. The Spirit does not
in this dispensation regenerate and strengthen man by
Himself, as it were, but by the very life and strength of
the Second Adam, Jesus Christ—Christ, not as God merely,
for as God He is everywhere, but Whole Christ—the Christ
who is " perfect God and perfect man, of a reasonable
soul and human flesh subsisting." (John xiv. 16—20 ;
xv. 1—10.)

Christ, not *merely* present in the heart, as one friend's
image is in the heart of another friend. This is a figurative and, in a certain sense, an unreal presence. It is a
human way of speaking to denote love for one absent ;
whereas the Scripture speaks of a presence over and above
this—a presence, it is true, to bring about Christ's love
in the heart, but still a presence besides it—over and
above it.

What mean you, then, by this presence ?

I mean a mystical and supernatural presence,—a presence for the most wondrous and gracious of purposes, to
make us partakers of a new life,—but, withal, a presence
infinitely above our comprehension, because the presence
of the nature of One infinitely above our comprehension ;
because, again, the presence within us of the nature of a
spiritual body, of which spiritual body we know nothing.

I mean a presence above nature, and brought about
in a way infinitely above nature, through the power and
working of God's Almighty Spirit.

But, secondly, Why should this be ? Why should we
not be saved by having Christ presented to our hearts

only in His offices of love? Why should there be such an unspeakable mystery as the diffusion of His whole life-giving nature?

I answer,—Because Christ is *the Second Adam*.

This mystery of our salvation by Christ's nature imparted to us, though unspeakable, is shadowed out by, and analogous to, our ruin by the first Adam's nature, transmitted to us as the seed of spiritual death.

If God, in His word, calls His Son the Second Adam, I am led to expect a communication of His nature that I may be restored, because it is by the communication of the first Adam's nature that I am lost.

We are lost, not because we imitate Adam, but because we are born in Adam, and so partake of that from Adam which is the cause of sin and death in us.

Now, seeing that God has provided us with a Second Adam in His Son Jesus Christ;

Seeing that He has provided in this Christ, this Second Adam, an undefiled human nature;

Seeing that the diffusion of this nature, though impossible by way of nature, MAY be possible by way of grace to Him who once brought about the Incarnation, and will bring about, in due time, the general resurrection;

Seeing all these things cannot be gainsaid, I am ready to receive with all thankfulness, and I pray God to give me His grace to live as one who receives, such a mystery.

The mystery of the transfusion of Adam's evil nature by natural means, prepares me for the diffusion of Christ's holy nature by grace.

It appears to me to be in accordance with all God's dealings, that the recovery should be analogous to the ruin.

The mystery is very deep that Christ should in this inconceivable way be communicated to us; but I see an

c

ample reason for it in the needs of my nature—my threefold nature of body, soul, and spirit, to which the whole nature of the first Adam was the source of sin and death.

But thirdly, Has the doctrine of the two Adams ever been drawn out in this way? Is this a new doctrine, or has it ever been held?

I will here adduce the testimony of two divines—one, unrivalled as the defender and expounder of the doctrine and discipline of the Church of England; the other, one of the greatest names amongst the Protestants of the Continent—Hooker and Calvin.

Hooker, in his "Ecclesiastical Polity," Book v. chap. lvi. sec. 7, thus comments on the truth we are considering:

"To all things He (Christ) is life, and to men light *as the Son of God;* to the Church, both light and life eternal, by being made the Son of Man for us, and by being in us a Saviour, whether we respect Him as God, or as man. Adam is in us as an original cause of our nature, and of that corruption of nature which causeth death: Christ as the cause original of restoration to life. The person of Adam is not in us, but his nature, and the corruption of his nature derived into all men by propagation; Christ, having Adam's nature as we have, but incorrupt, deriveth not nature, but incorruption, and that immediately from His own person, into all that belong unto Him. As, therefore, we are really partakers of the body of sin and death received from Adam, so, except we be truly partakers of Christ, and as really possessed of His Spirit, all we speak of eternal life is but a dream."

And again: "Doth any man doubt but that even from the flesh of Christ our very bodies do receive that life which shall make them glorious at the latter day, and for which they are already accounted parts of His blessed body?

Our corruptible bodies could never live the life they shall live, were it not that here they are joined with His body which is incorruptible, and that His (body) is in ours as a cause of immortality, a cause by removing through the death and merit of His own flesh that which hindered the life of ours. Christ is therefore, both as God and as man, that true Vine whereof we both spiritually and corporally are branches. The mixture of His bodily substance with ours is a thing which the ancient Fathers disclaim. Yet the mixture of His flesh with ours they speak of, to signify what our very bodies, THROUGH MYSTICAL CONJUNCTION, receive from that vital efficacy which we know to be in His; and from bodily mixtures they borrow divers similitudes, rather to declare the *truth* than the *manner* of coherence between His sacred (body) and the sanctified bodies of saints." (Eccles. Polity, Book v. chap. lvi. sec. 9.)

Reader, these words require no comment. I would, however, earnestly ask you whether you have read carefully what Hooker has written on the two-fold nature of our Lord, as bearing upon this. If you have not, you are not acquainted with an exposition of Christian truth unrivalled in the whole scope of English theological literature.

If you are not a Churchman, and profess not to agree with this great divine on Church discipline or government, still read his words for the sake of building yourself up in a truth that, if a Christian at all, you must profess, and if a spiritual Christian, you must delight in, viz the doctrine of Christ, the God-Man, your Covenant Head. Nowhere else, believe me, will you find it so wondrously expounded.

It is all contained in about forty or fifty pages, from the 50th to the 60th chapters of the fifth book of his work on Ecclesiastical Polity.

But I must hasten to my other witness, Calvin, a man of equal note amongst his followers, pre-eminent among them as a commentator on Scripture, of great critical acumen, well acquainted with the original languages of the Bible, and, moreover, the bitterest and most determined opponent of the Church of Rome that the world has ever seen.

These are his words, in his "Institutes of the Christian Religion," Book iv. chap. xvii. sec. 9:

"The flesh of Christ, however, has not such power *in itself* as to make us live, seeing that by its own first condition it was subject to mortality, and even now, when endued with immortality, lives not by itself, Still it is properly said to be life-giving, as it is pervaded with the fulness of life for the purpose of transmitting it to us. In this sense I understand our Saviour's words as Cyril interprets them: 'As the Father hath life in Himself, so hath He given to the Son to have life in Himself.' (John v. 26.) For there properly He is speaking, not of the properties which He possessed with the Father from the beginning, but of those with which He was invested in the flesh in which He appeared. Accordingly, He shows that in His humanity also fulness of life resides, so that every one who communicates in His flesh and blood, at the same time enjoys the participation of life. The nature of this may be explained by a familiar example. As water is at one time drunk out of the fountain, at another drawn, at another led away by conduits to irrigate the fields, and yet does not flow forth of itself for all these uses, but is taken from its source, which, with perennial flow, ever and anon sends forth a new and sufficient supply; so the flesh of Christ is like a rich and inexhaustible fountain, which transfuses into us the life flowing forth from the Godhead into itself. Now, who sees not that the communion of the flesh and blood of Christ is necessary to all who aspire to the heavenly life? Hence those passages of the Apostle: The Church is the 'body of Christ;' His 'fulness.' He is the 'Head,' 'from whom the whole body, fitly joined together, and compacted by that which every joint supplieth,' 'maketh increase of the body.' (Ephes. i. 23 ; iv. 15, 16.) Our bodies are 'the members of Christ.' (1 Cor. vi. 15.) We perceive that all these things cannot possibly take place unless He adheres to us wholly in body and spirit. But the very close connexion which unites us to His flesh, he illustrated with still more splendid epithets, when he said that 'we are members of His body, of His flesh, and of His bones.' (Eph. v. 30.) At length, to testify that the matter is too high for utterance, he concludes with exclaiming, 'This is a great mystery.' (Ephes. v. 32.)"

I quote these two passages to show that the analogy of the two Adams has been thus drawn out by men of deep knowledge of Scripture, and amazing clearness and grasp of mind. They would not have so expressed themselves, unless they thought they had good reason, both from the letter and the whole analogy of Scripture, to do so. And if all this be new or strange to you, may it not be because you have not entered into the force of Scriptures which they strove to realize in all their fulness?

CHAPTER III.

SECTION I.

REGENERATION, A BIRTH OF WATER AND OF THE SPIRIT.

union with Christ

WHAT, then, must we call this incorporation into Christ—this grafting into Him as the True Vine?

It is Regeneration. The grace of Regeneration is that, in the kingdom of God, which answers to original sin in the kingdom of evil.

As original sin is the partaking of Adam's nature, so regeneration is the partaking of Christ's.

The means for the communication of this gift, its effects, and the essential difference between it and all other changes, however important, and, above all, the blessedness, on the one hand, of so partaking of Christ, and the responsibility, on the other, we must now consider.

Before, however, we examine the means whereby we obtain this gift of God, let us remember how we are made partakers of the old nature of sin and death, of which Regeneration is to be the antidote.

We receive the first Adam's nature with our being, our life, our human nature, at our birth, and we receive it in a state of unconsciousness.

We receive it, not through our souls, by any temptation addressed to them, but passively, through our flesh and blood, which we derive from our parents. By our generation and birth we are made partakers of the first Adam. We may expect something corresponding to all this in the means which God has ordained to make us partakers of the Second Adam.

The mystery of our regeneration or new birth is enunciated by our Lord in John iii. 1—5. "There was a man of the Pharisees, named Nicodemus, a ruler of the Jews: the same came to Jesus by night, and said unto Him, Rabbi, we know that Thou art a teacher come from God ; for no man can do these miracles that Thou doest, except God be with him. Jesus answered and said unto him, Verily, verily, I say unto thee, Except a man be born again, he cannot see the kingdom of God. Nicodemus saith unto Him, How can a man be born when he is old? can he enter the second time into his mother's womb, and be born? Jesus answered, Verily, verily, I say unto they Except a man be born of water and of the Spirit, he cannot enter into the kingdom of God."

Our Lord in these words explains Regeneration, or the being "born again," by the being "born of water and of the Spirit." By so doing, He teaches us when this new birth takes place, and how it is to be distinguished from every other change in a man's spiritual state.

Nicodemus was a pious, God-fearing Jew, who had been struck with the power displayed in the miracles wrought by our Lord. He came to Jesus, acknowledging Him to be a teacher come from God. "Rabbi, we know that Thou art a teacher come from God."

Jesus assures him that something more is required of those who would be in His kingdom, than merely listening to His words, and submitting to Him as a teacher. There must be a living union with Him, a new birth into Him: "Except a man be born again, he cannot see the kingdom of God."

Nicodemus does not understand this ; and asks, "How can a man be born when he is old? can he enter the second time into his mother's womb, and be born?" Our Lord explains His meaning by His reply: "Except a man be born of water and of the Spirit, he cannot enter into the kingdom of God."

The most careless reader cannot but perceive that our Lord's second answer, "Except a man be born of water and of the Spirit," must be taken as explaining His first, —"Except a man be born again."

A birth is *one thing*, always taking place at one definite point of time. If our Lord then explains (which He unquestionably does) the phrase, "being born again," by the corresponding phrase, "being born of water and of the Spirit,"—if He means one thing, occurring but once, by being "born again," He must of necessity mean one thing, occurring but once, by "being born of water and of the Spirit." [1]

To separate what He has joined,—the "water" and the "Spirit,"—is to question His wisdom in having joined them. Whensoever, then, a man is "born again," there and then he must be "born of water and the Spirit." The two must be together, or you have not the birth indicated by the Saviour.

No other time can be imagined when this takes place, except the time of our initiation into the Church of Christ by Baptism.

The Holy Spirit works on the heart of man by various means. Sometimes He uses the written word of God, sometimes the word preached, sometimes affliction, sometimes the near prospect of death, as His instruments for awakening a man to the realities of the eternal world; but at only one time does He work through the agency of

---

[1] "There is no other way of being born again of Water, as well as of the Spirit, but only in the Sacrament of Baptism."—BISHOP BEVERIDGE.

water, and that is when He grafts a man by Baptism into Christ's body.

That our Lord speaks here of a change of some sort which must pass on a human being, if he is to be received into Christ's kingdom, is allowed on all hands. There never was a controversy respecting the nature of this change, or the time at which it takes place, till three hundred years ago.

At that time the question was raised, whether the change spoken of was that grafting into Christ's body which takes place at Baptism, or that change of hopes, views, affections, desires, aims, and principles of action which comes upon a nominal Christian when he realizes his sinfulness in God's sight, and the adaptation of the whole work of his Saviour to the needs of his moral nature.

I do not think that our Lord can possibly allude in this place to this latter change, (considered by itself, apart from the Baptismal entrance into His kingdom,) for two reasons. First: If He did allude to this conscious apprehension of Himself, and His work, and His claims on the heart, *why should He have connected such a change in any shape or way with water?* "Except a man be born of *water* and of the Spirit." Let any true Christian now reading these words think of the time when, after leading a life careless of the claims of His Saviour, those claims came with power to his heart.

What had the application of water (I mean at the time) to do with this change? A thousand things may have led you to serious consideration of your state before God; perhaps a sermon, perhaps a religious book, perhaps a deep affliction, a bereavement, a fit of sickness that brought you to death's door; certainly not, I will venture to say, the application of water to your body. Supposing that you have received Baptism at some time in your riper

years; then weeks, months, probably years, passed between
your turning to God and your being "born of water."
Supposing that you were baptized in infancy, the probability is, that many years intervened between your experience of what you (perhaps) have been in the habit of
calling your regeneration, and your baptism in water. Do
you not see, then, that to apply the term "regeneration,"
to your "conversion," or "Christian repentance," or
"realization of God and Christ and eternal things," is a
mistake, and a mistake of no ordinary importance? for to
apply the word regeneration, as is ordinarily done, to conversion, is systematically to ignore that *initial* grace which
is given to men as the foundation, so to speak, the root of
future "newness of life," of continual daily turning to God.
In the words of St. Paul, "So many of us as were baptized
into Jesus Christ, were baptized into His death; therefore
we are buried with Him by Baptism into death, that like
as Christ was raised from the dead by the glory of the
Father, even so we also should walk in newness of life."

I do not intend now to enter at large into the meaning
of these words. I would only have you observe, that the
Apostle appeals to a Baptismal union with Christ in His
death and resurrection, *i.e.* regeneration, as bringing a
man under the most solemn obligation to walk in "newness of life."

Again, Regeneration and Conversion are two different
terms, differently derived, presenting two different ideas,—
the one *birth*, at the commencement of a life; the other,
turning in the middle of a walk. They are never inter-
changed in Scripture. I do think these considerations, if
realized, shut us up, as it were, to the one change which the
Church has always associated with these words,—the Baptismal grafting into Christ.

Another reason why our Lord cannot mean by the

change He indicates that change of heart and life rightly called conversion, appears from the way in which He speaks to Nicodemus about " the new birth " being a *mystery*, a *new* privilege, the entrance into a *new* state of things, the kingdom of God.

If our Lord had meant by the new birth sincere repentance, or the change of heart which a worldly man undergoes when he becomes a true Christian, He could, I think, at once have made this plain to a sincere inquirer like Nicodemus.

Certain Psalms, such as the twenty-fifth, the fifty-first, the eighty-sixth, abound with expressions of sorrow for sin, and aspirations after God and holiness, which would have indicated to Nicodemus something of the nature of regeneration, if it be the same as conversion, or realizing our sinfulness and God's free grace in Christ Jesus.

Conversion is simply " turning,"—turning from sin, and turning to God. The Hebrew word answering to it is one of the most common in the Old Testament. It occurs in the fifty-first Psalm, " Sinners shall be *converted* unto Thee ; " and in the short compass of this Psalm, (as well as in many others,) we have all the characteristics of conversion. " Against Thee, Thee only, have I sinned ; " here we have the confession of sin as being an offence against God : " Hide Thy face from my sins ; " here is shame and sorrow on account of it : " Create in me a clean heart, O God, and renew a right spirit within me ; " here is the soul's desire for cleansing and deliverance. Conversion is also a *turning to God ;* and one half of the Psalms abound with expressions indicating such a state of soul ; the sixty-third, for instance : "O God, Thou art my God ; early will I seek Thee. My soul thirsteth for Thee, my flesh also longeth after Thee, in a barren and dry land, where no water is."

Here, then, is the doctrine of conversion pervading the whole of the most important book of the Old Testament. Not one Psalm can be realized or understood without it. All, more or less, imply that the man who lifts up his soul to God in the words they furnish, is turned to God. If, then, our Lord meant simply to direct Nicodemus to seek a new heart, is it likely that He would have expressed so old a truth in such new terms ? and when Nicodemus (to all appearance a sincere inquirer) asks for an explanation, still more strange does it seem that our Lord should have increased the difficulty a thousandfold, by connecting *water* with the Spirit as a needful element in bringing about such a change.

Take the definition of modern popular writers, such as Witherspoon, who identifies it with conversion ; for he says (Works, vol. ii. p. 119), " It appears that regeneration, repentance, conversion, call it what you will," &c.

He proceeds, shortly after, to describe it thus : " The change in regeneration doth properly consist in a strong inward conviction of the vanity of worldly enjoyments of every kind, and a persuasion that the favour and enjoyment of God is infinitely superior to them all."

Can any one suppose that our Lord merely meant this when He said, " Except a man be born of water and of the Spirit, he cannot enter into the kingdom of God ? "

The necessity of a thorough change of heart before a sinful or worldly man can abide God's presence, is no mystery. It is a most *unpalatable* truth to the sinner, not a *difficult* or a *mysterious* one. The worldly man does not say with Nicodemus, " How can these things be ? " he rather says, " Depart from me, for I desire not the knowledge of Thy ways." It is, in fact, because he understands something of the nature of conversion, as a thing which will for ever separate him from what he now sets his heart upon, that he forcibly excludes all thoughts of it from his mind.

The writings of at least one great and useful Christian (Chalmers), describe so lucidly the implantation of a new affection ; its expulsive power ; its persuasive, controlling, transforming efficacy ; its giving a new bent to the whole inner man, that an unconverted man, by reading his sermons, cannot but understand the nature of conversion.

There is no mystery in conversion, beyond the mystery which attaches to the acting of one spirit on another,—the Spirit of God on the human heart.

But, in Regeneration, if it be the conveyance of Christ's new nature, for the purpose of counteracting and renewing the old nature, there is an inconceivable mystery ; for it is the miraculous implanting of that new and holy nature, which is, both in soul and body, the seed of life.

But some persons have interpreted this passage so as to exclude Baptism by water.

They have ventured to say, that when our Lord used the *word* water, He did not really mean any such thing.

They affirm, that when our Lord said, " Except a man be born of water and of the Spirit," He meant, " Except a man be born of the cleansing Spirit," " the Spirit acting like water." Now, of course, on such a mode of interpre- tation, the words of Incarnate Wisdom may be made to bear any meaning. No Socinian gloss ever more effectually perverted the words of Scripture.[1]

---

[1] Something like this is actually the interpretation of Socinus in his treatise " De Baptismo Aquæ." Cap. iv. p. 46. " All are not agreed upon what is here to be understood by the word ' water.' That opinion commends itself most to my judgment which explains this word (water) as signifying ablution from the filth of sin, or the repentance by which we are washed from sin."

It may be well for those who would explain away our Lord's men-

And such an interpretation is the more daring, when
we consider that in the immediate context of this discourse
we have continual reference made both to Baptism, and
to water " as its outward element." The two verses which
follow the conclusion of this discourse with Nicodemus
are : "After these things came Jesus and His disciples into
the land of Judæa ; and there He tarried with them, and
baptized. And John also was baptizing in Ænon, near to
Salim, because there was much *water* there : and they
came, and were baptized." Does it not strike you,
reader, that the Holy Spirit guided the Apostle to insert
these words, in which there is such an unmistakeable
allusion to material water, immediately after the discourse
with Nicodemus, for the purpose of guarding Christ's
little ones against this falsely spiritual interpretation?

Still it may be asked, " If Regeneration be a new thing,
the conveyance of a new nature, the peculiar blessing of
a new kingdom, why should our Lord ¿have evidently
expected some knowledge of it in Nicodemus, as it is clear
that He did from His exclamation, ' Art thou a master in
Israel, and knowest not these things?' "

To which we answer, As a master in Israel (that is, one
supposed to be well acquainted both with the Scriptures
and the Jewish traditions respecting the Messiah), Nicodemus had much to prepare him for the doctrine of the
new birth.

From what he knew from the Hebrew Scriptures of the
first Adam, and the entrance of sin through him into the
human family, and its hold upon man's old nature, he
should have been ready to welcome, rather than to stumble

tion of water in this place, to remember that in doing this they are
also at one with Grotius and the Arminians, the precursors of
Rationalism in Germany, and of the "Latitudinarian" school
which so long blighted the Church in this country.

at, the mystery of a new stock from God into which human nature was to be grafted, and by which it was to be renewed.

That the ancient Jews understood their need of this, and that the Messiah should supply this need, is evident from the old Rabbinical proverb, "The mystery of Adam is the mystery of the Messiah." [1]

And another consideration, to which I think its due weight has never been attached, is decisive.

Our Lord here evidently lays down what is to be the gate, the entrance into His kingdom; a thing which a man has to pass through at the outset; that, just as circumcision was the initiation into the Jewish, so this birth of water and of the Spirit was to be the initiation into the Christian state.

This kingdom was formally set up on the day of Pentecost. During the great forty days between our Lord's Resurrection and His Ascension, we are told that He was speaking of the "things pertaining to the kingdom of God." Now, He had spoken to Nicodemus some time previously of something which He called "a new birth,— a birth of water and of the Spirit;" being the entrance into His kingdom: but in the sayings of Christ between

[1] Our Lord may also have had in view the types of Baptism in the Old Testament and the Baptism of proselytes, which among the Jews was so accounted their new birth, that the very relationships they had had as heathens were supposed to be annulled. According to Chrysostom's exposition, our Lord seems also to reprove a want of faith in God's power to produce it. "What, one may say, has this birth in common with Jewish matters? Tell me, rather, what has it that is not in common with them? For the first created man, and the woman formed from his side, and the barren woman, and the things accomplished by water . . . . . all these proclaimed beforehand, as by a figure, the birth and the purification which were to be."

His Resurrection and Ascension, though these were all
respecting the kingdom of God, nothing is said, in so many
words, of the new birth of water and the Spirit. But,
though we do not find any direct mention of it, we do find
our Lord ordaining Baptism as the rite of initiation into
His kingdom : " Go ye and disciple all nations, baptizing
them " (and this is, in the original, equivalent to " Go ye
and disciple all nations BY baptizing them ") " into the
name of the Father, and of the Son, and of the Holy
Ghost." [1]

Again, the terms of entrance into the kingdom of God
were proclaimed by St. Peter, on the day of Pentecost, in
these words,—" Repent, and be baptized every one of you
in the name of Jesus Christ for the remission of sins."
Throughout the record called " the Acts of the Apostles,"
whenever the kingdom of God is extended, mention is
expressly made of Baptism *as the entrance into it.* Nowhere, throughout the Acts, have we mention made, in so
many words, of the birth of water and of the Spirit as
the entrance into the kingdom.

Those, then, who do not believe that our Lord alluded
to Baptism, when He expressly mentions water in His
discourse with Nicodemus, are under the necessity of

---

[1] " βαπτίζοντες.] The μαθητεύειν consists of two parts—the *initia-
tory,* admissory *rite* and the *subsequent teaching.* It is much to be
regretted that the rendering of μαθητεύσατε, 'teach,' has, in our
Bibles, clouded the meaning of these important words. It will be
observed, that in our Lord's words, as in the Church, the process of
ordinary discipleship is *from Baptism* to *instruction,* i.e. admission
in infancy to the covenant, and growing up into τηρεῖν πάντα, κ.τ.λ.
—the exception being, what circumstances rendered so frequent in
the early Church, instruction before Baptism, in the case of adults.
On this we may also remark, that Baptism, as known to the Jews,
included, just as it does in the Acts (ch. xvi. 15—33), whole households—wives and children."—ALFORD, on St. Matt. xxviii. 19.

believing that a thing, which He laid down as the entrance into His kingdom, was, within a very short time after, entirely passed over, both by Himself and His inspired Apostles, when they came actually to admit men into His kingdom.

Another mode of doing away with the express mention of water in our Lord's words, it may be well here to notice, as, by the correction of a miserable mistake, we may call attention to a most important view of Christ's ordinance. You hear continually, "the water," and "the Spirit," opposed, as it were, to one another. When a man thinks and asserts that His Saviour had wise reasons for joining "water" and "the Spirit," and that His words are to be taken in their plain acceptation, he is told that there is no intention to depreciate *water* Baptism,—that it is a very edifying ceremony ; but that, after all, the Baptism of the Spirit is the paramount consideration.

All this is said with an air of condescension to his weakness, in taking into any real account his Saviour's mention of water ; the falsely spiritual man forgetting, it is to be charitably hoped, Who it is Who connects the "water" with the "Spirit."

This disjoining of "the water" and "the Spirit," this contrast between *water* and *Spirit* Baptism, is said in extreme ignorance of some of the plainest declarations of Scripture, respecting the *diversity* of the operations of the Holy Ghost.

It is assumed that, because the Holy Ghost is a *Spirit*, therefore His operations can only be mental or moral workings on the spirit of man ; but what saith the Scripture ? The first operation of the Holy Spirit mentioned in God's Word, is in the second verse of the first chapter in the Bible,—"The Spirit of God moved on the face of the waters." Is this what *we* call a *spiritual* work?

D

The next reference to His working *is* with respect to
what we call a spiritual work ; where God says (Gen. vi. 3),
"My Spirit shall not always strive with man." Here is
His work on the conscience.

The next operation of the Spirit that we shall notice is
of another kind. God tells Moses that he has filled
Bezaleel with the *Spirit of God ;* to devise cunning works,
to work in gold, and in silver, and in brass, to make the
tabernacle. (Exod. xxxi. 3.) Here is a work of the Spirit
solely on the intellect, perhaps on its lower functions.

The next which we shall notice is very fearful to contemplate ; for it is God endowing a man with one of the highest
gifts of a purely spiritual nature, and not working any
corresponding work upon his heart. It is when the Spirit
of God came upon the apostate prophet Balaam, and he
took up his parable, and foretold the glories in which he
was to have no part. (Numb. xxiv.)

The next is diverse still. The *Spirit* of the Lord came
upon Samson, and endued him with supernatural strength
of body for the deliverance of God's people. (Judges xiv.
6—19 ; xv. 14.) Here, then, the moving on the waters,
the striving with men's consciences, the skill of Bezaleel,
the prophecy of the reprobate seer, and the strength of
Samson, are equally the work of God's Spirit.

Turn we now to the New Testament. The first work
of the Spirit of God there, is the greatest work of God
on record—greater than the creation of the worlds. It
was the creation in the womb of the Virgin of that
undefiled human nature in which the Eternal Word
was to dwell for ever and ever. "The Holy Ghost shall
come upon thee, and the power of the Highest shall
overshadow thee ; therefore also that holy thing which
shall be born of thee shall be called the Son of God."
(St. Luke i. 35.)

Was this an operation on the *mind* of the Virgin only ?
Was it what many would call a spiritual work at all ?

Then we find that our Lord, *as a man*, did His mighty
works—not His work of conversion of sinners only, but
such works as the casting out of devils—by the Spirit of
God. " If I, by the Spirit of God, cast out devils."
(Matt. xii. 28.)

On the day of Pentecost, the Holy Ghost was given to
gather out and build up the Church of Jesus Christ. Then
commenced that dispensation of the Spirit in which we are
now living. Are His works now works on the heart or
mind only ? Turn to the twelfth chapter of St. Paul's
First Epistle to the Corinthians, and you will see that
every gift on which the existence and well-being of the
Church depends is a gift of God's Spirit, from the first
rudimentary gift of faith, which enables a man merely to
profess Christ's name (1 Cor. xii. 3), to the " charity that
never faileth :" all are works of the Spirit :—the word of
wisdom, the word of knowledge, faith, gifts of healing,
working of miracles, prophesying, discerning of spirits,
tongues, interpretation of tongues :—all these, some in
their operation affecting the mind, some the moral faculties, some the heart, some the body, are equally works of
God's Spirit.[1]

[1] " We are to observe that the Spirit of God is the great ministry
of the Gospel, and whatsoever blessing evangelical we can receive,
it is the emanation of the Spirit of God. Grace and pardon, wisdom and hope, offices and titles, and relations, powers, privileges,
and dignities,—all are the good things of the Spirit ; whatsoever
we can profit withal, or whatsoever we can be profited by, is a gift
of God, the Father of Spirits, and is transmitted to us by the Holy
Spirit of God. For it is but a trifle and a dream to think that no
person receives the Spirit of God but he that can do actions and
operations spiritual."—JEREMY TAYLOR : *Liberty of Prophesying,*
vol. v. p. 578. Eden's Edition.

Every work of God on the individual Christian, from the first infusion of the mere rudiment of faith which enables him to say that Jesus is the Lord (1 Cor. xii. 3), to the quickening of his mortal body at the last day (Rom. viii. 11), all are operations of the Spirit.

Now, amongst these operations of the ever-blessed Spirit, and to be carefully distinguished from all the rest, are His Sacramental operations; *i. e.* His operations in making effective to the end of the world the words and promises of Christ with reference to the two Sacraments; for to these ordinances Christ has annexed a blessing of their own, a grace peculiar to themselves, and one not (ordinarily) to be sought for or obtained through any other means—the blessing of union with Himself as the Second Adam.

Just, then, as it is one work of the Spirit to convince a man of sin, another to draw his heart to his Saviour, and another to raise up his dead body, so it is another at Baptism to graft a man into Christ's mystical body; for the Apostle says, " By one spirit are we all baptized into one body." (1 Cor. xii. 13.)[2]

---

[1] " By Baptism therefore we receive Jesus Christ, and from Him that saving grace which is PROPER UNTO BAPTISM."—HOOKER: *Eccles. Pol.* v. ch. lvii. sec. 6.

[2] Calvin has this remark on this passage : " Paul comprehends the whole Church, when he says that it was cleansed by the washing of water. In like manner, from his expression in another place, that by Baptism we are engrafted into the body of Christ (1 Cor. xii. 13), we infer that infants, whom He enumerates among His members, are to be baptized in order that they may not be dissevered from His body." And he adds these words : "See the violent onset which they (Anabaptists) make with all their engines *on the bulwarks of our faith.*"—CALVIN's *Institutes*, Book iv. chap. xvi. vol. iii. p. 372. Calvin Soc. Translation.

"This visible Church, in like sort, is but one continued from the first beginning of the world unto the last end. Which company being divided into two moieties, the one before, the other since the

Let us remember that the two Sacraments differ essentially from all else in Christianity, in the fact of their being covenant acts, and so derive their efficacy not only

coming of Christ; that part which since the coming of Christ partly hath embraced, and partly shall hereafter embrace, the Christian religion, we term as by a more proper name, the Church of Christ. And, therefore, the apostle affirmeth plainly of all men Christian (1 Cor. xii. 13) that, be they Jews or Gentiles, bond or free, they are all incorporated into one company, they all make but one body. The unity of which visible body and Church of Christ consisteth in that uniformity which all several persons thereunto belonging have, by reason of that one Lord whose servants they all profess themselves, that one faith which they all acknowledge, that one Baptism wherewith they are all initiated."—HOOKER : *Eccles. Pol.* iii. chap. i. sec. 3.

" ' By one Spirit are we all baptized into one body,' that is, the Spirit of God moves upon the waters of Baptism, and in that Sacrament adopts us into the mystical body of Christ, and gives us title to a co-inheritance with Him."—JEREMY TAYLOR : *Liberty of Prophesying*, vol. v. p. 580. Eden's Edit.

I believe that the interpretation of these divines is the only one consistent with a common sense view of this passage in connexion with its context. It can only have one of two meanings, either that of a grafting of all the Corinthians by a specific work of the Spirit in and by Baptism into the Church, or a grafting them by a true and genuine conversion into the (so-called) invisible Church of the true elect. Now the whole context of the passage and the whole analogy of the Epistle is against the latter meaning. St. Paul is bringing certain considerations to bear upon the whole body, because all are in the body, and so all ought to be influenced by these considerations. And the whole of the rest of the Epistle shows that the moral and spiritual state of this Church was such, that the Apostle stood in great fear of the final salvation of very many of its members; so that, on the principle of our opponents, we should rather have expected him to say, " By one Spirit ye have not all been baptized into one body ; ye have need to be baptized by the Spirit into the true invisible Church." Into all this I shall enter more fully when I examine the Epistle to the Corinthians in Chapter VI.

from the promise of Christ, but are to be considered His acts.

Luther recognises this fundamental principle with respect to them :—

" You should not regard, therefore, the hand or mouth of the minister who baptizes,—who pours over the body a little water, which he has taken in the hollow of his hand, and pronounces some few words (a thing slight and easy in itself, addressing itself only to the eyes and ears, and our blinded reason sees no more to be accomplished by the minister) ; but in all this you must behold and consider the word and work of God, by whose authority and command Baptism is ministered, who is its Founder and Author, yea, who is Himself the Baptist. And hence has Baptism such virtue and energy (as the Holy Ghost witnesseth by St. Paul), that it is the laver of Regeneration (Titus iii. 5), and of the renewal of the Holy Ghost ; by which laver the impure and sentenced nature which we draw from Adam is altered and amended." [1]

Calvin also recognises the same principle :—

" It ought to be sufficient for us to recognise the hand and seal of our Lord in His Sacraments, let the administrator, be who he may." And again : " Against these absurdities we shall be sufficiently fortified, if we reflect that by Baptism we were initiated not into the name of any man, but into the name of the Father, and the Son, and the Holy Ghost ; and, therefore, that Baptism is not of man, but of God, by whomsoever it may have been administered." [2]

I have now, I hope, made it sufficiently clear that it is

[1] Homily on Baptism. Luther's Works. Witt. 1558, vol. vii. p. 377.

[2] Calvin's Institutes, Book iv. chap. xv. sec. 16, vol. iii. p. 340. Calvin Society's Translation.

repugnant to every principle of right interpretation to explain these words of our Lord to Nicodemus otherwise than as asserting the necessity of the change to be wrought in a man by God's Spirit in the Sacrament of Baptism.

One more objection remains to be considered. It has been often gravely asserted that our Lord could not allude to Baptism, because His (*i. e.* Christian) Baptism was not then instituted; as if He, to whose foreknowledge all the future was present, could not refer to a thing which He was about shortly to enjoin as the visible entrance into His kingdom.

It seems incredible that men can affect to persuade themselves that our Lord does not allude in this place to the one Baptism into His body, and still more that they can bring forward such a reason for this opinion. For does not our Lord, in this very discourse, speak of things future as if they had already been, or were on the very eve of being, accomplished? He speaks, in verse 13, of His Ascension as an event already past: "No man hath ascended up to heaven but He that came down from heaven, even the Son of man which is in heaven." Again, He speaks, in verse 14, of "the Son of man being lifted up, that whosoever believeth on Him should not perish." Here both "the lifting up" and the eye of faith turned to it are things future.

Again, what are all our Lord's parables but delineations of a kingdom shortly to be set up, as if it were already established? Our Lord constantly speaks of His future kingdom as if it were already present; of the things of that kingdom as if it were already come; of its gifts as if already in possession. A very distinct case of this occurs in St. John vii. 37, 38 : "If any man thirst, let him come to Me and drink. He that believeth on Me, as the Scripture hath said, Out of his belly shall flow rivers of living

water." These words seem to refer to the time in which
our Lord was then speaking, and to offer a gift to be
received at once by those who heard Him. But if we
refer to the context, we shall find that the gift held out
was not a *present* but a *future* one : " This spake He of the
Spirit which they who believe on Him should receive ;
for the Spirit was not yet given, because that Jesus was
not yet glorified." In several places He speaks of the
duty of watching and waiting for His second coming, as
a duty then incumbent on His followers ; whereas, of
course, it could not be their duty till after His ascension.
" Let your loins be girded about, and your lights burning,
and ye yourselves like unto men that wait for their Lord,
when He shall return from the wedding." (St. Luke
xii. 35.) [1]

In accordance with the analogy of Scripture, this new
birth of water and of the Spirit has been expounded from
the earliest times, and by almost every great scripturist,
as having but one meaning. There is an allusion to it
in the writings of Justin Martyr, a man who lived in
the country of our Lord, and within a century after His
death : he consequently could have conversed with those
who knew the Apostles, and he sealed his testimony by
suffering martyrdom.

This man writes an apology, or defence of the Christian
religion, and in this he describes the rite of initiation
in these words : " As many as are persuaded and believe
that the things taught and affirmed by us are true,
and undertake to live accordingly,—these are taught to
pray, and to beseech with fasting, remission of their former
sins at God's hands ; we also praying and fasting along

---

[1] I owe the substance of the preceding page to a kind and able
correspondent.

with them. Afterwards, they are brought by us to a place
where there is water; and after the same manner of regeneration that we were regenerated by, are they also rege-
necated ; for they then receive the laver in water in the
name of the Father of all things, and our Lord and Saviour
Jesus Christ, and the Holy Spirit. For Christ said, 'Unless
ye be regenerated, ye shall not enter into the kingdom of
heaven.'" (Justin Martyr, Apol. I. § 61.)

This passage is decisive on the opinion of the early Christians, as to the essential difference between regeneration
and conversion. The persons here alluded to by Justin
gave every evidence of conversion : they believed the
Gospel, they undertook to live accordingly ; they were
taught to pray, and to beseech with fasting, remission of
sins at God's hands ; but not till they came to the water
were they regenerate.

We have precisely the same procedure in the ministration
of Baptism to those of riper years, in the Book of Common
Prayer. The rubric enjoins the minister to take every
pains to instruct them. They, in the service, make solemn
profession of repentance and faith ; but not till they are
actually baptized are they " born again." [1]

---

[1] " Unless as the Spirit is a necessary inward cause, so water were
a necessary outward means to our regeneration, what construction
should we give unto those words wherein we are said to be new-
born, and that ἐξ ὕδατος, even of water ?"—HOOKER : *Eccles. Pol.*
Book v. chap. lx. sec. 3.

" ' Unless a man be born of water and of the Spirit.' This precept was in all ages expounded to signify the ordinary necessity of
Baptism to all persons . . . This birth is expressed here by water
and the Spirit, that is, by the Spirit in baptismal water ; for that
is, in Scripture, called the laver of a new birth, or regeneration."—
JEREMY TAYLOR : *Liberty of Prophesying*, vol. v. p. 572. Eden's
Edition.

SECTION II.

EXAMINATION OF INTERPRETATIONS OF JOHN III. 3--5.

IT may be well here to review carefully, and at some length, the various interpretations which have been assigned to these words of Christ to Nicodemus. (John iii. 3—5.)

But three interpretations of these words have ever been suggested. Only one is possible. The three are :—

I. An interpretation which excludes all reference to water baptism. According to this, our Lord, in these words, asserts the necessity of a new heart, or of real spiritual religion, and bids Nicodemus seek it as being yet a worldly, unconverted man.

II. The second interpretation supposes our Lord to assert the necessity of two distinct births, a birth of water in Baptism, and a birth of the Spirit in conversion : which latter may be, and in point of fact, generally is separate from the former.

III. The third interpretation is that of the Church. That our Lord here asserts the necessity of a certain specific change of spiritual relationship and condition designed and intended to bring about, here and hereafter, a renewal of the whole man, which change the Holy Spirit works at the time of the due reception of Baptism.

Let us carefully examine into the reasons for each of these interpretations.

They who adopt the first exclude all reference to water Baptism, except perhaps by way of remote typical allusion, and suppose our Lord by these words to impress upon His

followers the need of a heart renewed in its affections
Godward.

The objection utterly fatal to the soundness of this
interpretation is, of course, our Lord's express mention
of water.

If our Lord meant merely to urge Nicodemus to seek a
new heart, the mention of water seems altogether out of
place.

It brings misunderstanding and confusion of ideas into
the simplest and plainest matter possible : for nothing can
be more plain than the idea of conversion or repentance,
or the new heart,—it is that a man should be turned in
heart and soul from the world and sin to God through
Christ. Nothing can be plainer than its necessity. To
connect such a change with water seems to put a gratuitous stumbling-block into the way of sincere inquirers
apprehending clearly that first truth of Christianity, the
nature of evangelical repentance.

It is absurd to suppose that there is anything difficult
or mysterious in the doctrine of the nature and necessity
of a change of heart. The simplest idea of heaven, as the
place of a holy God and holy angels engaged in holy
occupations, carries on the face of it the necessity for a
worldly, sin-loving man being thoroughly changed before
he could enjoy such a state, or even bear to be in it. A
man must love God, and love goodness, and love worship,
and delight in praise and thanksgiving, if the eternity set
before us in the Bible is not to be to him a dreary
eternity in occupations for which he has no taste. For a
man then to enjoy heaven, he must have a new heart.
Now, what is this new heart? Why, mystify it as men
will, it can only mean new affections and inclinations—for
I suppose it is not meant that the bodily organ, the centre

of the circulation of the blood, is to be renewed. The word "heart" in the phrase, "a new heart," can only stand for the affections and desires.

When then we consider that our Lord had the whole future of His Church naked and open to His searching glance, is it likely that He would have encumbered His enunciation of the paramount need of evangelical repentance with the use of a word which must of necessity be the fountain-head of a stream of misunderstanding respecting such a very plain matter?

This word "water" at once introduces, and apparently for no purpose, a new set of ideas connected with an outward form or rite—a form or rite to which the Saviour Himself, in His last words on earth, assigned a remarkable position in His spiritual system; but a form or rite which (on the strict principles of those who deny baptismal regeneration) it is the most dangerous delusion possible to mix up with Regeneration.

Our Lord must have foreseen that this His express mention of water would put, for many hundred years, His whole Church collectively, and the best and humblest souls in it, on a wrong track as to His meaning.

Consider the persons who have stumbled at this one word "water," and have been naturally led by it to interpret this important place as asserting the need of a change connected with water baptism:—Hermas, Justin Martyr, Irenæus, Clement, Tertullian, Origen, Cyprian, Athanasius, Ambrose, Chrysostom, Augustine, Bernard, Luther, Melancthon, Bucer, Cranmer, Ridley, Jewel, Hooker, Bishop Hall, Mede, Barrow, Jeremy Taylor, Beveridge.

All the Fathers of the first three centuries, without exception, i.e. the champions of the faith of Christ, in ages when to be a Christian was to be ready at any moment to surrender goods, reputation, family, liberty, life itself, for Christ. All the great leaders of the Reformation in Germany and England almost without exception ;—all the great and good men whose names are household words in the Church of England ;—that Church itself, in all her three authorized Baptismal Services, and in her Order of Confirmation, formularies every word of which has been weighed, sifted, and assented to by the first theologians and scripturists of their day,—all these have, on the strength of our Lord's mention of water, interpreted this text as an enunciation of the need of Baptismal engrafting into Christ's Church.[1]

But it has been said that to be "born of water and of the Spirit" may possibly mean to be born of the Spirit alone in His capacity as the purifier of the heart. Now, if such be the meaning of our Lord's words, then His second or explanatory answer increases, and apparently gratuitously, and without reason, the difficulty of His first ; for our Lord, if He meant simply this, need only have said, "Except the heart of man be thoroughly cleansed and renewed, he cannot enter into the kingdom of God." And on this mode of interpretation there is a great confusion of ideas; in fact, a confusion of two distinct notions, "birth" and "cleansing." Begetting, or birth, is the commencement of *life* within, cleansing is the washing away of *filth*. The Holy Spirit does not beget a man anew by cleansing him, but by infusing life into him. A man is not *born again* of the Spirit as the " cleanser" or " purifier," but as the " giver of life." To support this confusion of ideas, miscalled an interpretation, the prophecy of the Baptist is appealed to : " He shall baptize you with the Holy Ghost

---

[1] See the list of quotations from these writers at the end of this section.

and with fire." But this latter text affords no ground for such an interpretation, for Christ did literally baptize with the Holy Ghost, and with fire, on the day of Pentecost. There were then seen cloven tongues as of fire, which was the outward and visible sign of the Spirit's presence ; for, I suppose, that none will say that men saw with eyes of flesh the Holy Ghost Himself. To explain "the Holy Ghost and fire" to mean the Holy Ghost inflaming the heart with zeal or love, is an interpretation for the nonce having no parallel in the figurative language of the rest of Scripture.

The natural meaning of St. John the Baptist's words is, that they are a prophecy of what actually took place on that great day of the Lord, when the kingdom of God came with power. To purchase the gift shed abroad on that day Christ had died. The outward visible sign of that gift was a tongue of fire on each Apostle.[1] As sure as the flame sat upon him the Holy Ghost was in him. How perilous, then, to explain away a plain allusion to material " water " in one Scripture, by so gratuitous and forced an interpretation of "fire" in another.

I say such a plain allusion to material water, for in the chapter immediately preceding this discourse with Nicodemus, we have our Lord changing actual water into wine, and in the same chapter, iii. 23, we have a distinct reference to the outward element, " John was baptizing in Ænon, near to Salim, because there was much water there."

---

[1] That St. John referred to the Pentecostal fiery sign is also to be inferred from our Lord's words in Acts i. 5, alluding to those of his forerunner and indicating their speedy fulfilment : "John truly baptized with water, but ye shall be baptized with the Holy Ghost not many days hence." When thus baptized with the Holy Ghost, they were actually baptized with fire.

It is then in the very highest degree improbable that our Lord, if He merely intended to lay down the need of a new heart, should introduce into His enunciation a figurative allusion so calculated to mislead.

II. The second interpretation suggested is that in which our Lord is supposed to lay down the necessity of two distinct births, a birth of water in Baptism, and a birth of the Spirit in conversion, which latter may be, and, in point of fact, almost always is, separate from the former.

In the case of infants in a Christian country, the birth of water, according to this interpretation, takes place first, and the birth of the Spirit may (or may not) take place many years afterwards. In the case of heathen in India or China the birth of the Spirit, or genuine conversion (according to this interpretation), must take place first, and the birth of water comes afterwards as a sign of profession. A man, according to this, is to be first born of God, and then *born of a mark of profession !* Christ, then, according to this interpretation, is made to assert the co-ordinate necessity of two distinct things : Baptism in its place as an outward seal of Church membership, and the Holy Spirit in His place as the renewer and purifier of the heart.

The objection absolutely fatal to this gloss is that our Lord's second answer to Nicodemus is an explanation of His first. By the words " being born of water and of the Spirit," in verse 5, our Lord explains the " being born again " of verse 3.

Now, we necessarily and unavoidably attach the idea of simple unity to " a birth." A birth, by its very nature, is one thing. It cannot possibly be divided, so as to take place at two different times. If our Lord, then, explains the phrase " being born again " by the corresponding phrase " being born of water and of the

Spirit," if He means one thing by being "born again," He must mean but one thing by being "born of water and of the Spirit."

Again, if the birth of water is but an outward profession, and the birth of the Spirit is an inward work distinct from it, why should our Lord join together two things so utterly asunder in their respective importance? The birth of the Spirit in producing a change of heart is so unspeakably great, and the birth of water as a profession, or an arbitrary sign or seal, or instructive type, is so exceedingly small a matter in comparison, that no satisfactory explanation can possibly be given why our Lord should thus link the two together. The most unscriptural, by far, of the two interpretations which we have been considering, is this one, according to which our Lord asserts the necessity of Baptism *per se*, and of a conversion by the Spirit *per se*, which two are both called births, and yet *may*, and in the vast majority of cases *do*, occur at different times, and so are different things ; for by thus dissociating Baptism from its spiritual grace, men actually make their Saviour exalt the mere outward rite to a level with that spiritual reality which they call the new birth; for they make, on this principle, Christ assign to both the appellation "birth," by His saying, "Except a man be born of water and of the Spirit." Is it not plain, then, that if we disjoin "water" from the Spirit Who works in and by it, and then, from this mention of it in this place as a needful birth, proceed to insist upon its necessity, we, by so doing, make a mere empty substitute for circumcision a needful supplement to Christ's work! We introduce a mere *ceremonial* observance as the entrance into a *spiritual* religion. We bring a mere typical rite into a system of realities. We fall into the deadly error of the Galatians ; for when men have begun by conversion in the Spirit, we insist upon their being perfected by a Baptism which, on such principles, only touches their flesh.

III. The third possible interpretation, and the only one consistent with the analogy of faith, and with a common-sense view of the passage and its context, is that of the Catholic Church, and of the greatest minds, and holiest and humblest hearts, in her fellowship.

It is that our Lord here asserts the necessity of that peculiar work of the Holy Spirit with which it is His gracious pleasure to accompany the due administration and reception of the Sacrament of Baptism.

This specific operation is the grafting a man into Christ's mystical body; the bringing him into a new spiritual relationship to the Second Adam, answering in the kingdom of grace to his natural relationship to the first Adam in the kingdom of evil.

God in the highest wisdom has ordained that this great change of spiritual relationship should take place at a certain definite time, and with certain outward sensible circumstances of washing with water, and the invocation of the name of the Ever-blessed Trinity.

He has done this, we may reverently surmise, because we, His creatures, as compound beings, are subject to the conditions of time and sense; so that we may each one of us know that our relationship to Him does not depend upon certain lively feelings, which may possibly pass away, and are always fluctuating, but upon our having at a certain time come in contact with an outward and visible instrumentality, ordained by Him for the diffusion of His kingdom among men; at which moment we underwent that baptism which His incarnate Son ordained as the means of incorporating men into His Church—which Church is no human society, but His mystical body, the

E

branches of Himself, the true Vine, having root in the mystery of His holy Incarnation ; which Church, too, is designed by its Divine Founder to embrace all the world, and every creature in it.

Here, then, we have an intelligible *rationale* of those words of our Lord, in which He speaks of a new birth of "water, and of the Spirit." He is referring to initiation into the *kingdom* of God, which kingdom is outward and visible, and yet inward and spiritual—outward as regards its signs and tokens, by which we discern it among the things of time and sense, spiritual as regards its gifts of grace and heavenly relationships. Like the Jewish state of things which it was intended to supersede, it was to be an outward and visible body, but it was to be endued with gifts of grace of which the Jewish were but a shadow.

Our Lord thus ordains, as the entrance into His kingdom, a rite or sacrament corresponding to the twofold character of that kingdom. It is outward, for water is to be applied with certain words, "of the one of which," as Luther says, "our eyes take note, our ears the other." But with all this, it has a spiritual operation attached to it. "By the one Spirit we are ALL then baptized into the one body," for the kingdom of which it is the entrance has all throughout an unseen and spiritual relationship to the Second Adam, the New Head of humanity.

Here, then, we have a rational interpretation of these words of Christ—rational in the highest and best sense of the word ; one which corresponds with the eternal fitness of things ; an interpretation, however, by which the outward sign, being the mere channel of grace, cannot possibly be exalted *per se ;* and one which yet tallies with, and affords an explanation of, the extraordinary spiritual gifts ascribed to, or associated with, the reception of that outward sign in the rest of the New Testament—that it should be called a death, burial, and resurrection with Christ (Rom. vi. 3, 4 ; Col. ii. 11, 12)— a putting on of Christ (Gal. iii. 27)—a means for obtaining remission and cleansing through Christ's blood (Acts ii. 38 ; xxii. 16 ; Ephes. v. 26)—the bath of new birth instrumental to salvation (Tit. iii. 5)—a spiritual deliverance corresponding to that of Noah in the ark (1 Pet. iii. 21), and that of the Israelites in the passage of the Red Sea (1 Cor. x. 1—10).

Except on the Church interpretation of our Lord's words—that in and through Baptism the Holy Spirit works the specific work of grafting a man into Christ— the twelve or thirteen texts which so unequivocally connect Baptism with salvation (and which are some of them most important for their evangelical, and others for their practical application), cannot be harmonized with the whole scope and tenor of the Christian Revelation.

It seems foreign to the whole Christian scheme, as the Puritan understands it, to connect salvation in any way with a typical or figurative ordinance. It grates against one's so-called spiritual perception to take these remarkable texts unreservedly, as they stand. And so evangelical bodies of men have habitually explained these texts away by rationalistic glosses and comments of a precisely similar character to those by which the Scripture testimonies to our Lord's Divinity and Incarnation have been deprived of all real meaning.

This, of course, cannot be done without grievous injury to the submissive faith of those who put forth, and those who receive, such misinterpretations of God's word.

Explaining away on rationalistic, or falsely spiritual grounds, one set of express Scripture assertions, paves the way for a similar treatment of all others. A supposed

internal spiritual sense or faculty is made the judge of
the written word itself,—so far as to decide what assertions of that word are to be received unreservedly, and
what to be practically ignored.

And so we find that bodies or schools of Christians,
who began their career with a godly protest against the
corruptions and superstitions of the Church of Rome,
have ended with an absolute denial of such eternal
verities as vicarious Atonement and the Divinity of the
Saviour, which that corrupt branch of the Church yet
bears witness to. I am afraid that at the great day it
will be found to have been no small spiritual sin for men
with open Bibles to condemn, under the common name of
Popery or superstition, the unreserved reception of the
Saviour's own words respecting His Sacraments, and the
glosses of mediæval tradition respecting purgatory, or
the worship of the Virgin, or the assumptions of the
Bishop of Rome.

NOTE.—The following Christian writers quote or allude to this
passage (John iii. 3, 5) as implying a spiritual change wrought in
Baptism—a new birth in that Sacrament :—

Hermas, Pastor. lib. iii. Simil. ix. cap. xvi. (Migne). "That
seal is water, into which persons go down liable to death, but come
out of it assigned to life. For which reason this seal was preached
to these also, and they made use of it that they might enter into
the kingdom of God."

Justin Martyr, A.D. 148, Apol. i. 61. Quoted in Blunt on
"Right Use of Early Fathers," p. 533. "Then they are led by
us to the water, and are regenerated by the same process of regeneration by which we were ourselves regenerated ; for they then
receive the laver in the water in the name of God the Father and
Master of the universe, and of our Saviour Jesus Christ, and of the
Holy Ghost. For Christ says, 'Unless ye be born again, ye cannot
enter into the kingdom of heaven.'"

Irenæus, A.D. 167, Contra Hæreses, lib. iii. chap. xvii. 1

(xix.) Migne. "When He gave His disciples the commission of regenerating unto God, He said unto them, 'Go and teach all nations, baptizing them,'" &c.

Clement of Alexandria, A.D. 192, Pædag. i. chap. xii. (Blunt's Right Use of Early Fathers, p. 536). "He seems to me to form man of the dust, to regenerate him by water, to make him grow by His Spirit, to instruct him by His Word."

Tertullian, A.D. 200, De Baptismo, 13. ("Library of Fathers," p. 272.) "When with this law is compared that limitation, 'Except a man be born of water and of the Spirit, he shall not enter into the kingdom of God,' this hath bound down faith to the necessity of Baptism."

Origen, A.D. 210, Homil. xiv. in Lucam, tom. iii. p. 948, Benedictine edition. Quoted in Gibson's "Testimonies," p. 103. "And because, through the Sacrament of Baptism, the pollutions of our earthly origin are removed, so it is, also, that infants are baptized; for, 'Except a man be born of water and of the Spirit, he cannot enter into the kingdom of God.'"

Hippolytus, A.D. 230, Homilia, in Theophania, § viii. (Blunt, p. 545.) "How shall we come? it is said. By water and the Holy Spirit. This is the water, in communion with the Holy Spirit, by which Paradise is watered, the earth enriched, the plants are nourished, animals are generated, and, in a word, man is born again and quickened, in which Christ was baptized," &c.

Cyprian, Epist. lxxii. 1. "For then may they at length be fully sanctified, and become sons of God, if they be born of each Sacrament, since it is written, 'Except a man be born of water and of the Spirit, he cannot enter into the kingdom of God.'" Page 240 in Oxford Translation.

All these are ante-Nicene testimonies. They are, i.e. the testimonies of men, every one of whom lived in continual danger of his life from his profession of Christ. From what remains of the writings of these men they all appear to have been men of a true, realizing faith, and also men of great intellectual power.

Athanasius, Epist. iv. ad Serapion, tom. ii. p. 705, Benedictine edition. Quoted in Gibson, p. 125. "He who is baptized puts off the old man, and is made a new man, being born again by the grace of the Spirit."

Ambrose, A.D. 397, De Myst. iv. 20, tom. ii. p. 330. Quoted in Gibson, p. 185. "Nor, again, does the mystery of regeneration take place without water ; for, 'Unless a man be born of water and of the Spirit, he cannot enter into the kingdom of God.' "

Chrysostom, A.D. 407, Homilies, on St. John iii. 5. "The first creation, then—that of Adam—was from earth ; the next, that of the woman, from his rib ; the next, that of Abel, from seed : yet one cannot arrive at the comprehension of any one of these, nor prove the circumstances by argument, though they are of a most earthly nature. How, then, shall we be able to give account of the unseen generation by Baptism, which is far more exalted than these, or to require argument for that strange and marvellous birth ?"

Augustine, A.D. 430. " Let us rather hold the sound doctrine of God our Master in both things ; that there be a Christian life in harmony with Holy Baptism, and that eternal life be promised to no man, if either be wanting. For He who said, 'Except a man be born of water and of the Spirit, he shall not enter into the kingdom of God,' Himself also said, 'Except your righteousness shall exceed the righteousness,' &c."—De Fide et Operibus (xxvi.) 48.

Luther, in Joelem iii. 28. Quoted in Abp. Lawrence, on "Doctrine of Church of England on Efficacy of Baptism," p. 88. "Christ says, 'Unless a man be born again by water and the Spirit.' This view is manifest that the Holy Ghost wills, by means of Baptism, to exert His influence with efficacy on the soul."

Melancthon, Loci Theologici. See Appendix B at the end of this work. "The command respecting Baptism is of universal application, and belongs to the whole Church. 'Except a man be born of water and of the Spirit, he cannot enter into the kingdom of God.' It belongs, therefore, to infants that they may become a part of the Church."

Cranmer, Works on "Lord's Supper." (Parker Society, p. 304.) "As in our spiritual regeneration, there can be no Sacrament of Baptism if there be no water. For as Baptism is no perfect Sacrament of spiritual regeneration without there be, as well, the element of water, as the Holy Ghost spiritually regenerating the person baptized, which is signified by the said water."

Ridley, "Works." (Parker Society, p. 238.) "Baptism is ordained in water to our spiritual regeneration."

Jewel, "Treatise on Sacraments." (Parker Society, p. 1104.) "For this cause are infants baptized, because they are born in sin.

and cannot become spiritual, but by this new birth of the water and the Spirit."

Hooker, Eccles. Pol. Book v. chap. lx. sec. 3. "Unless as the Spirit is a necessary inward cause, so water were a necessary outward means to our regeneration, what construction should we give unto those words wherein we are said to be new-born, and that ἐξ ὕδατος, even of water?"

Bishop Hall, "Paraphrase on hard Texts." John iii. 5. "Works," vol. iv. p. 225. "Except a man be born again by the effectual working of God's Spirit, as by the author of this new birth, and in the ordinary course of God's proceedings in His Church by the water of Baptism, as the sign appointed by God in the Sacrament of our regeneration, he cannot enter into the kingdom of God."

Mede. See quotation from him in Appendix B.

Jeremy Taylor, "Liberty of Prophesying," vol. v. p. 572, Eden's edition. "This birth is expressed here (John iii. 5) by water and the Spirit, i.e. by the Spirit in baptismal water; for that is, in Scripture, called the laver of new birth or regeneration."

Beveridge, Sermon xxxv. vol. ii. ("Lib. of Anglo-Cath. Theol.") "There is no other way of being born again of water as well as of the Spirit, but only in the Sacrament of Baptism."

CHAPTER IV.

REGENERATION OF INFANTS IN HOLY BAPTISM.

I COME now to consider, "Who are the proper recipients of that Sacrament of Regeneration which our Lord has ordained to be the means whereby men are to be engrafted into His body?" To which I answer, All those who partake of the nature of the first Adam. "If through the offence of one many be dead, much more the grace of God, and the gift by grace, which is by one man, Jesus Christ, hath abounded unto many. As by the offence of one, judgment came upon all men to condemnation; even so by the righteousness of one, the free gift came upon all men to justification of life." (Rom. v. 15—18.)

All, then, who partake of the condemnation of the first Adam, have a title to "the gift;" but are they all in a condition to receive it? Certainly not. Two classes of persons are in this condition: first, infants; then those persons of riper years who, not having been baptized in infancy, repent and believe.

Many persons would put the latter class first, and the reason they give is, that in the New Testament we have more prominently brought before us the Baptism of adult persons.

I cannot consent to this, for I do not see the validity of the reason. For in the first place, if anything can be gathered from our Lord's words and acts, respecting Infants, it is that they are in a better position for receiving

grace from Him than believing adults are. Our Lord not
only permits Infants to be brought to Him, but severely
blames those that would keep them from Him, thereby
asserting that they can come to One whose greatness and
love they are unconscious of, and receive a blessing from
Him in an outward rite, even though they may not
be able to realize what they are receiving.

Then our Lord gives us a reason why children should be
brought, "Of such is the kingdom of God." And He says
again, that unless adult believers become conformed to
the image and likeness of little children, they cannot enter
into the kingdom of God. (Matt. xviii. 3.)

And He says this to such believers as His Apostles.
They who had already consciously accepted Him, were
told that a further conversion was necessary in their case ;
which conversion was that they should become like infants,
i.e. they must have the same mind to receive unhesitatingly
the deep mysteries of His kingdom (no matter how contrary to their prejudices and above their understanding)
as little children have to receive whatsoever is taught them
though they may not understand it at the time.

Our Lord then evidently considers infants to be in a
better spiritual position for receiving the grace of His
kingdom than such believing adults as the Apostles were
at that time.

In the next place, the religion of Jesus Christ was
then being spread and propagated amongst those who
were hearing of it for the first time. Such persons must
both receive the Gospel and be baptized as adults, because
when they were infants Christ's very name was unknown.

But this surely was not to be the *normal* state of things.
So far from this, the more rapidly Christianity spread in
any country, or among any people, the sooner must such a
state of things give way to one in which persons, instead

of hearing of Christ and believing in Him for the first time as adults, would, from their earliest years, hear of Him, and believe Him to be their Saviour.

I believe, then, that the New Testament was written not for the age of the Church in which the Gospel was preached to unbelievers, but for those many successive ages which have succeeded it, in which the children of the Church have been taught more or less of its truths from the earliest dawn of their consciousness.

When, then, the New Testament mentions frequently the baptism of adults, it does precisely what any other missionary record would do.

Such a record would naturally dwell upon remarkable cases of conversion, in which the steps that led to Baptism would be noticed rather than the Baptism itself.

The Book of the Acts of the Apostles is the only inspired record we have of the Church's earliest missionary work. The first notice of Baptism there is in the sermon of St. Peter on the day of Pentecost. "Repent, and be baptized every one of you . . . . for the promise is to you, and to your children." They were to be baptized BECAUSE *of the promise;* but the promise belonged to their children, as well as to them, consequently Baptism, the seal of the promise, would equally belong to their children. We may be quite sure that they, being Jews, would naturally consider that such a seal of promise as Baptism would belong to their children, for they had been educated in a religion of which the first principle was, that children must receive a seal of God's promises on their eighth day.

After the notice of the first Baptism on the day of Pentecost, very few instances of the actual administration of it are mentioned. Two of these, that of the Ethiopian eunuch and that of Cornelius, are recorded for a specific purpose, viz. to mark the development of God's design with respect to the conversion of the Gentiles; the sole reason for their Baptism being alluded to at all being, that they were baptized as Gentiles. In the case of two others, Lydia and the jailor at Philippi, the Baptism of their *households* is expressly mentioned.

But in addition to all this, it must ever be borne in mind that Christianity was by no means a new religion. Neither the ideas which it had to deal with, nor the language in which it expressed them, were new. Its germs, and far more than its germs, were contained in the system which it superseded. The God was the same, and His moral law was the same. There were the same ideas of atonement and sacrifice, only in the new Dispensation all centred in the Divine Antitype. The Incarnation, the One Sacrifice for all sin, the coming down of the Spirit, His work both in outward miracles and on the heart, were all foretold in very plain terms, in the book of the Old Covenant.

Even the two Sacraments, the especial badges of Christianity, were not new. The Lord's Supper was a part of the Paschal solemnity, sanctified by our Lord to higher purposes; and it had long been the practice, at the admission of a proselyte, to baptize both himself and all that belonged to him.

But it was a fundamental principle of the Old Covenant that children should be admitted to its privileges, and a rite was ordained for the purpose. This rite was superseded by another, Baptism, as the form of entrance into the grace of the New Covenant. This latter rite, then, would *naturally* be administered to infants, because those first converted were educated in the religious principle, that infancy, so far from being a disqualification, was *the* qualification for covenant blessings.

If there was to be a difference between the Old Cove-

nant and that which superseded it, with regard to what
was in the Old Covenant so fundamental a point, we should
certainly have heard of it. We should certainly have been
told, for instance, that in the three households, of the
Baptisms of which we have the record, there were no
children, or that the children in them had their Baptism
deferred.

We should have been told this, because the New Testament is written for those who are expected to be
acquainted with the principles of the Old, and amongst
them with the principle of infant membership. If Infant
Baptism be practised at all, it must, of necessity, soon
supersede, in a Christian community, the practice of
Adult Baptism. If, then, it be contrary to the will of
the Divine Founder that infants should be baptized, we
should certainly have been warned against it. For instance, there are three Epistles called the Pastoral Epistles,
full of principles and rules for the regulation of the Christian community. Some of these regulations are on what
we should call minor matters. In the First Epistle to
Timothy, the Apostle directs that a widow should not be
admitted into the number of those who were on the roll
of the Church's arms till she was threescore years old,
and till she had given evidence of Christian character.
(1 Tim. v. 9.)

Now, if the children of Christians were debarred from
receiving Baptism in unconscious infancy, and seeing that
they must be admitted into the Church at some time, we
should have expected some regulation respecting the age
and the amount of consciousness of Christian truth which
was indispensable in their case. Some such injunction
would be quite as needful as that respecting the admission
of widows to Church alms.

We should have expected some such rule as this: "Let

not a child be baptized till he is of such an age; till he
has had such and such instruction; till he has shown that
he has profited under it by genuine signs of conversion."
If, then, the Baptism of Infants be contrary to Christ's
will, the omission of all warning against so universal a
custom—a custom which so rapidly and so naturally
superseded Adult Baptism—is inconceivable.

I have made these observations on infants being the
primary and most suitable subjects for Baptism, not so
much for the sake of those who deny Infant Baptism, as
of those who profess to hold it; for if the New Testament
contemplates the Baptism of infants, it unquestionably
contemplates their Regeneration in that Baptism; that, in
fact, Baptism is to them what Christ ordained it for—the
communication of Himself as the Second Adam.

It is one thing to baptize children, and another to
believe that God there and then makes them partakers of
the life-giving nature of the Second Adam. The doubt
continually occurs, Does not their want of consciousness,
which, of course, hinders them from exercising repentance,
prevent us from pronouncing with certainty that they are
there and then engrafted into Christ?

One consideration will, I think, if duly realized, for
ever set this doubt at rest; for it will convince us that
it is both reasonable, and in accordance with the mercy
and grace of God, that unconscious infants should be in
Baptism made partakers of the Second Adam. It is this.
In what condition are infants made partakers of the
nature of the old Adam? They are made partakers of
his deadly nature in a state of perfect unconsciousness.
When they can commit no actual sin—for they are in
the mere germ of existence—they are made partakers of
Adam's nature of sin and death.

If, then, God has provided a Second Adam (which,

ly Name, He has done), why should not
state of unconsciousness receive in Bap-
this Second Adam, in order to counteract
ew the nature, which they have helplessly
and un........ received from the first Adam?

"Regeneration," as has been well said, "is the correlative and opposite to original sin. As original sin is the
transmission of a quality of evil, so regeneration is the
infusion of a quality of good; as original sin is inherited
without the personal act of us who are born of the flesh,
so regeneration is bestowed without personal merit in us
who are born of the Spirit; as in the inheritance of original
sin we are passive and unconscious, so in regeneration,
when we are baptized as infants, we as passively and as
unconsciously receive a new nature.[1]   If it were not so,
Christ would not be AN ADAM, a Head of a race in the sense
that the first Adam was; for the first Adam transmits his
nature to all unconscious infants, who are born into him.
Seeing, then, that the Second Adam is not a man only, but
THE GOD-MAN, and remembering what He has said about
infants, can we dare to make unconsciousness any bar to
the reception of His nature through the means which He
has appointed?

But this most important view will require further consideration, though I may have to repeat some truths I
have before stated.

When our Lord rebuked His Apostles because they
supposed that unconsciousness in infancy was a bar to
the reception of blessing from Him, He said of infants,
"Of such is the kingdom of God." [2]

[1] "The gift of Baptism, which hath been granted against original
sin, that what by our generation hath been drawn to us, by our
regeneration may be taken away from us."—AUGUSTINE, *Enchi-
ridian*, sec. 17.

[2] "We can hardly read our Lord's solemn saying, without seeing

What is this kingdom of God?

It is not a mere system of doctrine, or a religion. It is a heavenly, spiritual state of things, instituted by our Saviour for the purpose of counteracting a carnal, sinful state of things, introduced into the world by the sin of the first Adam.

This carnal, sinful state of things has its roots in that mysterious transmission of sin from father to son, whereby, in the words of the Apostle, " we are, by nature, children of wrath."

Here, then, is a kingdom of sin and death, into which every man is introduced by his natural birth.

He is brought into the world with a prospect of never-ending existence before him, and the world into which he is brought is a state of trial, on his right or wrong use of which the happiness or misery of his eternity depends.

But he is brought into this state with a seed of evil

---

that it reaches further than the mere then present occasion. It might one day become a question whether the New Christian Covenant of repentance and faith could take in the unconscious infant, as the Old Covenant did,—whether, when Jesus was no longer on earth, little children might be brought to Him, dedicated to His service, and made partakers of His blessing? Nay, in the pride of the human intellect, this question was sure one day to be raised, and our Lord furnishes the Church, by anticipation, with an answer to it for all ages. Not only may the little infants be brought to Him, but in order for us who are mature to come to Him, we must cast away all that wherein our maturity has caused us to differ from them, and *become* LIKE THEM. Not only is Infant Baptism justified, but it is (abstractedly considered,—not as to the preparation for it, which from the nature of the case must be exceptional) the NORMAL PATTERN OF ALL BAPTISM; none can enter God's kingdom, except *as an infant*. In Adult Baptism, the exceptional case, we strive to secure that state of simplicity and childlikeness, which in the infant we have ready and undoubted to our hands."—DEAN ALFORD on Mark x. 14.

within him which makes the trial unequal; for it is a strong innate propensity to sin, a natural aversion to God and holiness in the heart's core of the unconscious infant, as the latent seeds of hereditary disease may be in his body.

If uncounteracted by divine grace, this latent evil will grow with his growth, and expand as the faculties of his soul expand; and when he comes out into the world, it will there find the appropriate sphere of its development. Whatever position he occupies in the world, whether high or low, rich or poor, it matters not, he will have continually presented to him those lusts of the flesh, those lusts of the eye, and that pride of life, which will tend to alienate him still more from God, till he passes into eternity, having spent his time of probation in strengthening that evil principle which he had received at his entrance into it.

Such would have been the state of all mankind without exception, had not God mercifully interposed.

By this interposition a Second Adam was provided to be to us for life, righteousness, and salvation, what the first Adam had been for sin, death, and condemnation.

The new state of things introduced by this Second Adam to counteract and destroy the power of sin and death, is called "the kingdom of God;" and the Word made flesh, the Head of this spiritual kingdom, asserted the right of infants to a part in it when He said, "Of such is the kingdom of God."

By so saying He pronounced that they were fit subjects of that kingdom of grace which He had come upon earth to establish.

But He had before decreed that there should be but one entrance into this kingdom of grace: "Except a man be born of water and of the Spirit, he cannot enter into the kingdom of God." If then, owing to any cause, each infant is not, when baptized, grafted into the Second Adam, the kingdom of God's dear Son would, in the conveyance of its good things, fall far short of the kingdom of sin and death in the conveyance of its curse. It would fall short in the case of the very beings whom Christ had pronounced best fitted to be its subjects. Unless at Baptism all infants can be grafted into Christ, it cannot be said that in Christ's dispensation "where sin abounded grace does much more abound;" for where *original* sin abounds, regenerating grace falls short. In the kingdom of God's dear Son there would be no transmission of grace to coincide with and counteract the transmission of original sin, which every infant receives at his entrance into the kingdom of evil. The Second Adam, in the transmission of His new and better nature, would fall short of the first Adam in the transmission of his sin; for whereas the first Adam transmits his nature to all brought into *his* kingdom, the Second (unless Baptism be regeneration to *all* infants) would not transmit His better nature to all brought into His.[1]

Now this cannot be, for the first kingdom of sin and death had for its source of evil a mere man, in no respect above the sinful beings derived from him; whereas the new and better state of things has for its Head one equal in dignity to God, being the Incarnate Word, God manifest in the flesh.

---

[1] "It is all the reason of the world that since the grace of Christ is as large as the prevarication of Adam, all they who are made guilty by the first Adam should be cleansed by the Second. But as they are guilty by another man's act, so they should be brought to the font to be purified by others: there being the same proportion of reason that by others' act they should be relieved, who were in danger of perishing by the act of others."—JEREMY TAYLOR, *Liberty of Prophesying*, p. 541. Eden's Edition.

F

On this account we should expect, in the kingdom brought in by Him, an overflowing of grace.

We cannot imagine that the laws of the kingdom of God's dear Son would, in the conveyance of its good things, be outdone by the laws of the kingdom of darkness, in the conveyance of its curse.

We see, then, in the true view of Infant Baptism, its true defence ; nay, rather, its necessity.

If it be only a significant rite, typifying certain benefits, but not the instrument of their conveyance, it had better surely be postponed till the child, the person most interested in the ceremony, be capable of entering into its meaning ; but if it be the means of union with Christ the Second Adam, in order to destroy the baneful effects of his union with the first Adam, the sooner he is made partaker of such a benefit the better.

NOTE.—It is not my purpose, in this book, to examine the testimony of the Fathers and later ecclesiastical writers to the regeneration of infants in Holy Baptism.

As, however, attempts are made to prove that infant Baptism is not primitive, it may be well to show how some of the earliest writers regard it as a matter of course that in their day infants should receive the laver of regeneration : besides, if the principles set forth in the preceding chapter are right, they are likely to have been embodied from the first in the practice of the Church.

Here it may be well to remind the reader that the silence of an author is no argument against the existence of a practice in his day ; and the more common and the more a matter of course any practice is, the less likely is it to be noticed.

It would be very suspicious if we found in every writer of a small book an allusion to every doctrine or practice of Christianity.

It will be only needful to cite some few of the earlier writers of whose works any *considerable* remains have come down to us. About the testimony of later writers, such as St. Augustine (A.D. 380—430), there can be no difference of opinion, as the reader will see by referring to the extracts from his voluminous writings in Appendix C at the end of this volume.

Again, when we go back to the age of Cyprian (150 years earlier than Augustine), we can be in no doubt as to the universal practice of infant Baptism in his days, seeing that under his presidency a council of bishops was held in Carthage, in which it was debated whether a child should be baptized before his eighth day (that being the day appointed for circumcision), and (on the broad ground that Christ had come to seek and save the lost) it was decided that a child might be baptized as soon as born. Cyprian's words in declaring the decree of the council are : " But as to the case of infants : whereas you judge that they must not be baptized within two or three days after they were born, and that the rule of circumcision is to be observed ; so that none should be baptized or sanctified before the eighth day after he is born, we were all in our assembly of the contrary opinion. For as to what you thought fitting to be done, there was not one that was of your mind, but all of us, on the contrary, judged that the grace and mercy of God was to be denied to no one that is born. For whereas, our Lord in His Gospel says : ' The Son of Man came not to destroy men's lives, but to save them,' as far as lies in us, no soul, if possible, is to be lost." (Quoted in Cotton's Edition of Wall, vol. i. p. 129.) And again (next page) : " Unless you will think that the grace itself which is given to baptized persons is greater or less according to the age of those who receive it ; whereas the Holy Ghost is given, not by different measures, but with fatherly affection and kindness equal to all."

There are four writers of a date previous to this, who allude to the Baptism of infants :—

Irenæus (A.D. 167) writes : "He (Christ) came to save all persons by Himself : all, I mean, who by Him are regenerated unto God ; infants and little ones, and children and youths, and elder persons." When we consider how uniformly the Fathers of that age, not only connect, but, as it were, identify, regeneration with Baptism, there can be no doubt that Irenæus means here "regenerated in Baptism." An instance of such connexion or identification I have given in the quotation from this Father in the note at the end of Chapter III.

Clement of Alexandria (A.D. 192) alludes to "children lifted, or taken out, of the water" (Pædagog. lib. iii. c. 2), in a passage which is inexplicable except it be taken as referring to their being "taken out" of the font. (Cotton's Wall, 84.)

Origen (A.D. 210) distinctly recognises it in the passage I have quoted in page 53. Also in Homily viii. on Leviticus, c. 4: "Besides all this, let it be considered what is the reason that whereas the Baptism of the Church is given for forgiveness of sins, infants also are by the usage of the Church baptized, when, if there were nothing in infants that wanted forgiveness and mercy, the grace of Baptism would be needless to them." (Wall, page 104.) Also in Origen's Homily on the Romans: "For this also it was that the Church had from the Apostles a tradition (or order) to give Baptism to infants." (Wall, "History of Ancient Baptism," vol. i. p. 106, Cotton's Edition.)

I have reserved to the last the testimony of Tertullian (A.D. 210), because, though it is exceedingly decisive in favour of the fact that infant Baptism prevailed in his time, yet still an inference has been drawn from it exactly the opposite to that which sound criticism appears to me to warrant. The principal passage is from his treatise on Baptism, xviii. (page 277, Oxford translation): " Wherefore the delaying of Baptism is more profitable according to the condition and disposition, and moreover the age of each person, but especially in the case of children. For why is it necessary, if the thing be not so necessary, that the sponsors also be brought into danger ? for both they themselves may, from their mortal nature, fail of their promises, and they may be disappointed by the growing up of a bad disposition. The Lord, indeed, said, ' Let them come unto Me.' Let them come, then, when they are of riper years. . . . *With no less reason unmarried persons should also be put off*, within whom temptation is already prepared, as well in virgins by reason of their ripe age, as in widows by reason of their wandering about (or widowhood), until they either marry or be confirmed in continency. They that understand the weighty nature of Baptism will fear its attainment rather than its postponement."

It is as clear as possible from the above extract that infants were commonly baptized in Tertullian's time : he in part disapproves of it, and would rather have delay ; but on what ground does he recommend delay ? On the ground of the exceeding danger of post-baptismal sin, and the difficulty of obtaining forgiveness for it ; for, let the reader observe that Tertullian recommends the postponement of Baptism, not only in the case of infants, but in that of unmarried persons.

There can be no doubt whatever but that we have in this passage indications of the beginning, at least, of the prevalence of that most pernicious opinion that sin after Baptism is next to unpardonable, and consequently that the later the period of life to which Baptism is deferred the safer for the baptized person.

That this is the reason for the recommendation of delay is clear from this, that not infants alone, but all unmarried persons, are to have their Baptism delayed till "they either marry or be confirmed in continency."

They, then, who affirm that we have here an indication that infant Baptism had not yet been fully accepted by the Church are altogether, it seems to me, mistaken in their inference, for the same reasoning necessarily requires us to believe that unmarried persons were not then, in the eyes of the Church, accounted as safe and proper recipients of Baptism.

Such a passage is not an indication that a post-apostolic practice was getting slowly established, but rather that a very decidedly post-apostolic and pernicious opinion, tending to narrow the efficacy of the forgiving grace of God, was gaining ground. An opinion, be it remembered, of which the natural result is to make men defer their Baptism ; for if there be but one perfect cleansing, it seems only natural to defer it till there can be little or no risk of further pollution.

CHAPTER V.

THE OLD TESTAMENT ANTICIPATES THE SACRAMENTAL
TEACHING OF THE APOSTLES.

IF what I have said respecting the grace conferred by
God in Baptism be in accordance with His word, so that
each member of the Church has been, at his Baptism into
it, in some sort made a partaker of Christ, we should
naturally expect that this will be assumed in the teaching
by which he is to be nourished to life eternal.

Such we find to be the language universally adopted by
the inspired writers. The baptized Christian, whether he
be a nominal or a true believer, is always spoken of as
having already received grace for the improvement of
which he is answerable, and in a position which he has
not to acquire, but to maintain. The Old Testament, the
Bible of the preparatory dispensation, ever addresses the
whole circumcised nation as in *real* covenant relationship
with God ; and the New Testament, in dealing with the
Church with which *it* has to do, adopts a mode of speaking
answering in all respects to that of the Old, without any
limitation or qualification whatsoever.

Let us begin with the Old Testament. It is almost
exclusively occupied with the history of God's dealings
with one nation. For above a thousand years God was
continually manifesting Himself to them, and interfering
with the natural order of things for their benefit. And,
all through their course, God, by His prophets, spoke both
of them and *to* them, as persons whom He had loved, and

chosen, and brought into a state of nearness to Himself, such as was enjoyed by no other people.

When they were in bondage in Egypt, God said to Pharaoh, "Israel is *My son, My firstborn:* and I say unto thee, Let My son go, that he may serve Me : and if thou refuse to let him go, I will slay thy son, even thy firstborn." (Exod. iv. 22.) Here God speaks of the whole nation collectively, as His children. Similarly, in Deut. xiv. : "Ye are the *children* of the Lord your God ;" and in Deut. xxxii. 19,—" And when the Lord saw it, He abhorred them, because of the provoking of *His sons* and of *His daughters*."

Again, in Isaiah He speaks of the whole nation, when He says, " I have nourished and brought up *children*, and they have rebelled against Me." (Isa. i. 2.)

In what sense were the children of Israel thus called " God's children " ?

Evidently in a much higher sense than that in which all the rest of human beings were at that time ; for the very words of all these passages imply that God had made them His children in a sense in which no other people were. And yet the children of Israel were certainly not, as a body, God's children in that higher and better sense implied by our Lord in the Sermon on the Mount, where He says, " Love your enemies ; bless them that curse you ; . . . . that ye *may* be the children of your Father which is in heaven."

They were certainly not God's children in the sense of loving, fearing, and obeying God ; or God would not have complained of "the *provoking* of His sons and of His daughters," nor that " He had nourished and brought up *children*, and they had *rebelled* against Him." [1]

In what way, then, were the nation, the majority of

[1] For further instances, see Appendix A, sec. 1.

whom were always rebellious, God's children, seeing that they were evidently His children in a higher sense than if they had only been made by Him, yet not in the still higher sense of bearing His image ?

St. Paul tells us that they were God's children by adoption. "My kinsmen *according to the flesh*, who are Israelites, to whom pertaineth the adoption." (Rom. ix. 3, 4.) Observe that in this passage St. Paul is not speaking of the spiritual Israel who accepted the Saviour, but of the great body, Israel after the flesh, who rejected Christ, and respecting such St. Paul expresses his great heaviness and continual sorrow of heart.

Again, the children of Israel were from first to last called God's *chosen*, i.e. elect people; thus Deut. xiv. 2 : "Thou art an *holy people* unto the Lord thy God; and the Lord hath *chosen* thee to be a *peculiar people* unto Himself, above all the nations that are upon the earth."

This is unquestionably the usual mode adopted by the inspired prophets of addressing their countrymen; and let the reader notice how invariably, in so doing, they addressed *all* the body, the circumcised nation, without distinction. Thus in Deut. xxxii. 9, in the midst of a context full of upbraiding and reproof for their having forgotten God, we have the words, "The Lord's portion is His people; Jacob is the lot of His inheritance."

Again, in 1 Sam. xii. 22 : "The Lord will not forsake *His people*, for His great Name's sake; because it hath pleased the Lord to make you His people." In what sense were the persons here spoken to the "people of God"? Were they the people of God in the sense of truly loving God and serving Him? So far from this, the chapter begins,—"And Samuel said unto *all* Israel." In this better sense, the "*all* Israel" of the time of Saul could not be the people of God; and yet in one most important sense (by no means to be ignored because it is not the highest) they assuredly were *all* the people of God.

Again, in the Book of Psalms (Ps. lxxxi. 11—13): "*My people* would not hearken to My voice; and Israel would none of Me. So I gave them up to their own hearts' lust, and they walked in their own counsels. Oh that *My people* had hearkened unto Me!"

Again, Isa. i. 3: "Israel doth not know, *My people* doth not consider."

Again, Jer. ii. 13: "*My people* have committed two evils; they have forsaken Me, the fountain of living waters, and have hewed them out cisterns, broken cisterns, that can hold no water." [1]

The whole point of these three appeals, it is obvious, consists in this, that the rebellion of the children of Israel was the more detestable in that it was the rebellion of the "people of God."

If the term "people of God," throughout the Old Testament, meant only the elect remnant,—the seven thousand men who bowed not the knee to Baal,—those, in fact, who had not forsaken God,—could such a mode of speaking to the body of the Israelites have been adopted?

But again, the inspired prophets upbraid the Israelites in terms which imply a still nearer relationship of the whole circumcised nation to God—viz. that of a wife to her husband.

Thus Jer. ii. 2: "Go and cry in the ears of Jerusalem, saying, Thus saith the Lord; I remember thee, the kindness of thy youth, the love of *thine espousals*, when thou wentest after Me in the wilderness."

[1] For further instances, see Appendix A, sec. 2.

And, above all, the sixteenth and twenty-third chapters of Ezekiel.

Ezek. xvi. 6—12, 14 : " And when I passed by thee, and saw thee polluted in thine own blood, I said unto thee when thou wast in thy blood, Live ; yea, I said unto thee when thou wast in thy blood, Live. I have caused thee to multiply as the bud of the field, and thou hast increased and waxen great, and thou art come to excellent ornaments : thy breasts are fashioned, and thine hair is grown, whereas thou wast naked and bare. Now when I passed by thee, and looked upon thee, behold, thy time was the time of love ; and I spread my skirt over thee, and covered thy nakedness : *yea, I sware unto thee, and entered into a covenant with thee*, saith the Lord God, *and thou becamest mine.* Then washed I thee with water . . . . I clothed thee with broidered work . . . . I decked thee with ornaments . . . . I put a jewel on thy forehead . . . . And thy renown went forth among the heathen for thy beauty : for it was perfect through my comeliness, which I had put upon thee, saith the Lord God."

Then the Almighty proceeds to upbraid the person thus loved and cherished for her wantonness and infidelity, and in the thirtieth verse accuses her, not of simple fornication, but of adultery : " How weak is thine heart, saith the Lord God, seeing thou doest all these things, the work of an imperious whorish woman, ... as a wife that committeth adultery, that taketh strangers instead of her husband :" and (ver. 38), " And I will judge thee, as women that break wedlock and shed blood are judged." [1]

In this remarkable passage the Jewish Church is judged . and condemned, not for simple fornication, but for *adultery.* Now, adultery is the sundering of the dearest of human

[1] For further instances, see Appendix A, sec. 3, *a, b, c.*

ties, and the closest of human relationships. By this, then, the closeness as well as reality of the relationship subsisting between God and the Jewish Church is implied, or the prophet would have spoken of *fornication only*, not adultery. Now this relationship must have been established by God between Himself and the whole visible body, for it was the visible Jewish Church as a whole which so departed from God as to call forth from the prophet the strong language I have cited.

Again, we find that God promises that He will dwell amongst the children of Israel ;—after this He tells them continually that He does dwell among them, notwithstanding all appearances to the contrary ; and that this His presence amongst them enhanced exceedingly the guilt of their repeated defection from Him.

They did not merely disobey a law or testament given in time past, but they disbelieved in, and made nought of *a real perpetual presence and indwelling*, whereby He made their temple His house and sanctuary, and their chief city "the city of the great King."

Exodus xv. 17 : "Thou shalt bring them in, and plant them in the mountain of Thine inheritance, *in the place, O Lord, which Thou hast made for Thee to dwell in ;* in the sanctuary, O Lord, which Thy hands have established."

Exodus xxv. 8 : "And let them make Me a sanctuary, *that I may dwell among them.*"

Exodus xxix. 45 : "And *I will dwell among the children of Israel,* and will be their God."

Numbers xxxv. 34 : "Defile not therefore the land which ye shall inhabit, *wherein I dwell : for I the Lord dwell among the children of Israel.*"

Deut. vi. 15 : "The Lord thy God is *a jealous God*

among you—lest the anger of the Lord thy God be kindled against thee."

1 Kings viii. 13 : "I have surely built Thee an *house to dwell in, a settled place for Thee to abide in for ever.*"

2 Kings i. 3 : "But the angel of the Lord said to Elijah the Tishbite, Arise, go up to meet the messengers of the king of Samaria, and say unto them, Is it not because there is not a God in Israel, that ye go to inquire of Baalzebub, the god of Ekron ? "

2 Chron. xxxvi. 15 : "And the Lord God of their fathers sent to them by His messengers, rising up betimes, and sending ; because He had compassion on His people, *and on His dwelling place.*"

Psalm lxxvi. 2 : "In Salem also is His tabernacle, *and His dwelling in Zion.*" [1]

Here is a presence of God amongst them, which continued all through the darkest parts of their chequered and eventful history. It was a real presence, though an unseen one ; for it continued through long ages, when there appears to have been no Shechinah, or visible glory above the mercy-seat. It was a presence which did not overbear the moral nature and responsibility of those amongst whom it had established itself. It did not compel them to be good and righteous. God was verily and indeed amongst the people of Israel, and yet after such a sort that they could disbelieve in, and even insult, His presence. Once He was, as it were, seen to take possession of His sanctuary. The house was filled with His glory, so that the priests could not abide in it ; but this was only once—for centuries afterwards His presence had to be realized by faith.

In remarkable accordance with this, we find that when God denounces the severest judgments against the children

---

[1] For further instances, see Appendix A, sec. 4.

of Israel and Judah, as harlots, who had broken their marriage vows with Him, the name that He gives to Judah is "Aholibah"—"*My tabernacle in her.*" (Ezekiel xxiii, 4.)

Again, because of this dwelling of God among them, the whole nation of Israel are "holy." Deut. vii. 6 : "Thou art *an holy people unto the Lord thy God :* the Lord thy God hath chosen thee to be a special people to Himself above all people that are upon the face of the earth." We have the same words in Deut. xiv. 2, 21.

In what sense were the children of Israel all of them "holy?" Certainly not in the highest sense of having their hearts cleansed from sinful lusts. These very people who are in some places called "holy to the Lord," are in other places called "stiffnecked, and uncircumcised in heart and ears." They could only be "holy" or "saints" in the sense of "*dedicated to God,*" "*separated,*" "*set apart*" *for His service:* whether they truly and faithfully served Him being quite another matter. Let the reader also observe that this signification of "holy" as "*dedicated,*" "*separated,*" "*set apart,*" is almost the only meaning which this word and the kindred verb "sanctify" has throughout the Old Testament. It first occurs in Genesis ii. 3, where it evidently signifies simply "separation," or "dedication :" —"And God blessed the seventh day, *and sanctified it.*" So we find that throughout the books of Exodus, Leviticus, and Numbers, the terms "sanctify," "hallow," "holy," are applied to the vessels of the tabernacle,—to the flesh of the sacrifices,—to everything, in fact, rational or irrational, set apart to the worship of God. Above all, we find these terms applied to the priests, Aaron and his sons, without the remotest reference to their internal purity of heart. Thus, Exodus xxix. 37, 43 : "Seven days shalt thou make an atonement for the altar, and sanctify it, and it shall be an altar most holy : whatsoever touches the altar shall be holy." (Compare Matthew xxiii. 17, 19 : "The altar which sanctifieth the gift.") "And there will I meet the children of Israel, and the *tabernacle shall be sanctified by My glory*. And I will *sanctify* the tabernacle of the congregation and the altar. I will *sanctify* also both Aaron and his sons, to minister to Me in the Priests' office." [1]

Again, the whole circumcised nation are addressed as redeemed, purchased, saved.

Exodus xv. 13,—"Thou in Thy mercy hast led forth *the people which Thou hast redeemed :* " 16,—"till the people pass over *which Thou hast purchased*." Deut. ix. 26,— "O Lord God, destroy not Thy people, and Thine inheritance *which Thou hast redeemed :* " xxxii. 6, 9,—"Do ye thus requite the Lord, O foolish people and unwise ? is He not thy Father that hath *bought* thee ? . . . For the *Lord's portion* is His people ; Israel is the *lot of His inheritance ;* " xxxiii. 29,—"Happy art thou, O Israel : who is like unto thee, *O people saved by the Lord !* " [2]

No terms can be applied more absolutely to the whole nation than these, and yet this goodness and grace was not in such sense theirs that it could not be forfeited, for God says, Psalm cvi. 40,—"Therefore was the wrath of the Lord kindled against *His people*, insomuch that He abhorred *His own inheritance*." Isaiah xlvii. 6,—"I was wroth with My people, *I have polluted Mine inheritance*." Jeremiah xii. 7,—"I have forsaken Mine house, *I have left Mine Heritage ;* I have given the *dearly beloved of My soul* into the hand of her enemies."

Again, the whole circumcised nation are *chosen* by God. They are His "called," His "elect."

[1] For further instances, see Appendix A, sec. 5.
[2] For further instances, see Appendix A, sec. 6.

Deut. vii. 7, 8,—"The Lord did not set His love upon you *and choose you,* because ye were more in number than any people ; . . . but because the Lord loved you, and because He would keep the oath which He had sworn unto your fathers : " x. 15,—"Only the Lord had a delight in thy fathers to love them, and *He chose their seed after them, even you above all people,* as it is this day." [1]

But though thus chosen, their whole history shows that they were not so elected that they could not fall away. They had to " continue in God's goodness," and this they failed to do.

In no case do we find that the election is limited to the godly amongst them. Nowhere have we the least hint that all these great things, all these words of grace, are said of an invisible few.

Let the reader observe also how God's election of His people is in one sense unconditional, in another conditional. It is unconditional, because God chose them *in their fathers,* not for their foreseen righteousness or goodness, but of His mere love and mercy : and yet their election was conditional, for they had to " continue in God's goodness," to " abide in His love." (Rom. xi. 22 ; John xv. 1—10.) " Ye have seen what I did unto the Egyptians, and how I bare you on eagles' wings, and brought you unto Myself. Now therefore, *if ye will obey* My voice indeed, and keep My covenant," (*i.e.* in New Testament language, " If ye make your calling and election sure," 2 Pet. i. 10,) " then ye shall be to Me a kingdom of priests and an holy nation." (Exod. xix. 4, 5.) Again, Deut. xxviii. 9,—"The Lord shall establish thee an holy people unto Himself, as He hath sworn unto thee, if thou shalt keep the commandments of the Lord thy God." This place is very remarkable, for the children of Israel are in other places said to be holy, an

[1] See Appendix A, sec. 7.

holy people to the Lord, and yet here God promises if they obey Him, *to establish them* as such. They were already His people, but still in such a sense as to be *on their trial.*

Let me now draw the reader's attention to three similitudes, showing, in a way which no other language can reach, the love that God had to this nation, the care that He took of them, and the exceeding closeness wherewith He had bound them to Himself.

In Deut. xxxii. 9—12, under the figure of a bird tending her young, God reveals the tender and affectionate solicitude He had for His people Israel. "The Lord's portion is His people; Israel is the lot of His inheritance. He found him in a desert land, and in the waste howling wilderness; He led him about, He instructed him, He kept him as the apple of His eye. *As an eagle stirreth up her nest, and fluttereth over her young, spreadeth abroad her wings, taketh them, beareth them on her wings: so the Lord alone did lead him.*" And yet this care and love was in a measure lost on the ungrateful people, for we read, a few verses further, respecting this very people, "He forsook God that made him, and lightly esteemed the rock of his salvation."

Again, on account of the exceeding care which He had bestowed upon them in order that they might bring forth fruits of righteousness, God speaks of them, in Isaiah v. 1—7, as His vineyard, fenced, cleared of stones, planted with the choicest vine. He asks, " What could have been done more for My vineyard that I have not done in it? Wherefore, when I looked that it should bring forth grapes, brought it forth wild grapes? The vineyard of the Lord of Hosts is the house of Israel, and the men of Judah His pleasant plant: and He looked for judgment, but behold oppression; for righteousness, but behold a cry."

Again, under the similitude of a girdle, which He commanded Jeremiah to put round his loins, and afterwards to hide by Euphrates till it was "marred," God teaches us how very closely He had bound the children of Israel to Himself, and His intention in having done so. Jeremiah xiii. 11,—"As the girdle cleaveth to the loins of a man, *so have I caused to cleave unto Me the whole house of Israel*, that they might be to Me *for a people*, and *for a name*, and *for a praise*, and *for a glory :* but they would not hear."

But it may be said that in these expressions of His love and care, God had, after all, some secret reservation. It may be said that He really intended His goodness to reach some only, not all who were called by His name.

Such an idea cannot be reconciled with His expressed wish and desire in Deut. v. 29,—" O that there were such an heart in them, that they would fear Me, and keep all My commandments alway, that it might be well with them." Again, in Deut. xxxii. 29,—"O that they were wise, that they understood this." Again, in Psalm lxxxi. 13,— "Oh that My people had hearkened unto Me, and Israel had walked in My ways ! "

It is a depth of infinite mystery that God should allow human beings to repel His love, and frustrate the intentions of His mercy ; that they should, in the words of His Son, be suffered to reject the counsel of God against themselves ; but if we are to take His word in its plain sense, it is so.

What mean the tears of the Saviour over Jerusalem ? "If thou hadst known, even thou, at least in this thy day, the things which belong to thy peace." " How often *would* I have gathered thy children together, as a hen gathereth her chickens under her wings, and ye *would* not."

From all these passages one cannot fail to observe how uniformly God spake to the Church of the Old Testament.

G

No matter what the period of their history, and no matter what their character as a nation, in the brightest as well as in the darkest times, He inspired the prophets to address them as His children, His people, His chosen, His bride.

It is quite conceivable that the Holy Spirit might have inspired the prophets carefully to restrict such terms of love and honour, as God's people, chosen, &c. to those amongst the Jews who responded to God's call and love, and walked in His truth.

But the mode of address actually adopted is not so. They are told by the prophets that because they actually *are God's people*, therefore their sin is the greater, and their need of repentance the more urgent.

That the majority of them had fallen into idolatry did not disannul the fact that they had been once made God's people.

But how did they become God's people ? how did the men of each successive generation enter into the bonds and obligations of God's covenant ? By circumcision, administered to each one on his eighth day ; for so God ordained at the beginning when He chose them in their forefather. "Thou shalt keep My covenant therefore, thou and thy seed after thee in their generations. . . . Every man-child among you shall be circumcised. . . . He that is eight days old shall be circumcised among you, ... and My covenant shall be in your flesh for an everlasting covenant." (Gen. xvii. 9, 10, 12, 13.)

And this continued in force to the end. When the dispensation, as a way of access to God, was broken up, St. Paul witnessed respecting circumcision, "I testify to every man that is circumcised, that he is a debtor to keep the whole law." (Gal. v. 3.)

CHAPTER VI.

THE APOSTLES HOLD ALL BAPTIZED CHRISTIANS TO BE MEMBERS OF CHRIST.

SECTION I.

EXAMINATION OF THE FIRST EPISTLE TO THE CORINTHIANS.

THE dispensation, the privileges of which we have been considering, was temporary. It was to pass away when He came to Whom all its types bare witness, and in Whom they were all fulfilled.

In the fulness of time, Jesus Christ, the promised Seed, the Second Adam, was revealed. He came to introduce a new state of things—the kingdom of God. He came, not merely to found a religion, or to make an atonement, but to establish a kingdom, of which He was to be the King.

And it was to be more than a mere kingdom. It was to be THE CHURCH, a company of men believing in Him, and baptized into His body. And these persons, so blessed, were not merely to be under Him as their King, or instructed by Him as their Prophet, or reconciled through Him as their Priest ; but, over and above all these things, they were to be supernaturally joined to Him by a union so intimate, so close, that it could only be illustrated by the union which subsists between the limbs of a human body and its head, and between a vine and the branches which form part of it.

G 2

Now He, the King of this new kingdom, the Head of this new body, was no other than God's Only-Begotten Son. To set up this new kingdom, the most stupendous miracle was wrought that the universe had ever seen. God became man, without ceasing to be God. The manhood was taken into God.

What, then, must be the nature of the new kingdom which Christ introduced? If we had only known the fact that He, the Son of God, had founded it, we should have said that it must be a state of unmixed good; that it must be paradise on earth; that nothing which defileth can possibly enter into it. I think that if we had lived before the times of Christianity, and had realized that the Eternal Son of God was to become incarnate, in order to inaugurate a new kingdom, we should have said, that such a Saviour must introduce a sinless state of things, a perfect Church. But from the lips of the great Head Himself we have intimations of what the real state of His Church will be; and how contrary are they to what we should have expected! Instead of being a state of unmixed righteousness, it is a field sown with mingled wheat and tares: "The kingdom of heaven is like unto a man which sowed good seed in his field; but while men slept, his enemy came and sowed tares among the wheat, and went his way," &c. (Matt. xiii. 24, 25.)

Again, He compares it in the same chapter to a net cast into the sea, and gathering of every kind, good and bad, which were not to be finally separated till the end of the world. And, lest it should be said that all these are descriptions of a merely external state of things, an outward and visible Church only, He uses another figure or parable, asserting the same mixed state of things of the Church, *considered as His mystical body:* "I am the true Vine, and my Father is the Husbandman. Every branch *in Me* that beareth not fruit He taketh away. If a man abide not in Me, he is cast forth as a branch, and is withered," &c. (John xv. 1—6.)

In due time this Church was founded, and then faith and holiness, such as the world had never seen before, began to grow and flourish in the earth. The Holy Ghost was poured forth, and men were gathered into the fellowship of Christ's body.

But no sooner had the Church gained a footing in the world, than the view of it given by our Lord Himself was seen to be the true one; there were tares mingled with the wheat; the net inclosed fish of all sorts; the vine had branches, some fruit-bearing, some barren, and some withering. And this, not in times of prosperity and comparative quiet, but in times of persecution.

The proof of this is to be found in the Apostolical Epistles, especially in those of St. Paul.

From his Epistles we gain a far deeper insight into the actual state and character of the early Church, than we do from any other parts of the New Testament, for several of these were written to Churches which he himself had planted and watched over; such were the two Epistles to the Corinthians, and those to the Galatians, Ephesians, Philippians, and Thessalonians.

I would ask the reader to give his most earnest and prayerful attention to the evidence which I shall now bring forward of the way in which the Apostle addresses the subjects of Christ's kingdom, the members of the several Churches to which he wrote his letters.

He addresses them *all* as in a *real* state of grace, as all partakers of the Holy Spirit, and baptized *by Him* into Christ's body—not into a mere outward society, but into His *mystical body*. He upbraids some of them with actually committing, and warns all of them against committing, very gross and deadly sins.

And he makes the sinfulness of those amongst them who thus sinned, enhanced by the fact of their being *really* and *truly* in the state of grace in which he assumed them to be. He, in fact, addresses Christians exactly in the same way in which, as we have seen, the inspired prophets addressed Jews ; with this difference, that, whilst the Jewish prophets assumed that the evil Jews were the large majority of the Jewish Church, the Apostle assumes (except, perhaps, in the case of the Corinthian and Galatian Churches) that the evil were, at present, the minority. Still, the mode of speaking adopted in both cases is exactly similar.

The prophets upbraided the majority of the Israelites, because that, after God had made them His people, they revolted from Him. The Apostle tells the minority (as we charitably hope) of wilful sinners amongst the Corinthians, that by their sins they wounded Christ the more deeply, because they had been grafted into His body.

For the proof of this let us first examine one of the longer Epistles, and we will take the First Epistle to the Corinthians, one in which the Apostle enters most fully into the character and circumstances of his converts.

He addresses it to the " Church of God which is at Corinth," those who are " sanctified in Christ Jesus, called to be saints." [1] And all through the Epistle he addresses all the members of this Church as in one and the same state of grace. The following are instances :—

" Of Him," *i.e.* God, " are ye in Christ Jesus." (1 Cor. i. 30.)

" Ye are God's husbandry," 1 Cor. iii. 9, (compare our Lord's parable of " The field," Matt. xiii. 24,) " ye are God's building " (comp. Ephes. ii. 21, 22). " Know ye not that ye

---

[1] For apostolic meaning of word "*saints*," see Chapter VIII.

are the temple of God, and that the Spirit of God dwelleth in you ? If any man defile the temple of God, him shall God destroy ; for the temple of God is holy, which temple ye are." (1 Cor. iii. 16, 17.)

In chap. v. 12, he speaks of those "within" and those "without," meaning by the former the whole Church, and by the latter the heathen, and he counsels them to put out from among them (excommunicate) a certain very gross sinner.

In chap. vi. 11, "Ye are washed, ye are sanctified, ye are justified in the name of the Lord Jesus and by the Spirit of our God." Again, ver. 15, "Know ye not that your bodies are the members of Christ ?" Again, "Know ye not that your bodies[1] are the temples of the Holy Ghost ?" Again, "Ye are not your own ; ye are bought with a price."

Again, in chap. viii. 11, 12, he considers the weakest and most ignorant among them as so far a member of Christ, that sinning against him was sinning against Christ.

In the beginning of the tenth chapter, he insists on a very remarkable analogy between the Baptism of the whole body of the Corinthians into Christ, and that of the whole body of the Israelites into the dispensation of Moses, in the cloud and in the sea. This he does for the practical purpose of warning the Corinthian converts that the final benefit resulting from their election and their covenant privileges was, like that of the Israelites, conditional. Just as God had brought *all* the Israelites into a state of comparative liberty and salvation by the passage through the Red Sea, so had He brought all the Corinthians into a corresponding state of salvation at their Baptism ; but as the one miserably failed of obtaining the end of *their* deliverance, so must the other take heed lest

[1] The best reading is τὰ σώματι.

they fall after the same example of unbelief. (2 Cor. vi.
1 ; Heb. iii. iv. *passim ;* Jude 5.)

The point of comparison is between the *whole body* of
Israel, and the use they made of their common privileges,
in the one case ; and the *whole body* of the Church, and
the use or abuse of their common privileges, in the other.

As the passage of the Red Sea made all Israel partakers
of a common redemption from bondage, so Christian Baptism (or the parallel would not hold good) brought all the
Corinthians into a common state of grace in Christ.

In the twelfth chapter St. Paul speaks of the Church as
the body of Christ. He begins with noticing the great
variety of spiritual gifts in the Church, and, after enumerating some which were not general, he notices a work of
the Spirit *common to all.* " By one Spirit are we all baptized into one body "[1] (ver. 13) ; and after drawing a wonderful and beautiful analogy between the human body and
the mystical body of Christ, he concludes, " Now *ye* are
the body of Christ, and members in particular."

Such is the language of the Apostle to the whole body
of the Corinthian Church. Do such expressions imply
that all those to whom he wrote were walking worthy
of their calling ? So far from this, the whole Epistle is
full of reproof of them, not for shortcomings, or sins of
infirmity, but for gross and deadly sins.

" Ye are carnal : for whereas there is among you envying, and strife, and divisions, are ye not carnal, and walk
as men ?" (1 Cor. iii. 3.) And in the seventeenth verse,
to which I before alluded, he speaks of their defiling (or
destroying) the temple of God, " *which temple,*" he says,
" *ye are.*"

In the fifth chapter he speaks of their countenancing
very gross sin. " It is reported commonly that there is

[1] See note 2 in page 36.

fornication among you, and such fornication as is not so much as named among the Gentiles, that one should have his father's wife."

"Ye do wrong, and defraud, and that your brethren. Know ye not that the unrighteous shall not inherit the kingdom of God?" (1 Cor. vi. 8, 9.) Again, the whole of the latter part of chap. vi. is full of expressions implying that the Corinthian Christians were all of them members of Christ, and yet that some of them were actually falling into very deadly sins.

"Know ye not that your bodies are the members of Christ? shall I then take the members of Christ, and make them the members of an harlot? God forbid. . . .

What! know ye not that your bodies are the temple of the Holy Ghost which is in you, which ye have of God?" (1 Cor. vi. 15, 19.)

In the eighth chapter we find a statement showing the extremely imperfect spiritual state of some of these Corinthians, in that they were so weak in the faith as not yet to realize fully the nothingness of a heathen idol : "Howbeit there is not in every man that knowledge" (viz. of God the Father and of Jesus Christ) ; "for some" (*i.e.* some Christians) "with conscience of the idol unto this hour eat it as a thing offered unto an idol ; and their conscience being weak is defiled." And yet such brethren, though so miserably weak in spiritual perception, are, in the twelfth verse, identified by the Apostle with Christ : "When ye so sin against the brethren, and wound their weak conscience, ye sin against Christ."

In the tenth chapter the Apostle warns his converts by the example of the Israelites perishing in the wilderness through repeated sin, lest they also fall from Christ through idolatry, fornication, tempting Christ, and murmuring.

From the eleventh chapter we gather that some among them very grossly abused the Lord's Table.

From the fifteenth we gather that some (v. 12) denied the resurrection of the body; that on others (v. 32) the hopes of the Gospel had so little hold that they said with the heathen, "Let us eat and drink, for to-morrow we die;" and that others (v. 34) were in such a state of insensibility, that the Apostle had to arouse them with the words, "Awake to righteousness, and sin not, for some have not the knowledge of God: I speak this to your shame."

Before proceeding to examine the language of other Epistles, I would earnestly entreat the reader to notice two or three obvious deductions from the preceding.

First, then, let it be observed that St. Paul's mode of addressing nominal Christians exactly answers to the way in which the prophets treated nominal Jews. In both the one case and the other, the real communication of the privileges of the respective covenants was insisted on, to convince those under the covenant of their greater sin in not living to the covenant blessings and obligations.

The covenant blessing of which the Corinthian Christians had been made partakers, viz. an engrafting into Christ's body in Baptism, was an infinitely greater spiritual blessing than that received by the Jewish child at his circumcision; and yet, in one important respect, they answered to one another,—they laid the recipient, in each case, under obligations of which he could never divest himself, and which he might receive to his greater condemnation.

Then observe, what was St. Paul's fear respecting his converts. It was not lest any should deem themselves to be members of Christ when they were *not*, but lest those who had been *all* made members of Christ should fail to realize it. He casts not the shadow of a doubt on the reality of their engrafting into Christ ; on the contrary, he holds all responsible for grace, because all had been engrafted.

Now, it is quite conceivable that he might have spoken in very different terms to the nominal Christians among the Corinthians. He might have said to them : "By your divisions, and the unreproved fornication of some among you, and the idolatry of others, and by your scandalous profanation of the Lord's Table, and by your want of charity, and your vain-glorious display of spiritual gifts, and by your denial of such a fundamental article of the faith as the resurrection, you plainly prove that many among you are not the members of Christ, and never have been. By one Spirit ye have evidently *not* all been baptized into one body. Ye may have been baptized with water, but that has clearly never brought such as you into the body of Christ."

What a contrast do his actual words present ! We find no expressions of doubt or hesitation respecting the Corinthians having all received grace : "Know ye not, that your bodies are the temples of the Holy Ghost which is in you," "Ye are the body of Christ," &c.

The reader will observe, also, how impossible it is to suppose that the Apostle addressed his converts on some unreal hypothesis, or imaginary charitable assumption, that they were members of Christ, when in reality they were not ; for he intimates in all the expressions to which I have directed attention, that the sin of the Corinthians was immeasurably enhanced by the fact of their actually having been made members of Christ. The charitable assumption or hypothesis would have been to assume that they were, in reality, *not* in that state of grace which made their sin the more sinful.

When we hear of a person bearing a honourable name, and belonging to a noble family, disgracing himself, we charitably hope and assume (till we are made sure one way or another) that such a person is not a scion of the noble stock. When a person disgraces the Christian name, the *charitable* hypothesis would be to assume that such a person neither is, nor has been, in a state of grace, for the more he has received the more he is answerable for.

SECTION II.

EXAMINATION OF THE EPISTLES TO THE ROMANS AND THE COLOSSIANS.

THE same mode of speaking is adopted by St. Paul in two other of his Epistles, those to the Romans, and the Colossians.

In both these Epistles, the grace of union with the Second Adam is presented to us as a Burial and Resurrection with Christ. We are united to Him, not only as an Adam, but as a crucified, buried, and risen Adam. By having been engrafted into Him, we partake both of His Death and Resurrection ; so that the same Baptism which grafts us into Him, is the means by and in which we are buried and raised up again with Him.

In the fifth chapter of the Epistle to the Romans, the analogy between the two Adams, and the condemnation and justification they respectively confer, are drawn out at large.

In the twelfth verse, " As by one man sin entered into the world, and death by sin, and so death passed upon all men, for that (or, in whom) all have sinned." Then in the fifteenth, "If through the offence of one many be dead, much more the grace of God, and the gift by grace, which is by one man, Jesus Christ, hath abounded unto many." Then again, in the seventeenth verse, "If by one man's offence death reigned by one; much more they which receive abundance of grace, and of the gift of righteousness, shall reign in life by one, Jesus Christ." Again, in the eighteenth, "As by the offence of one judgment came upon all men to condemnation, so by the righteousness of one the free gift came upon all men to justification of life." Again, in the nineteenth, "As by one man's disobedience many were made sinners, so by the obedience of one shall many be made righteous."

In these verses, the death and condemnation derived from the first Adam are described as more than counter-balanced by the righteousness and life derived from the Second.

But then the question immediately occurs to the Apostle: Is not such a doctrine dangerous to the holiness of Christians?—if, where sin (under the first Adam) abounded, grace (under the Second Adam) does much more abound, may we not continue in sin, so that God's grace may be more magnified in our final acceptance ? [1]

---

[1] Augustine, in commenting on this passage, notices particularly the bearing of the doctrine of the fifth chapter on that of the sixth. (*Enchiridion de Fide, Spe, et Caritate*, Oxford Translation, p. 116.) His words are : "The Apostle says, 'Not as by one man sinning, so is the gift also, for the judgment, indeed, was of one unto condemnation, but the grace of many offences unto justification.' Because assuredly that one sin which is derived by way of descent, even if it be alone, makes men liable to condemnation: but the grace justifies from many offences the man who, beside that one which in common with all he hath derived by way of descent, hath added many of his own likewise. However, that which he says a little after, 'As by the offence of one upon all men unto condemnation,

No, he answers, such a thought must not be entertained
for a moment ; for the Second Adam, into whom we have
been baptized, was *crucified* for *sin*. He submitted to
death to expiate sin, and rid us of it, and shall we live
under the dominion of that evil thing which nailed Him
to the cross? We must not, for our Baptism was a
grafting into Christ, Who died for sin, and was buried for
sin, and rose again to apply to us the virtues of His death
and risen life, to the *destruction* of sin within us. Such is
the meaning of the wonderful words—"How shall we, who
are dead [or rather " who died "] to sin, live any longer
therein? Know ye not, that so many of us as were baptized into Jesus Christ were baptized into His death?
Therefore we are buried with Him by Baptism into death :

so by the righteousness of one upon all men unto justification of
life,' sufficiently shows that no one born of Adam is otherwise than
held under condemnation, and that no one is freed from condemnation
otherwise than by being born again in Christ."

" Of which punishment through one man, and grace through One
Man, having spoken as much as he judged sufficient for that part of
his epistle, next he commended the great mystery of Holy Baptism
in the Cross of Christ, in such manner as that we understand that
Baptism in Christ is none other than the likeness of the death of
Christ ; and that the death of Christ crucified is none other than
the likeness of the remission of sins : that, as in Him, true death
had place, so in us true remission of sin ; and as in Him true resurrection, so in us true justification. For he says, ' What shall we
say then? Shall we continue in sin, that grace may abound?' For
he had said above, ' For where sin abounded, grace did much more
abound.' "

The continuation of this remarkable passage, with its distinct
application to the case of infants, the reader will find in Appendix
C at the conclusion of this volume. It is the first of the quotations
from Augustine I have given there.

The reader will observe that Augustine holds the "death to sin "
in Baptism to consist in remission of past sin, not in the complete
internal mortification of sinful desires.

that like as Christ was raised up from the dead by the glory of the Father, even so we also should walk in new-ness of life." (Rom. vi. 1—4.)

Before proceeding further, let the reader observe :—

First, that the Apostle contemplates the Baptism of all the Roman Christians, without exception, to be a union with Christ, a grafting into Him as the Second Adam, a co-burial with Him in His burial, and a rising again with Him in His resurrection. He uses the most *inclusive* term, "So many of us as," and he appeals to it as an indisputable truth, "*Know ye not*, that so many of us as were baptized into Jesus Christ were baptized into His death ?"

Observe, also, that the words of the Apostle here exactly answer to his mode of speaking to the Corinthians, and have the same practical force.

Just as he says to the Corinthians, "Know ye not that your members are the members of Christ?" "By one Spirit are we all baptized into one body ;" "Ye are the body of Christ :" so he says to the Romans, "Know ye not, that so many of us as were baptized into Jesus Christ were baptized into His death ? . . . that we should walk in *newness* of *life*."

But a difficulty has always clung to this most important practical chapter, from a misconception concerning the "death to sin" mentioned at its commencement : "How shall we, who are dead to sin, live any longer therein ?" and in the eleventh verse, "Likewise reckon ye yourselves to be dead indeed unto sin, but alive unto God through Jesus Christ our Lord." Death is a state of perfect apathy. The dead corpse, or the dead limb, are alike in-sensible to pleasure or pain. And further, natural death is a thing that admits of no degrees ; a man must be either dead or alive.

Now, a moment's consideration will convince us that the *death to sin* to which the Apostle here alludes cannot be a state of apathy towards sin, for the Apostle warns those who were *dead to sin* (or had died to sin) against *falling into it.*

You cannot warn a dead man against a danger.

Yet the Apostle says,—" Reckon ye also yourselves to be dead indeed unto sin, but alive unto God through Jesus Christ our Lord." And to these persons *thus dead* he says in the next verse,—" Let not sin reign in your mortal body, that ye should obey it in the lusts thereof. Neither yield ye your members as instruments of unrighteousness unto sin : but yield yourselves unto God, as those that are alive from the dead." (Rom. vi. 11—13.)

Here, then, is a past death to sin in the very persons who are in danger of falling under its dominion, or who are, at least, liable to be seduced and overcome by it.

In what respect could it be a " death "? It was a *sacramental* death, a union with Christ in His death *to the intent* that by the virtue of His death and risen life (of which each baptized person had been made a partaker), the baptized man might effectually, and in very deed, mortify sin by denying it ; not at all *necessarily* implying that it had been already mortified in this latter sense, in each one of the baptized.[1]

---

[1] The view here taken is, in the main, that of one of the first (though by no means the best known) of the divines of the 17th century, Dean Jackson. (Works, vol. x. p. 334.)

" He (the Apostle) speaks not of such a death to sin as was peculiar to himself, or to some few, but of such a death as was common to all these Romans, and to every true member of the visible Church. He doth not suppose, nor was it imaginable, that all of them to whom he wrote were thus actually dead to sin, or that sin did not or could not reign in some of them ; at least, it may and doth to this day reign in many which have by Baptism been

Observe, then, how general the language of the Apostle is : " Likewise reckon ye also yourselves to be dead indeed unto sin, but alive unto God through Jesus Christ our Lord." And to what intent were they so to reckon themselves ?——" Let not sin *therefore* reign in your mortal body, that ye should obey it in the lusts thereof. Neither yield ye your members as instruments of unrighteousness unto sin : but yield yourselves unto God, as those that are alive from the dead, and your members as instruments of righteousness unto God." [1]

admitted into the visible Church ; whereas our Apostle's reason equally concerns all that are baptized. All and every one of them are in his sense and meaning in this place dead to sin; and yet are not all of them dead to sin, or sin dead to them, or in them, either by a natural or civil death."

And then, after showing that this death could not possibly be merely a promise and vow to forsake sin, he explains it to be their receiving in Baptism an antidote from God, by which the rage and poison of it might easily be assuaged or expelled. . . . "So we may say that any popular disease is quelled or taken away, after a sovereign remedy be found against it, which never fails, (if) so men will seek for it, seasonably apply it, and observe that diet which the physician upon the taking of it prescribes unto them."

[1] As I believe that our ability to apply this remarkable passage, as the Apostle did, to the furtherance of holiness amongst Christians, depends upon our rightly understanding the force of the term "dead to sin," which is its keynote ; and as its true meaning seems to be lost sight of by many of our leading commentators, I ask the reader's indulgence for appending here a note which I have given in another publication, entitled "Church Doctrine Bible Truth :"—

" In this sense Baptism is a 'death to sin' because it unites the baptized with Christ in His ' death to sin ;' and makes him partaker in Christ's risen life ; but whether sin is actually mortified in any particular baptized man, so that he loathes it, and is delivered altogether from its power, is another matter.

" The death to sin here, then, cannot mean a death to sin in the sense of sin being annihilated, or rendered powerless in the person

H

The more general, then, the application of the words, "Reckon yourselves dead," the more general the application of the precept of holiness which follows, "Let not sin therefore reign." If the words, "Reckon yourselves dead," spoken by the Apostle to all the Romans baptized into Jesus Christ, are limited in their application, or said hypothetically, so is also the precept of holiness, "Let not sin reign," limited in *its* application.

We see from this how exceedingly dangerous to men's souls it must be to absolve them from their Baptismal obligations, by throwing the faintest doubt on the reality of their Baptismal grace.

For the Baptismal obligation to holiness is the consequence of the grace received at Baptism; because so many of us as were baptized into Jesus Christ were buried with Him therein; *therefore*, as He was raised to a new and exalted life, the power of which has been vouchsafed to us in Baptism, so are we bound to walk in newness of life.

---

so dead, and for this reason, that a few verses further on St. Paul writes to these very persons who are thus asserted to be 'dead to sin' in Baptism, to exhort them 'not to let sin reign in their mortal bodies that they should obey it in the lusts thereof.' If sin were dead in them, or if they had *died to sin* in the sense of being effectually delivered from its presence and power, there would be no sense in writing to them to bid them not to suffer sin to *reign* in their mortal bodies, for in such a case sin, so far from *reigning*, would scarcely be *felt* in them.

" The whole context of the passage shows that the persons thus addressed as 'dead' were dead *sacramentally* only [in Baptism], and not dead to sin in heart and affections, or they would have needed no exhortations of the sort contained in this chapter. Their sacramental death was a step to the complete internal mortification of sin, and a reason why they should mortify sin, not the actual complete mortification of sin. They were to *reckon* themselves dead to sin in *order that* sin might not reign in them."

If we examine the remainder of this Epistle, we shall find the terms used throughout it in complete accordance with the Apostolic assertion that *all* the Baptized have been buried and raised again with Christ in Baptism. The terms by which the Apostle holds all the Roman Christians to be partakers of grace are as inclusive as can well be conceived. There is not one intimation throughout it that the Apostle thought that some to whom it would be read were partakers of the characteristic blessing of the Christian covenant, and some not.

It is addressed to "all that are in Rome, beloved of God, called to be saints" (chap. i. v. 7). Just before, he had said, " In whom are ye also the called of God."

Throughout the whole of the latter part of the fifth chapter, as I before noticed, there is an analogy drawn between the two Adams, evidently for the one purpose of showing the largeness and freeness of the grace proceeding from the Second Adam ; how—to say the least—it was *capable* of embracing, and cleansing, and renewing all lost in the first Adam.

Then we have the Baptismal passage in the commencement of the sixth chapter with its distinct, unqualified assertion, that " so many of us as were baptized into Jesus Christ were baptized into His death, and (consequently) buried with Him by Baptism into death,"—and so all, as I have shown, *sacramentally* " dead to sin."

Then, following upon this, he says, without any limitation, " Reckon ye also yourselves to be dead indeed unto sin." " Let not sin therefore reign in your mortal body." "Yield yourselves unto God, as those that are alive from the dead." " Ye are not under the law, but under grace."

Then, in the next chapter (vii.), " Wherefore, my beloved brethren, ye also have become dead to the law by the body of Christ [with which ye have been buried and raised

H 2

again in Baptism], that ye should be married to another [compare 2 Cor. xi. 2, 3], that ye should bring forth fruit unto God." Again, in chapter viii., he hints not obscurely that it might not be well with them all, for he speaks of the "carnal mind being at enmity with God," and says to them, "Ye are not in the flesh, but in the Spirit, *if so be* that the Spirit of God *dwell* in you," and yet he distinctly seems to lay down that the Spirit was given to all. "Ye have not received the spirit of bondage again to fear, but ye have received the Spirit of adoption." Then, in the eleventh chapter, in very plain terms, he singles out some supposed sinner among them, *evidently as a type of what any one of them might be*, and, instead of denying that such an one had ever been in grace, he distinctly asserts the fact of the past reception of grace by this supposed sinner, in order to make him fear the more. "If some of the branches were broken off, and thou, being a wild olive tree, wert grafted in among them . . . Well, because of unbelief they were broken off, and thou standest by faith. Be not high minded, but fear." "For if God spared not the natural branches, take heed lest he also spare not thee." "Behold, therefore, the goodness and severity of God : on them which fell, severity ; but toward thee, goodness, if thou continue in His goodness : otherwise thou also shalt be cut off." (Chap. xi. 17, 20, 22.)

Then, in accordance with all this, we have the Apostle calling upon *all* to present their bodies living sacrifices to God, and, in conjunction with this, we have his broad unqualified assertion that God had dealt some measure of faith to *every* man, and that *all* were to be accounted as members of Christ's body. "I say . . . . to every man that is among you . . . . according as God hath dealt to *every man*, the measure of faith. For as we have *many* members in one body, and all members have not the same office : so we, BEING MANY, are one body in Christ, and EVERY ONE members one of another."

In accordance with this, *all* are to love all, " Be kindly affectioned one to another."

Then, chapter xiii. commences with so general a precept as, " Let *every* soul be subject to the higher powers," and ends with warnings in equally general terms, and of the same character as those we have noticed in the Epistle to the Corinthians, implying that these Roman Christians, though once all grafted into Christ, might need rousing out of the sleep of sin, and so must "walk honestly, not in rioting and drunkenness, not in chambering and wantonness, not in strife and envying."

Again, from chapter xiv. we gather that none were to look down on *any one* who had the least pretension to be a brother. " Let not him that eateth not despise him that eateth, for *God hath received him.*" (v. 3.) " Who art thou that judgest another's (that is, Christ's) servant ?" (v. 4.) Again, " Why dost thou judge thy *brother ?*" (v. 10.) Again, "Destroy not him with thy meat for whom Christ died." (v. 15.) Again, "For meat destroy not the work of God" (v. 20)—the work, unseen, it may be, by you, which you are to acknowledge in the feeblest, dullest, most unpromising, and most inconsistent.

Such a continuous vein of inclusive expressions cannot be accidental. The reader will notice how exactly it accords with the Apostle's mode of addressing the Corinthian Christians. If St. Paul had held the modern Calvinistic or Puritan view of the restriction of Baptismal grace, could he have so written ? St. Paul distinctly recognises that some of these Roman Christians might fall from Christ through sin. He meets their case not by denying their Baptismal Regeneration, but by reasserting it, and bidding them remember it and CONTINUE in it.

We now turn to St. Paul's Epistle to the Colossians.

In the third chapter there is exactly the same remarkable use of the term "death," to which we have drawn attention (v. 3) : "Ye are dead,[1] and your life is hid with Christ in God." Let us pause for a moment, and ask ourselves, Should we not have said that those persons must of necessity be in a very advanced state of personal holiness, of whom it could be said that "they are dead, and their life is hid with Christ in God?" But how does the Apostle proceed? By warning these very persons against falling into the grossest sin : "Mortify *therefore* [*i.e.* because ye are dead, or have died] your members which are upon the earth; fornication, uncleanness, inordinate affection, evil concupiscence, and covetousness, which is idolatry; for which things' sake the wrath of God cometh on the children of disobedience." Here, then, is a passage exactly answering to that in Rom. vi. : "Reckon yourselves dead indeed unto sin, but alive unto God through Jesus Christ our Lord. Let not sin therefore reign in your mortal bodies," &c.

And when we examine the context, we find that there is here also precisely the same reference to a Baptismal burial and resurrection. "Buried with Him in Baptism, wherein also ye are risen with Him through the faith of the operation of God, who hath raised Him from the dead." (Coloss. ii. 12.)

All the evangelical and moral precepts, then, with which the third chapter is so full,—precepts applicable, some to gross sinners, and some to persons living in all degrees of conformity to God's will,—are addressed to the Colossian Christians on the ground that they have all received the grace of Baptismal union with the Second

[1] Or rather, ye died, ἀπεθάνετε. The same tense of the same verb which is used in Rom. vi. 2

Adam; so that both in the one Epistle, and in the other, all the Baptized are assumed to have been sacramentally buried with Christ, and to have sacramentally risen with Him in Baptism.

But there is one precept in the third chapter addressed to *children:* " Children, obey your parents in all things; for this is well pleasing unto the Lord." Let the reader remember, that as *all* the holy precepts of the third chapter are addressed to persons in a state of Baptismal grace, so is this to children. It necessarily assumes that they, as well as their parents, had been buried with Christ in Baptism.

CHAPTER VII.

BAPTISMAL GRACE, AS SET FORTH IN THE EPISTLE TO THE GALATIANS.

IN his Epistle to the Galatians, the Apostle addresses the whole baptized body, in the same way as in that to the Corinthians.

It is written to a Church respecting which the Apostle stood greatly in fear, when he considered the walk and life of many of its members. We shall find, however, that the expressions in this Epistle, which include all the Galatian Christians in the net of Divine grace, are as absolute as possible.

It is addressed (chap. i. 2) to the Churches of Galatia.

The whole Church seems to have been in danger of falling; for he says, apparently to the whole body (ver. 6), "I marvel that ye are so soon removed from him that called you into the grace of Christ unto another Gospel." He again (chap. iii. 1) resumes his loud and piercing note of warning: "O foolish Galatians, who hath bewitched you?" In chap. iv. 11, still keeping in view the whole body, he says to them, "I am afraid of you, lest I have bestowed upon you labour in vain." In verse 19 of the same chapter, he uses still stronger language to express his anxiety: "My little children, of whom I travail in birth again until Christ be formed in you, I desire to be present with you now, and to change my voice; for I stand in doubt of you." And in the fifth chapter (ver. 4): "Christ is become of no effect unto you, whosoever

of you are justified by the law ; ye are fallen from grace."
Then, again, he warns them how a few, holding error,
may corrupt all : "A little leaven leaveneth the *whole
lump.*" Then, in verse 13, he cautions them, in words
which are addressed to all, against fleshly abuse of Christian liberty : "Ye have been called unto liberty ; only use
not liberty for an occasion to the flesh." Then again,
verse 15, he tells them, "If ye bite and devour one
another, take heed that ye be not consumed one of another"
—lest, by your unrighteous divisions, and consequent
uncharitableness, ye destroy one another's souls. In the
last chapter, he again speaks words of deep and solemn
expostulation, which was evidently not unneeded in the
case of many of those to whom he wrote : "Be not deceived ; God is not mocked : for whatsoever a man soweth,
that shall he also reap. For he that soweth to his flesh
shall of the flesh reap corruption ; but he that soweth
to the Spirit shall of the Spirit reap life everlasting."

Here, then, we have a body of Christians, many of
whom were fallen into the same spiritual condition in
which Christians are now. They had fallen from grace,
inasmuch as they had ceased to rely solely on their
Saviour ; and they needed to be solemnly reminded that
by working the works of the flesh—such as adultery, for·
nication, uncleanness, lasciviousness, idolatry, witchcraft,
hatred, variance, envying, murder, drunkenness, and such
like—they would reap everlasting destruction.

Such were the Galatian Christians. And yet the terms
are most absolute and explicit in which the Apostle
addresses all of them as partakers of grace—the peculiar
grace of Baptism : "Ye are all the children [or sons, *vioì*]
of God by faith[1] in Christ Jesus. For *as many of you*

---

[1] Or rather "the Faith" (διὰ τῆς πίστεως), referring not so
much to the internal realizing act of the mind as to the objective

[comp. Rom. vi. 3, 4] as were baptized into Christ put on Christ. There is neither Jew nor Greek, there is neither bond nor free, there is neither male nor female : for ye are *all one* [*i. e.* one body] in Christ Jesus." (Gal. iii. 26—28.) Again, in the beginning of the next chapter, there is the same allusion to Jews and Gentiles as two bodies or classes, the fact of whose former separation, and present union in one body in Christ, occupies so much of the Apostle's mind. "We [Jews], when we were children, were in bondage under the elements of the world : but when the fulness of the time was come, God sent forth His Son, made of a woman, made under the law, to redeem them that were under the law, that we might receive the adoption of sons. And because ye [Galatian Gentiles] are sons,[1] God hath sent forth the Spirit of His Son into your hearts, crying, Abba, Father. Wherefore thou art no more a servant, but a son." Observe how comprehensively the Apostle speaks : " Ye are all the children of God ; " "Thou art no more a servant, but a son."

The two next verses (Gal. iv. 8, 9) bear very remarkably on the subject of our present investigation. In them the Apostle contrasts the former with the present state of the Galatian converts. Speaking of their former state, he says, " When ye knew not God, ye did service unto them which by nature are no gods." Their present state he alludes to under the term "knowing God." " Now, after that *ye have known God*"—but here the Apostle pauses, and, as it were, corrects himself. He remembers the spiritual dangers they were in, the turning back to bondage,

truths, or creed, called The Faith. See Bishop Browne on Article XI. page 300. Sixth Edition.

[1] Observe that the Gentiles are made sons (see iii. 26, 27) before they so receive the Spirit as to realize the relationship.

perhaps the Antinomian tendencies of some among them, and, as I said, he corrects himself in the words, "*or rather are known of God.*" By this he evidently implies that God had "known" all the Galatians so far as to have gathered them from the heathen, and made them His Church by profession of faith in Baptism, and yet they might fall short of *effectually* knowing Him who had so known them. There is a mode of speaking exactly the same as this in the prophets Hosea and Amos. In Hosea xiii. 4 : "I am the Lord thy God from the land of Egypt, and thou shalt know no god but me. . . . I did KNOW thee in the wilderness ;" but the children of Israel did not respond to this knowledge which God took of them ; for the prophet goes on, " According to their pasture, so were they filled ; they were filled, and their heart was exalted ; *therefore have they forgotten Me.*" So also Amos iii. 2 : "You only have I known of all the families of the earth ;" and yet this people, thus "known of God," failed to know that God who had " known " them.

In Gal. iv. 26, we have the heavenly Jerusalem spoken of as " our mother[1] : " again, " Ye[2] brethren, as Isaac was, are the children of promise : " and again in the last verse, " So then, brethren, *we* are not children of the bond-woman, but of the free." There are, the reader will observe, no cautious limitations ; no qualifying terms are used here ; and that such are not intended to be implied is evident from the first verse of the next chapter—the fifth—" Stand fast in the liberty in which Christ has made us free." Stand fast ye that are tempted to quit your Christian standing. Stand fast, because " the Jerusalem which is from above is free, which is the

---

[1] The majority of manuscripts, versions, and editions omit πάντων. The expression, however, is not less general.

[2] ὑμεῖς is the best reading.

mother of us all." " Stand fast in the liberty wherewith
Christ hath made us free : " and so again (ver. 13),
" Brethren, ye [i. e. the whole body, those who are falling
and those who are safe] have been called unto liberty."
In verse 25 of the fifth chapter there is a remarkable
expression, implying that the dispensation of the Spirit
is upon all, and includes all, even many who do not profit
by it : " If we live in the Spirit, let us also *walk* in the
Spirit," *i. e.* " If we live in that Church, if we are members of that body, which has the Spirit, let us also *walk*
in the Spirit—let us live to grace pledged and given : we
are surrounded by signs and tokens that the Spirit is ours,
let us walk accordingly."

Here, then, we have a Church called to liberty ; but
some in it forgot their high calling, and returned to
bondage.   Here is a Church, every member of which had,
in Baptism, been clothed with Christ, so as to be in
His body; and yet St. Paul was exercised by doubt,
and anxiety, and care for them that Christ *might be
formed in them :* here is a body of men, all "known of
God," and yet they had, many of them, yet to acquaint
themselves with Him who had graciously "known" them.

The proof of Baptismal Regeneration which I have drawn
from these four Epistles is one, the importance of which
cannot be overstated.   The closer we examine these inspired documents, the more we shall find that it pervades
them.

The whole argument is so well and pointedly stated, in
a well-known publication by the late Archbishop of Can-
terbury, that I cannot forbear giving it to the reader.   He
will find it in " Archbishop Sumner on Apostolical
Preaching."   Eighth Edition (page 152).

" It cannot be alleged that St. Paul had no opportunity
of introducing the doctrine of partial grace, or particular

election, to the Churches which he addressed. Many of them had admitted gross errors into their practice : others, as the Galatians, had swerved widely from sound doctrine; many individuals were 'unruly, and vain talkers and deceivers, who subverted whole houses, teaching things that they ought not, for filthy lucre's sake' (Tit. i. 10, 11). *These corruptions, however, are nowhere attributed to the denial of grace, but always to the abuse or neglect of it.* The Corinthians had very imperfectly purged themselves from the immoralities of their heathen state ; but how does he reprove them ? 'Know ye not that your bodies are the members of Christ ? Know ye not that your body is the *temple* of the Holy Ghost *which is in you*, which ye have of God?' (1 Cor. vi. 16, &c.) This is evidently saying, that the wickedness of the Corinthians was not owing to the denial of grace on the part of God, but to the abuse of it on their own. '

Again (page 158): " Another practical evil of the doctrine of special grace, is the necessity which it implies of some test of God's favour, and of the reconcilement of Christians to Him, beyond, and subsequent to, the covenant of Baptism.[1] St. Paul, it has been seen, insists upon the necessity of regeneration : he declares that 'the natural man receiveth not the things of the Spirit of God, neither can know them :' he calls the heathen nations 'children of wrath,' and 'sinners of the Gentiles :' he speaks of the old man as being 'corrupt according to the deceitful lusts :' in short, he expresses, under a variety of terms, the assertion of our Saviour, that, 'Except a man be born again, of water and of the Spirit, he cannot enter into the kingdom of God.' (John iii. 3, 5.)

[1] "This is not meant to deny the necessity of a personal recognition of Jesus Christ as Redeemer as the mind becomes capable of receiving the mystery.' This is the Archbishop's note.

" With equal clearness, he intimates that the Christians he addresses were thus regenerate : as having ' put off the old man with its deeds ;' and having become the 'temple of the Holy Ghost' and ' the members of Christ ;' as having the spiritual circumcision, and being ' buried with Christ in baptism' (Rom. vi. 3 ; Col. ii. 12) ; and as being 'washed, sanctified, and justified, in the name of the Lord Jesus, and by the Spirit of our God.'   To the Galatians, ' bewitched,' as he says they were, ' that they should not obey the truth,' he still writes : ' Ye are all the children of God, by faith in Christ Jesus. For as many of you as have been baptized into Christ have put on Christ.' (Gal. iii. 26, 27.)   These addresses and exhortations are founded on the principle that the disciples, by their dedication to God in Baptism, had been brought into a state of reconcilement with Him, had been admitted to privileges, which the Apostle calls on them to improve. On the authority of this example, and of the undeniable practice of the first ages of Christianity, our Church considers Baptism as conveying regeneration, instructing us to pray, before Baptism, that the infant 'may be born again, and made an heir of everlasting salvation ;' and to return thanks, after Baptism, ' that it hath pleased God to regenerate the infant by His Holy Spirit, and to receive him for His own child by adoption.' "

Let the reader observe that I by no means quote these extracts as embodying the view of Baptismal grace I am giving in this publication, but as testifying to the legitimate character of a certain line of argument in its favour, which we derive from the language of the Epistles we have been considering, and which will be found as truly to be contained in other Epistles, which we shall now proceed to examine.

CHAPTER VIII.

SAINTS AND BELIEVERS.

THIS appears to be the proper place to consider the sense in which the Apostle applies to all the Christians to whom he addressed his Epistles the term "holy" or "saints" (ἅγιοι), and "faithful" or "believers" (πιστοί).

The word "saint," or "holy person," is now almost universally used as implying real purity of heart, and devotion to God's service. It is applied to Apostles, such as St. Peter or St. Paul; to eminent men who have been raised up by God in bygone times to contend for the faith, such as St. Athanasius or St. Augustine; or to men and women of very deep holiness and spirituality of mind.

In the New Testament, on the contrary, it is the common appellation of Christians. *In no one place is it used to distinguish Christians of very deep holiness and spirituality from those who have not attained to such a measure of conformity to God's will.* In only a small number of texts does it imply internal purity and spirituality, and in these places it has reference not to the present character of Christians, but to that which those will be found to possess at Christ's second coming who have *continued* in that service of Christ to which at Baptism they were solemnly separated and set apart.

Such places are 2 Thess. i. 10 : "When He comes to be glorified in His saints." Also 1 Thess. iii. 13 ; and perhaps one or two places in the Apocalypse.

In every other place it is applied to the whole body of baptized Christians in a city or district, and is the continuation of that mode of address which we find adopted by the prophets when they called all Israel a "holy nation"—a people, that is, *dedicated to God, and separated from all other people to serve Him.* Just then as the other appellations of God's ancient Church— such as "Israel," "children of God," "seed of Abraham," "God's people," "God's chosen"—were applied to all the members of the Christian Church, as taking the place of God's ancient Church ; so this one of "saints," or "holy persons," was similarly applied.[1] As it was of old addressed to all the circumcised nation, so comes now to be addressed to all the baptized Church implying, of course, that in some real sense Baptism separated each man to God's service, and that, if such one failed to live up to his profession, he was a livi lie. I will give a few instances, out of a multitu where this word "saint" is interchangeable with the wo "Christian." " Lord, I have heard by many of this m

[1] "The penmen of the Old Testament do often speak of th children of Israel as of an holy nation, and God doth often speak unto them as to a people holy unto Himself; because He had chosen them out of all the nations of the world, and appropriated them to Himself. Although, therefore, most of that nation were rebellious to Him which called them, and void of all true inherent and actual sanctity ; yet because they were all in that manner separated, they were all, as to the separation, called holy. In the like manner those of the New Testament, writing to such as were called, and received, and were baptized in the faith, give unto them *all* the name of *saints* as being in some manner such, by being called and baptized."—PEARSON *on the Creed.* Article, "Communion of Saints."

how much evil he has done to *thy saints* at Jerusalem."
(Acts ix. 13.) Again, in the same chapter (ver. 32), we
read of "Peter passing through all quarters," and so
coming down to "*the saints which dwelt at Lydda;*" and
again (ver. 41), "When he had called *the saints and
widows, he presented her alive.*" Again, "It hath pleased
them of Macedonia and Achaia to make a certain contri-
bution for *the poor saints which are at Jerusalem.*" (Rom.
xv. 16.) Again, "Now concerning the collection *for the
saints.*" (1 Cor. xvi. 1.)[1]

In all these places the word is evidently used in the
same broad sense as the word "Christians," when applied
to all who profess the name of Christ. It cannot possibly
be taken either as meaning the more spiritual members of
the Church, or as asserting the real purity of heart of all
whom it was applied. Archbishop Whately has a most
valuable passage on the apostolic use of this word, which
I here take the liberty of inserting, and which suggests
a practical application of the whole matter.

'You will observe that Paul constantly uses these
appellations, not as implying that his hearers *had* attained
superior Christian excellence, but as suggesting a *motive*
for their exerting themselves to attain it. He never tells
any of them to expect any '*call,*' but addresses them all
as called 'saints,' and exhorts them to '*walk worthy* of the
vocation whereto they are called.' He never speaks of
them *becoming* elect, but exhorts them, *as* the elect of God,
holy [or saints], to 'put on mercy, kindness, and humble-
ness' (Col. iii. 12), and to 'give diligence to make their
calling and election sure.' Never does he exhort them to
be saints, but to 'walk as *becometh* saints;' never to *enter*

[1] Other instances are 1 Cor. xiv. 33, xvi. 15 ; 2 Cor. viii. 4, ix. 1,
12, xiii. 13 ; Eph. vi. 18 ; Phil. iv. 21, 22 ; 1 Tim. v. 10 ; Philem.
5, 7 ; Heb. vi. 10, xiii. 24.

into any brotherhood, but to '*love as* brethren.' The titles, in short, which he applies, all denote their *privileges* and their *duties;* not their good *use* of those privileges, and faithful *performance* of those duties. It is to that use and that performance that he *exhorts* them. And he warns them (*e.g.* 1 Cor. x.), from the example of God's people of old, against neglecting or abusing their high privileges. All the Israelites were God's *chosen* (or elect), but with *most* of them (τοῖς πλείοσιν) God was not well pleased, as was shown by their being overthrown in the wilderness." [1]

The change in the use of this word "holy," or " saint," by its being never now applied to the baptized, but restricted to the godly Christian, has been productive of untold evil. The mass of Christians, never being reminded of the holiness of their state, have got to think that, as far as regards responsibility, they are, in all respects, as the heathen. And yet those who take the lowest view of Baptism—as a dedication to God, and separation of the person baptized to His service, ought to teach them far otherwise.

If men are habitually taught that they never begin to be in any sense " *God's people,*" or " *holy,*" till they are converted, at some time when they are grown to maturity; and when, along with this, they are reminded that they can do nothing to forward this conversion, so entirely is it the work of God; they, of course, under such teaching, hold themselves to be as completely out of the pale, and absolved from the obligations of the Christian covenant, as the heathen.

If children are dedicated to God in any real sense, *no matter how low that sense be,* at their Baptism—if it sepa-

[1] "Sermons on the principal Christian Festivals," 3d Edition, p. 340.

rates or sanctifies the nominal Christian only as much as circumcision separated the nominal Jew—it entails a fearful responsibility upon ministers of Christ and parents and teachers, to perpetually bring before their charge this holiness of their bodies. " If any man," says the Apostle, " defile the temple of God, him will God destroy ; for the temple of God is holy, which temple ye are." (1 Cor. iii. 17.)

What we have said respecting the term " holy persons," or saints (ἅγιοι), applies to the appellation "*faithful*," or "*believer*," (πιστός) : this term also is used almost always in its widest and most comprehensive sense by the Apostles. In New Testament language, πιστός, or believer, means one who believes the Divine nature and mission of Jesus of Nazareth, *quite independently of the effect which this belief has on his heart and life.* Thus, in Acts x. 45 : " They of the circumcision which believed." 1 Tim. v. 16 : " If any man or woman that believeth have widows." Similarly, ἄπιστος means an infidel or heathen, and by no means corresponds with our " mere nominal Christian." Thus, 1 Cor. vi. 6 ; vii. 12, 13, 14, 15 ; x. 27; xiv. 22, 23, 24; 1 Tim. v. 8. In modern Christian language, the word "believer" is generally used as synonymous with "real Christian"—one possessed of a lively realizing belief in God's love to us in His Son. This restriction in the application of this word is also most disastrous. The nominal Christian, finding that his belief, miserably in-operative though it be, is treated as so much infidelity, grows more and more careless about professing it, or even holding it ; whereas he ought to be reminded perpetually, that *the slightest acquiescence of his mind in any office or work of Christ is God's gift*—a hold which his God and Saviour has yet upon him, and which, if he but really and faithfully followed it out, would lead him to the most

unreserved acceptance of his Saviour in all His offices
of love towards him. So St. Paul treated even the
wretched Herod: "King Agrippa, believest thou the
prophets? I know that thou believest."

Every degree of faith, no matter how small, no matter
how mixed up with unbelief, is recognised in Scripture.
Thus it is said of the Israelites, when they came out
of Egypt, that "they believed the Lord." (Exod. xiv.
31; Psalm cvi. 12), and yet we know that they "fell
in the wilderness because of unbelief." Similarly it is
continually recorded of the Apostles and disciples, that
they *believed* (John ii. 11), and yet these very same
men, though they had seen one miracle in which our
Lord fed miraculously a vast multitude, yet believed not
that He was able to feed another and lesser multitude
under the same circumstances. (Matt. xiv. 15, 16, compared with xv. 33, and xvi. 8, 9, 10.)

Our Lord blesses one of them for his faith, and that
faith the gift of God, in that he confessed Him to be
"the Christ, the Son of the living God;" and yet, a few
minutes after, He reproves this same man for his unbelief
(and that the suggestion of Satan) in the very end and
purpose for which the Christ had come into the world—
to make, by His sufferings on the cross, an atonement for
sin. (Matt. xvi. 17, 23.)

CHAPTER IX.

BAPTISMAL GRACE——EPISTLE TO THE EPHESIANS.

In the Epistles of St. Paul which we have examined, we have seen how uniformly the Apostle addresses all the members of the Church as members of Christ; and as all, on that account, partakers of the distinguishing grace of the New Covenant.

But when we proceed to speak to the great body of the baptized now, as St. Paul unquestionably did in his day, men take exception. They say that the grace which St. Paul undoubtedly affirms to belong to the whole Christian Church, in reality belongs only to some in it; to a select few, who are restrained, by a secret decree of God, from receiving it in vain; to what is called in modern language the "invisible Church."

So that, according to this view, there are two Churches, ——one, the invisible, to which God has restricted Regeneration, and the Baptism of the Spirit, and the gift of incorporation into His Son; the other, the visible Church, consisting of all the baptized, composed of wheat and tares, holy and unholy, respecting any particular member of which it will be a matter of doubt, till the great day, whether he has really been engrafted into Christ at his Baptism.

Let us now review the Epistle to the Ephesians. We shall see that it yields the same testimony as the other

Epistles do, to the reality of the grace received by all the baptized, and the responsibility entailed upon the whole Church thereby.

Throughout the first three chapters we find the mind of the Apostle ever dwelling upon, and striving to embody in words, one great idea, which he calls a "mystery"— the "mystery of God's will,"—the "mystery of Christ." This mystery is, that God, for the accomplishment of His all-wise purposes, had for many ages divided mankind into two bodies; but that now at last, He had reconciled them both to Himself and to one another, and had made them one Church in His dear Son. These two classes or bodies are not, as we should perhaps have supposed, the two great divisions of good and bad men, or true and false believers. Much less are they two Churches—one visible, and the other invisible; but they are two visible bodies—Jews and Gentiles.

To the one class or body, the Jews, God had, during many ages, revealed Himself. They were His people, and He was their God. For nearly two thousand years they had been in the possession of His law, His service, and His peculiar presence. To the other body, on the contrary, God had only lately vouchsafed a share in these good things. They were still considered by the elder Church as unclean and unholy.

St. Paul writes to assure these Gentile Christians that they were "complete in Christ." By their incorporation into His Church they possessed every spiritual blessing which the elder election could possibly enjoy.

We will now examine the first three chapters in detail. We shall find that the Apostle adheres throughout to the idea of the Christian state being a corporate one—a body in Christ,—an "ecclesia;"—a number of persons, the consideration of whose individual responsibility is designedly sunk for the time in the idea of their union as *one body* under *One Head*.

The Apostle begins with this Divine Head. In the first part of the first chapter, he brings Christ before us as "*The Elect* ONE," in whom the *whole* Church is chosen. "*We* are chosen in Him before the foundation of the world." "*We* are blessed with all spiritual blessings in Him." "*We* have redemption through His blood." (Chap. i. 3—7.)

He then proceeds to assert that God's design in constituting Christ to be this elect ONE, is that He may eventually "gather together in *One* all things in Him."[1] Then he goes on to assert the participation of those to whom he writes his Epistle in these great things, inasmuch as they all had a common sealing of the Spirit: "In *Whom* ye also, when ye believed, were sealed with that Holy Spirit of promise."[2] Then the Apostle puts up to God, on behalf of these his converts, a prayer, the crowning petition of which is that they may fully realize the mighty power of God in exalting His Son to His right hand, to be the "head over all things to the Church, which is His body." (Chap. i. 10, 13, 22, 23.)

In the next chapter, the Apostle continues the same way of speaking of his converts, and of his fellow-Israelites. They were two aggregates or bodies of persons —at first involved in one common condemnation,—then saved by free grace,—God's workmanship, created in Christ Jesus unto good works. (Chap. ii. 2, 3, 8, 10.)

---

[1] The idea of oneness (under one head) is implied in ἀνακεφαλαιώσασθαι.

[2] Observe how this sealing is asserted to be the privilege of all, as no exception is made ; and we shall see when we come to consider another part of this Epistle, that it was in the power of those thus sealed to retain or efface the impress of the seal.

Then, still addressing the Gentiles as a body, he bids them contrast their former with their present state. "Remember, that *ye* being in time past Gentiles in the flesh . . . that at that time ye were without Christ : . . . but now, *in Christ* Jesus, *ye* who sometimes were far off are made nigh by the blood of Christ." (Chap. ii. 11—12—13.)

Then he proceeds to speak of all distinction between these two divisions of mankind being done away : "He is *our* peace, who hath made *both one* . . . having abolished in His flesh the enmity, even the law of commandments contained in ordinances." This of course means that one main design of the Jewish ordinances was to keep up a separation between God's chosen people and the rest of the world ; and as what was distinctly Jewish was abolished by Christ's sacrifice, so was the distinction or enmity it was designed to keep up. And He abolished this to "make in Himself of twain *one new man* . . . and that He might reconcile both unto God in *one body* by the cross . . . and came and preached peace to you who were afar off, and to them that were nigh." (Chap. ii. 14—17.)

Let us ask here in what sense were the Gentiles "afar off" from God, and the Jews "nigh" to Him ? Certainly not as His intelligent creatures, for all have equally their being in Him, and all will be impartially judged by Him. Certainly not as moral agents either, for the name of God was, through the wickedness of the Jews, blasphemed among the Gentiles. It could only be *ecclesiastically* that the Gentiles were afar off and the Jews nigh. As a body, or Church, possessing the law and the covenants, the Jews were "nigh ;" as not having these tokens of God's presence among them, the Gentiles were "afar off."

But this was now done away : "through Him *we both* have an access by *one Spirit* unto the Father." The remainder of the chapter is full of the same *general* and *inclusive* terms. "Now therefore *ye* are no more strangers and foreigners, but *fellow-citizens* with the saints, *and of the household of God;* and are built upon the foundation of the apostles and prophets, Jesus Christ Himself being the chief corner-stone; in whom *all the building fitly framed together* groweth unto an *holy temple in the* Lord: in whom *ye* also are *builded together* for an habitation of God through the Spirit." (Chap. ii. 18—22.)

Hitherto we have seen how steadily the Apostle has kept in view two collective masses, or bodies of persons; for two thousand years separate, but now made one Church in Christ.

Not one word has he spoken hitherto about any secret election in these two outward divisions. All that he has yet said respecting grace given, or grace withheld, has had reference to the whole visible body, whether Jew or Gentile.

He now asserts his claim to be the instrument of God for spreading far and wide the knowledge of a mystery hid from ages and generations. He calls himself "the prisoner of Jesus Christ for you Gentiles." He endured imprisonment, that is, not merely for preaching Christ, but for preaching the acceptance of the Gentiles on equal terms with the Jews in the Church of Christ. And this was a dispensation made known to him by a special revelation: "The dispensation of the grace of God which was given me to you-ward: how that by revelation He made known unto me the mystery." "The mystery of Christ, which in other ages was not made known unto the sons of men, as it is now revealed." (Chap. iii. 1—5.)

Let us here pause for a moment, and ask again, What is this matter which the Apostle dignifies with the name of "mystery of Christ"? Is it the Incarnation, or the

Atonement, or the Predestination of certain individuals
—quite irrespective of their ecclesiastical privileges—to
eternal salvation? The Apostle proceeds to tell us. The
mystery is, "that the Gentiles should be *fellow*-heirs, and
of the *same body*, and *partakers* of God's promise in Christ
by the Gospel." (Chap. iii. 6.)

Again the Apostle reverts to the personal honour God
had put upon him in making him the steward of such
a mystery : " Unto me, who am less tnan the least of all
saints, is this grace given, that I should preach *among the
Gentiles* the unsearchable riches of Christ ; and make all
men see what is *the fellowship of the mystery*, which from
the beginning of the world hath been hid in God."
(Chap. iii. 8, 9.)

Now we, simply because we have enjoyed all the blessings of the Gospel for so many hundred years, are under
very great difficulties in realizing the exultation of the
Apostle at his having been made the especial instrument
of God in making known such a mystery.

For that which was to him and to his fellow-countrymen
a mystery of such a nature that it hindered the ancient
people of God from receiving the Gospel, is to us no
mystery at all. We have had the kingdom and Church
of God transmitted to us from our fathers as a matter of
course—a thing to which we conceive that we have hereditary right and title. The reception of the Gentiles into
the Church of Christ is to us so plain and familiar a
matter, that it is difficult to understand how it could
ever have been a mystery in any sense.

On this account I suppose it is that some are led to
think that there must be in these three chapters some
more secret mystery,—as that of the invisible within the
visible Church; the election to life of a few persons, known
only to God, living in the midst of a visible assembly or

Church, of which the outward marks or badges are no pledges of grace received. But St. Paul has, as yet, dropped not the least hint of such being his meaning. His whole train of argument has been against such an interpretation of his words ; for he has been hitherto applying high terms of grace to large mixed bodies of men, considered not as good or bad, godly or ungodly, but as Jews and Gentiles, once two bodies, separated from, and at enmity with, one another, now made one mystical fellowship in Christ. [1]

If it had been the Apostle's object in writing these three chapters to enunciate the narrow or Calvinistic view of election [2]—the election of the invisible, as distinct from the visible Church, he certainly has only obscured his meaning and hampered his argument by such perpetual reference to the election of two such large and mixed classes of men as Jews and Gentiles, and their being made " of twain one new body in Christ." For these two classes are by their very nature outward, mixed, visible bodies, and the signs and tokens of their former separation and present union are outward and visible signs, and as comprehensive as can well be conceived.

We now come to the fourth chapter, in which the Apostle brings the doctrines of the first three chapters to bear upon the hearts and consciences of those to whom he was writing. We shall find that he never for a moment drops that ecclesiastical or inclusive way of speaking which

[1] Hooker in the first chapter of his third book, whilst contemplating the fact that there is an invisible Church known only to God, distinctly asserts that the Church recognised throughout this Epistle is the visible.

[2] Let the reader observe, that I am not denying for a moment that there is an inner or secret election ; I am merely showing that the Apostle is certainly not enunciating such a doctrine in his Epistle to the Ephesians.

he has hitherto employed.   His mind is to the end full of
the idea of the " one body."   All are addressed as one,—
one in grace, one in privilege, and *one in danger of falling
away.*   All are assumed to be *in* the Church—the body of
Christ—and yet all are warned against sins which would
certainly, if persisted in, cut them off from Christ.   The
whole body are warned against sins which it is impossible
to suppose that the members of an elect invisible Church
(as men now understand the term) would be guilty of.

First of all, he beseeches them to walk worthy of their
vocation, by each one being lowly, peaceable, forbearing ;
and they were to be all this, because of the divine gifts in
which *all* were *one.*   " Forbearing one another in love ;
endeavouring to keep the unity or [oneness] of the Spirit
in the bond of peace : [for] there is *one* body, and *one*
Spirit, even as ye are called in *one* hope of your calling ;
one Lord, *one* faith, *one* Baptism."   (Chap. iv. 2—5.)

" One Baptism."   If Baptism had been in the case of
some amongst these Ephesians a birth of water only, ad-
mitting to no real state of grace in Christ's body, it would
have been no seal of their vocation to lowliness and meekness as members of such a body.   How could the whole
body be called upon to walk worthy of their vocation, *because*
that vocation had been sealed by *one* Baptism, when this
solemn rite had failed in joining to Christ's body the very
persons who most needed the exhortation !

The Apostle then proceeds to speak in most express
terms of *all* being partakers of grace : " Unto *every one
of us* is given grace according to the measure of the gift
of Christ."   This grace is in part the grace of the Apostolic
ministry, which surely, if anything does, appertains to the
visible Church rather than to any invisible body.   " He
gave some, apostles ; and some, prophets ; and some, evangelists ; and some, pastors and teachers."   And this grace is

for the building up of the *whole* body : " For the edifying
of the body of Christ : till we *all* come in the unity of
the faith, and of the knowledge of the Son of God, unto
a perfect man." (Chap. iv. 7, 11—13.)

Can words express more clearly that God desires the
highest goodness of the whole visible Church, and has
given to each member grace to attain to it ?

Hitherto we have seen how general and comprehensive
are the terms in which the Apostle addresses all as included in the net of Divine grace.

Nothing whatsoever has as yet been written by him to
lead us to suppose that some of these Ephesians were in
grace, others not ; that there was a secret election which
embraced some as members of Christ's mystical body, and
passed over others.

We should now expect the Apostle to give some intimation of such a limitation of grace ; for at this place (ch. iv. 17)
he begins to warn them against the sins of that heathen
state from which they had come out. But let the reader
mark on what grounds the Apostle would have them put
off their old sins. He urges upon them their common
participation in the grace of their Divine Head, as a
reason why they should completely put away the sins of
their old nature. " This I say *therefore*,"—" therefore,"
that is, because of what I have just said respecting the ONE
HEAD of the mystical body from which the whole maketh
increase ; *on account of this*,—" I say and testify in the
Lord, that ye walk not as other Gentiles walk, in the
vanity of their mind, ... alienated from the life of
God. . . . . That ye put off as concerning the former conversation the old man, which is corrupt according to the
deceitful lusts." Then he proceeds to characterise these
lusts—these sins of their former state, which they were
to put away—" Wherefore putting away *lying*, speak

every man truth with his neighbour : for we are members one of another," *i.e.* in Christ. "Let him that *stole, steal no more.*" "Let no *corrupt* communication proceed out of your mouth." "Grieve not the Holy Spirit of God, whereby ye are sealed unto the day of redemption." Mark how inclusive are these expressions, "We are members one of another,"—"The Holy Spirit, whereby ye are sealed." Throughout the whole chapter there is not one limiting or narrowing word. It is taken for granted that all are in some sort partakers of the Spirit, because they are all members of Christ. And yet if there are Christians who are not in the (so called) invisible Church, they must be those who require to be warned against *lying*, and *stealing*, and speaking *corrupt words.* (Chap. iv. 17—30.)

The inspired Apostle warns members of Christ against sins the committal of which the Puritan puts down as a clear proof that such as are guilty of them have never been engrafted into the body of Christ's Church at all.

An examination of the fifth chapter leads to the same result. The persons to whom the Apostle speaks are "God's dear children ;" they are "light in the Lord ;" and because they are this, they must not even name among themselves certain gross and deadly sins, such as fornication, uncleanness, and filthiness. Those who are "light in the Lord," are very solemnly told, "Let no man deceive you by vain words : for because of these things cometh the wrath of God upon the children of disobedience." (Chap. v. 6—8.)

What vain words could possibly deceive them, except such as implied that those once in grace can never finally fall from it, or that the elect are in no danger from the infection of such evil things?

Those who are bidden to be followers of God, as "dear

children" (verse 1), are bidden "not to be deceived, lest, because of such things, the wrath of God come upon them as children of disobedience." And though, in one sense, these Ephesian Christians were *all* "light in the Lord," yet in the case of some among them that light might be unavailing, because they did not walk according to it. Some of them might have fallen into a sleep which might end in death, and so the Apostle speaks as if some among them needed a true awakening, for he strives to arouse them with such words as, "Awake, thou that sleepest, and *arise from the dead,* and Christ shall give thee light." [1] (Chap. v. 14.)

He bids these *saints,* in one verse, to " have no fellowship with the unfruitful works of darkness;" and in another, " not to be drunk with wine, wherein is excess." (Chap. v. 11, 18.)

In the latter verses of this chapter (21—33) the Apostle inculcates, in the same inclusive terms, the duty of mutual submission : " Submitting yourselves *one to another* in the fear of God;" and he then proceeds to bring the relationship of Christ to His Church, as a head to the members, to bear on the duties of mutual submission and love in each particular household. " Wives, submit yourselves unto your own husbands, as unto the Lord. For the husband is the head of the wife, even as Christ is the head of the Church: and He is the Saviour of the body." Is it conceivable that the Apostle should bring so stupendous a grace as the reason why each wife should fulfil such an every-day duty of common life, unless he considered that *every wife among them was bound to fulfil the duty, because she had been made a partaker of the grace ?*

---

[1] I am well aware that this quotation is not primarily addressed to the Ephesian Christians ; but it is no less evident that it was in the Apostle's mind that many among them might need it.

And so with respect to the duties of husbands to their wives : "Husbands, love your wives, even as Christ also loved the Church, and gave Himself for it ; that He might sanctify and cleanse it with the washing of water by the word."

Here, then, is the Church cleansed by the "one Baptism" to be the bride of Christ, which He nourishes and cherishes as His own body. Now, we have all submitted to this "one Baptism," and we are "members of His body, of His flesh, and of His bones." But this higher mystical union betwixt Christ and His Church is also typified by a lower mystical union, in which a man is "joined to his wife, and they twain are one flesh." Let then those amongst you who are joined to wives in this lower and earthly bond ever bear in mind that great mystery of Christ and His Church, so that "each one in particular may love his wife even as himself, and the wife see that she reverence her husband."

Such is the Apostle's argument. Could he possibly have grounded his reasons for the performance of such duties on an assumed union with Christ which some of these Ephesian Christians had never really entered into, and were, moreover, withheld from entering into by a secret decree of the Almighty?

Having thus shown how the great Church truth of union with Christ bears on the duties of husbands and wives, the Apostle sends a message to children. Now, in an Epistle like the present, which is written only to members of Christ, the Apostle can send no message to children, *except on the assumption that they too are in Christ's mystical body.* We have seen how, all through the Epistle, he has been careful to ground the performance of every duty on the fact of the past reception by each baptized person of this one privilege of union with Christ.

We have observed, also, how in the latter part of the
fifth chapter he has brought this to bear with great power
on the duties of husbands and wives in the marriage
state.

Now he sends a message to all the children of the
Ephesian Christians. "Children, obey your parents in the
Lord : for this is right." If the children of the Ephesian
Christians had not all been baptized, or if some of them at
their Baptism had not really been grafted into the body
of Christ's Church, the Apostle must have first laid down
how they were to be brought *into* Christ, before he could
say a word to them about their duties *in* Christ. But he
does no such thing. He says not one word about any of
these children having to seek an interest in Christ. He
says not one word about the necessity laid upon children
of being grafted into Christ at some future time, when
their faith might be more matured. He takes it for
granted that they were growing up in the Church as
members of Christ, and that the same motives to holiness
and goodness which were applicable to the older members
of Christ's body were applicable to them in their degree.

We gather exactly the same lesson from St. Paul's
message to fathers : " Ye fathers, provoke not your children to wrath : but bring them up in the nurture and
admonition of the Lord." Unless the Ephesian Christian
children were members of Christ, fathers would have
been told to see that their children were really " in
Christ," before they could bring them up in His nurture
and admonition.

These places (compared with Coloss. iii. 20) are decisive
both as regards the doctrine of Infant Baptism and the
way in which baptized infants are to be regarded. They
are found amongst precepts which are addressed to the
members of Christ's body as such ; which precepts, too,

K

derive all their force from the assumed fact of all to whom they are sent being " in Christ."

We are not, then, to wait for any change of views, or any deep conviction, in children, before we can regard them as members of Christ; but with the full assurance that each little one is dear to Him, and that He looks for the future holiness and eternal happiness of each one, we are to treat them as His; His as fully as those of riper years, who show that they belong to Him by having consciously come to Him, and surrendered themselves to His service.

CHAPTER X.

FURTHER EXAMINATION OF THE APOSTOLICAL EPISTLES.

WE have thus examined carefully the Epistles of St. Paul to the Galatians and Ephesians, and have seen how uniformly throughout these letters the Apostle takes for granted that all the baptized are partakers of the grace of the New Covenant. We have also noticed how impossible it is, on any fair ground of interpretation, to limit the application of this mode of address to some imaginary invisible Church, included in the visible body, whilst distinct from it.

We will now briefly draw attention to the evidence on this subject presented by other Epistles.

In his Epistle to the Philippians, the Apostle writes to the whole body as "saints." (Phil. i. 1.) He is confident that "He which hath begun a good work in them will perform it until the day of Jesus Christ." (Chap. i. 6.) He considers it "meet to think this of them all;" he "has them in his heart;" they are "all partakers with him of grace;" he "longs after them all in the bowels of Jesus Christ;" and yet, before he concludes, he gives no obscure intimation that some of those whom he thus longs after are losing their souls: "Mark them which walk so as ye have us for an ensample. For MANY walk, of whom I have told you often, and now tell you éven weeping, that they are the enemies of the cross of Christ: whose end is destruction." (Chap. iii. 17, 18.)

K 2

The Apostle cannot, in these words, allude to heathen persons ; he must mean those in the Church who were not abiding in Christ (John xv. 1—6), and who were being " cast forth as branches, and withered."

In accordance with this, he bids them to " stand fast in the Lord " (chap. iv. 1) ; as if such a warning were needed by all, for all were in Christ, but all might not, of necessity, adhere to Him.

The Epistles to the Thessalonians present us with the same mode of teaching.

They are written to the Church of the Thessalonians in God the Father, and in the Lord Jesus Christ. (1 Thess. i. 1.) He gives thanks for them all. (Chap. i. 2.) He knows their " election of God." (1 Thess. i. 4 ; 2 Thess. ii. 13, 14.) He speaks in the strongest terms of praise of their first reception of the Gospel; of their being his " hope, and joy, and crown of rejoicing." (1 Thess. i. 5—6, 7 ; ii. 19, 20.) And yet, in both these Epistles, the Apostle intimates that it may not be well with all among them. In the First Epistle he bids them to " warn the unruly." (Chap. v. 14.) He bids them also " not to quench the Spirit." (v. 19.) In the Second Epistle he commands them, " in the name of Jesus Christ, to withdraw from every brother that walketh disorderly." (2 Thess. iii. 6.) He " hears that there are such among them." (iii. 11.) Respecting such he gives command, " If any man obey not our word by this epistle, note that man, and have no company with him, that he may be ashamed. Yet count *him* not as an enemy, but admonish him *as a brother."* (iii. 14, 15.)

This needs no comment ; but I would now proceed to braw attention to another passage in the First Epistle especially bearing upon the subject. In the beginning of the fourth chapter of the First Epistle, the Apostle warns the members of this Church, of whose election he was assured, against fornication and adultery.

" This is the will of God, even your sanctification, that ye should abstain from fornication : . . . that no man go beyond and defraud his brother *in the matter* " (not " *any* matter," as our translation has it, but *the* matter he was then speaking of, *i.e.* adultery) . . . " For God hath not called us unto uncleanness, but unto holiness. He therefore that despiseth, despiseth not man, but God, who hath also given unto us His Holy Spirit." (1 Thess. iv. 3—8.)

Let the reader observe how Christians are here warned against gross sins of impurity, because of their calling, and because of the Spirit given to each. It is not said, " When ye have been effectually called, and have really received the Spirit, ye will not do such things." The calling, and the past reception of the Spirit, are taken for granted.

The passage is exactly parallel to 1 Cor. vi. 12—20, to which, in our examination of that Epistle, we have before called attention. The Apostle there warns Christians of the same age and country against the same sin, on exactly the same ground, viz. the covenant privileges of being members of Christ and partakers of the Spirit. " Know ye not that your members are the members of Christ ? shall I then take the members of Christ and make them the members of an harlot ? God forbid ! " " What ! know ye not that your body is the temple of the Holy Ghost which is in you, *which ye have of God ?* "

Here then is a sin which a modern evangelical preacher would pronounce to be incompatible with any effectual call and any gift of the Holy Spirit, which the inspired Apostle deprecates in the baptized on the very ground of their "call," and a gift of God's Spirit already vouchsafed.

I may remark, in passing, that a similar ground is taken by the Holy Spirit in the Book of Proverbs.

When God, in that Book, warns the young against this class of hardening and soul-destroying sins, He does it on the ground that the persons so tempted to fall were in covenant with Him. In the words of the Apostolic writer, calling particular attention to the language of this very Book of Proverbs, He speaks to the Jews, "*as to children*" (or "sons," *υἱοῖς*). (Heb. xii. 5.) "*My son—υἱέ μου—* attend to my wisdom, and bow thine ear to my understanding: . . . for the lips of a strange woman drop as an honeycomd, and her mouth is smoother than oil." (Prov. v. 1—3.) Again, "*My son*, keep my words, and lay up my commandments with thee . . . that they may keep thee from the strange woman." (vii. 1—5.)

Thus we see that both in the Law and in the Gospel, the calling of God, and the fact of a past reception into the bonds and grace of the covenant, are urged as the reason why men should pursue holiness, and avoid gross defiling sin.

God speaks to the Jew as to a *son*. He reminds him of the relationship he bears to Him, when He bids him keep the seventh commandment : and so with the Christian. By the mouth of St. Paul He reminds the Christian, in order to keep him holy, of his calling,—of his being *His* temple,—of God's Spirit in the Church and its members.

May not the awful prevalence of these sins in cities where the work of the Redeemer is faithfully preached, arise (in part at least) from the deliberate and systematic denial of the Divine truth we are now considering?

The Epistle to the Hebrews presents us with the same mode of addressing the whole body of the baptized.

In it God speaks to all the Hebrew Christians as "*holy brethren*, partakers of the heavenly calling." (iii. 1.) Surely no terms can be more characteristic of a state of grace; and yet, throughout the entire Epistle, we have solemn and repeated intimations that this state of grace did not imply the final perseverance of those once included in it.

These "holy brethren, partakers of the heavenly calling," have brought before them, as their Corinthian brethren had (1 Cor. x. 1—10), the fearful example of the Church in the wilderness; all of whom were brought into a comparative state of salvation at the hour of their baptism unto Moses in the cloud and in the sea; and yet the greater part fell in the wilderness because of unbelief.

The third and fourth chapters are full of this:— "Wherefore, as the Holy Ghost saith, To-day if ye will hear His voice, harden not your hearts, as in the provocation, in the day of temptation in the wilderness." "Take heed, brethren, lest there be in any of you an evil heart of unbelief, in departing from the living God." "We see that *they* could not enter in because of unbelief. Let us therefore fear, lest, a promise being left us of entering into His rest, any of you should seem [or be seen] to come short of it." (iii. 7, 8, 12, 19; iv. 1.)

Let the reader notice how exactly parallel, both in doctrine and warning, all this is with the words of the Apostle in 1 Cor. x. 1—10. "I would not that ye should be ignorant, how that all our fathers were under the cloud, and all passed through the sea; and were all baptized unto Moses in the cloud and in the sea: . . . but with many of them God was not well pleased." The whole force of the comparison in these two passages between the Church in the wilderness and the Christian Church, consists in this, that by their respective baptisms—the one thing common to the whole Church in each case—every man was separated to God and delivered to serve God,—had a present blessing and a present interest in God's promises, which he might either hold fast or lose irretrievably. Each member of the Church in the wilderness had been, in a sense, saved,[1] and this salvation took place at the moment of the passage of the Red Sea, when, in the words of the Apostle, *all* were baptized unto Moses in the cloud and in the sea. But the salvation was not final. It did not imply, or necessitate, the final perseverance of all who experienced it. It was a sign and sure token of God's merciful designs towards them, but it yet left in them power to frustrate His intention through their unbelief. This evil heart of unbelief yet remained in many who had even (to a certain extent) believed (Exod. iv. 31, xiv. 31 ; Ps. cvi. 12), and prevented them finally attaining to the rest God designed for each of them. Three times does the Holy Ghost bring the case of the *whole* Israelitish Church as a warning to the *whole* baptized Christian body ; necessarily implying, that all Christians are at Baptism brought into a state of salvation, which they have to work out and abide in. The very terms in which the Spirit bids men not to trust ignorantly and presumptuously in the mere fact of the past reception of grace in Baptism, are comparisons which imply its reality, and which would have no point in them unless Baptism were, in each case, the entrance into a state of *present* grace and salvation.

There are two other very fearful passages in this Epistle, in strict accordance with what the Apostle has hitherto been laying down, that men may be in the favour of God, and in a state of salvation, and yet fall from it. One of these we find in the sixth, another in the tenth chapter. Comparing these places together, it appears that there is

---

[1] See particularly Jude v : " I will therefore put you in remembrance, though ye once knew this, how that the Lord, having saved the people out of the land of Egypt, afterwards destroyed them that believed not."

no amount of grace from which it is not possible to fall.[1] The Apostle, beyond all doubt, contemplates the possibility of those falling away who were "*once enlightened*," who had "tasted of the heavenly gift," who had "been made partakers of the Holy Ghost," and "sanctified" (i.e. *dedicated to* God, and set apart to His service) by the "blood of the covenant." (Heb. vi. 4 ; x. 29.)

I cannot see how we are to evade the force of these awful passages, as implying the possible fall of those once in grace, except by the denial of their inspiration. I cannot see how the reality of the possession of grace can be described in more exalted, or the fall from that grace in plainer, terms.

And yet I would not assert that they are decisive against the doctrine of the final and necessary perseverance of some in the Church. It was the contemplation of places like these which forced St. Augustine to hold two gradations in the election of grace :[2] one of an election to grace which should infallibly end in final perseverance, another to every grace short of final perseverance.

The twelfth chapter is full of language analogous to that which pervades the first four. "Ye have forgotten the exhortation which speaketh unto you as unto children, My son, despise not thou the chastening of the Lord," &c. The exhortation to which the Apostle refers is taken from the Book of Proverbs. It is to be remarked how all through that Book the speaker addresses the hearer as his son. "My son" (see Prov. i. 8; ii. 1; iii. 1; iv. 1; v. 1; vi. 1; vii. 1). Now, the Apostle here asserts that this way of speaking adopted by the writer of the Book of

---

[1] See texts quoted in Chapter on Election and Final Perseverance.

[2] See note at commencement of Chapter XV.

Proverbs is not figurative or unreal; but that we are to
recognise in it the accents of God the One Heavenly *Father*
speaking to those whom He has adopted into His family.
In blaming the Hebrew Christians for having forgotten
these words of endearing relationship, the Apostle, by
implication, applies them to the whole Church of his
time, and, if so, to the Church at all times.

In verse 15 we have it implied that *all* those to whom
the Apostle wrote had been brought into a very high state
of grace : " Looking diligently lest any man fail of the grace
of God ; lest any root of bitterness springing up trouble you,
and thereby many be defiled ; lest there be any fornicator,
or profane person, as Esau, who for one morsel of meat
sold his birthright. . . . . For ye are not come to the
mount that might be touched, and that burned with fire,
nor unto blackness, and darkness, and tempest . . . but
ye are come (προσεληλύθατε) unto mount Sion, and unto the
city of the living God, the heavenly Jerusalem, and to an
innumerable company of angels, to the general assembly
and church of the firstborn, which are written in heaven,
and to God the Judge of all, and to the spirits of just men
made perfect, and to Jesus the Mediator of the New Covenant, and to the blood of sprinkling, that speaketh better
things than that of Abel. See that ye refuse not Him
that speaketh. For if they escaped not who refused Him
that spake on earth : much more shall not we escape, if we
turn away from Him that speaketh from heaven."

In verses 22 to 24 the most glorious things possible are
spoken of the state of grace. They who have come to it
(and the words of the Apostle imply that all whom he is
addressing have done so), have come to—have arrived at,
no earthly, but a heavenly state of things. It is in very
deed the kingdom of heaven upon earth. God, the good
angels, the saints in conflict as well as those at rest, Jesus

the Mediator,—all these are mingled, as it were, together, and all we (if this Epistle is addressed to the present Church) have come to this Sion, and have our birthright there (verse 16). Realized, or unrealized, we have come to these things. But though these things belong to us, are we necessarily enjoying them, or even believing them? No. The Apostle, immediately before he enumerates these glorious things, bids those who had *come* to them to "look diligently lest any man fail of the grace of God; lest any sell his birthright:" and immediately after enumerating them, in the same breath he says, "See that ye —ye who *have* come to these things, this mount Sion, this Jesus the Mediator—see that ye refuse not Him that speaketh."

It was quite possible, then,—nay, the probability was such, that it called forth the earnest and reiterated warning of the Apostle,—that they who had come to such things as the "mount Sion," the guardianship of angels, the fellowship of glorified saints, and the very sprinkling of the blood of Jesus, might yet refuse Him that speaketh, and involve themselves in a worse condemnation than those who had come to the mount Sinai, and had been baptized into the dispensation of Moses the servant, and had been brought into the older covenant only, which gendered to bondage.

Still, it may be asked, can the members of the present Christian Church—the Church of the baptized—be said with any propriety to have *come* to such things as the "city of God," the "heavenly Jerusalem," the "blood of sprinkling?" Can such things be possibly said of men in flesh and blood, and who are yet in danger of falling away? Yes, I answer, such things can be said just as much as it could be said to the members of the elder Church, because *the word of God came to them*, "Ye are GODS; and *ye are all the children of the Most High.* But ye shall die like men, and fall like one of the princes." (Ps. lxxxii. 6, 7.)

Our Lord draws especial attention to the reality of the truth this latter passage contains: " He called them gods to whom the word of God came, and the Scripture cannot be broken." (John x. 35.) If, then, the Church of the circumcision was put into so exalted a state by the mere coming of God's word to them, and that word the inferior covenant, why cannot the wondrous things in the verses we are considering be said of all the members of the Church of the better covenant, the Church of the *Incarnation ?*

It is a very great part of our probation, that we should know the greatness of the state of things in which we are. God, as of old, may be in the midst of us, and, like those of old, we may know it not.

The Apostle concludes with words which show that he meant what he said when he spake of such things being in the possession of those who could yet fall away. " Wherefore we receiving a kingdom which cannot be moved, let us have grace, whereby we may serve God acceptably with reverence and godly fear : for our God is a consuming fire."

The General Epistles of St. James, St. Peter, and St. Jude are full of instructions of a character exactly similar to that with which the Epistles of St. Paul abound,—instructions of a warning character, which proceed on the assumption that all to whom they are addressed have been received, by a past act of God's mercy, into a state of grace and a holy fellowship, which may yet be uncared for and unrealized, and so eventually lost. All are brethren, all are partakers of a calling and election, which they all must give diligence to *make sure.* The expressions implying the communication of grace to all are as general as possible. No limitation of them whatsoever to the members of an

imaginary invisible Church ; and yet some needed such
words as " Cleanse your hands, ye sinners ; and purify
your hearts, ye double-minded." (James iv. 8.) And St.
Peter finds it needful to say of some who lacked diligence
in adding virtue to virtue, " He that lacketh these things
is blind, and cannot see afar off, and hath forgotten that
he was purged from his old sins" (*i.e.* in Baptism—see
Acts xxii. 16). And the same Apostle speaks of others to
whom " it is happened according to the true proverb, The
dog is turned unto his own vomit again ; and the sow that
was washed to her wallowing in the mire." (2 Peter ii. 22.)
Similarly St. Jude reminds the Christians to whom he
wrote (and, of course, not needlessly) of the angels that
kept not their first *estate* ($\tau\grave{\eta}\nu$ $\dot{\epsilon}\alpha\upsilon\tau\tilde{\omega}\nu$ $\dot{\alpha}\rho\chi\grave{\eta}\nu$) ; and he speaks
of some as " trees whose fruit withereth, without fruit,
twice dead." Surely to have been "twice dead" they must
have once had some life, and the very fact of his comparing them to " trees whose fruit withereth, without
fruit," seems as if he had in view our Lord's parable of
the vine.

CHAPTER XI.

BAPTISMAL GRACE—GENERAL REVIEW OF THE TEACHING OF
THE EPISTLES.

ONE word more respecting the application to the Church
of our days of this mode of address so invariably adopted
by the Apostles in writing to the Church of their days.

It is alleged, I think very ignorantly and very irration-
ally, that the differences between the Church in those days
and the Church in ours are such, that what could be said
to the members of the Church *then* cannot with equal confidence be said now ; and so, that we have no warrant, from
what is said of their Baptism and its grace, to address our
congregations as having received in Baptism the same grace.

It is alleged that the members of the Galatian, Ephesian, and Colossian Churches were *all* baptized as "*converted men,*" who had each one for himself repented and
believed ; the bulk of the members of the Church now, on
the contrary, being baptized as unconscious infants.

Now what is meant by "*converted men*" ? If you mean
by "converted men" truly godly, spiritual Christians,
then the assertion that all the Apostolic Christians were
such is made in wilful ignorance of the contents of the
Apostolical Epistles. Throughout these writings we have
seen how constantly men who are assumed to have received
the highest grace are warned (and, of course, not needlessly) against the grossest sins.

If by "converted men" are meant men once heathen,

and afterwards, through hearing the preaching and seeing the miracles of the Apostles, converted to Christianity; then I deny that the Apostolic Churches were composed *wholly* of such men.

For, in the first place, there were amongst the Christians of these Churches, in the more populous cities, no inconsiderable number of Jews, who had been in covenant with the God of Abraham from their infancy, and had been brought up and educated in the national expectation of a Messiah. Here, then, would be persons in each Church whose education and religion had been preparing them for the reception of Christ's doctrine. They would be quite familiar with all the ideas of atonement, acceptance with God through sacrifice, repentance, faith, and obedience, which we derive as much from the Old Testament as from the New. Above all, they would be well acquainted with the principle of infant membership. In their case the contrast between what they had been as Jews and what they became as Christians would be by no means so sharp as we at first sight might suppose. They would have found Him whom before they had been looking for—"Jesus of Nazareth, of whom Moses in the law and the prophets did write."

Then, in the next place, I believe that we practise Infant Baptism on the authority of Christ and His Apostles; and so I believe, that whenever the father or head of a family was baptized, his children and dependants were baptized along with him. For I am forced, by common sense, if I accept the Apostolic warrant for Infant Baptism, to believe also, that *what we practise on their authority they practised themselves.* So I must, of course, believe that there was in every Christian Church a considerable number (viz. its due proportion) of baptized children of all ages, growing up into Christ by the teaching of the Church, just as ours are (or should be).

And we are not left to conjecture upon this point. The Apostle, in writing to two of his most advanced Churches, writes to the children among them as members of Christ, and sends a message to them just as if they were as much in Christ as their elders. He puts no difference between these children and those adult Christians about them, whose present faith, because their minds were fully expanded, would of course present a sharper contrast to their former unbelief, but was not on this account more acceptable to God than the tenderer and less developed Christianity of the child. And doing this, the Apostle only follows the leading of his Master. If we can gather anything from the memorable words of Christ respecting children, it is, that they are in a more favourable position for being grafted into Christ,—in a more fitting state to receive Baptism, than the conscious adult. Adults, to be received into God's favour, have to be made like to children, not children to adults : " Except ye be converted, and *become as little* children, ye shall not enter into the kingdom of heaven."

If what is said in Scripture respecting Baptism is to be our guide in our estimation of it, then Infant Baptismal Regeneration is a much more natural and easy thing to apprehend than that of adults. In adult Baptism the previous conversion seems to be all, and the rite of Baptism seems to come in as a mere formal appendage. Indeed, if we take the low popular or rationalistic view of it, we cannot help wondering why such stress is laid upon it by our Lord and His Apostles. So merely formal a matter seems quite out of place in such a system as Christianity. Infant Baptism, on the contrary, presents none of these difficulties ; the baptized infant receives the Second Adam in nearly, if not in exactly the same state of unconsciousness as he received the first.

And the reception of grace by infants, and their consequent education as members of Christ, is, of course, infinitely more in accordance with the constitution and course of nature, which proceeds from the same Author as Christianity; for men come into this world, not as Adam did, with the full use of every faculty both of mind and body, but as unconscious infants. Men come into the world members of a society, the duties and privileges of which they will not be conscious of till many years have passed over them. Is it not, then, in accordance with all this that children should be, in unconscious infancy, born again into a state of grace, the duties of which they will gradually realize as they grow to man's estate?

I cannot understand what can have given rise to the notion that the Christians to whom the Apostle wrote were all, in the modern sense, really converted; or that the Apostles, in writing their epistles, only addressed them to such as were so. And yet we find grave, sober-minded men, who are supposed to find their spiritual aliment more particularly in these parts of God's word, asserting this in order to make void the application of the sacramental terms used in them to the present visible Church.

How can such a notion be reconciled with the two Epistles to the Corinthians, particularly with 1 Corinth. x. 1—10, where the Apostle enumerates the sins by which the Israelites fell, and bids his converts avoid the wrath of God against such: "Neither be ye idolaters,—neither let us commit fornication,—neither let us tempt Christ,—neither murmur ye." Or, again (2 Cor. xii. 20, 21), "For I fear, lest, when I come again, I shall find you such as I would not . . . lest there be debates, envyings, wrath, strifes, backbitings, whisperings, swellings, tumults: and lest, when I come again, my God will humble me among you, and that I shall bewail many which have sinned

L

already, and have not repented of the *uncleanness* and *fornication* and *lasciviousness* which they have committed."

Or, again, would any minister now address a set of persons whom he believed to be really converted as St. Paul addresses the "elect" Ephesians? "Wherefore, putting away lying, speak every man truth with his neighbour. Let him that stole steal no more. Let no corrupt communication proceed out of your mouth." Or, the Colossians, "Put off all these, anger, wrath, malice, blasphemy, filthy communication out of your mouth"? Or, again, the Hebrews, "Lest there be any fornicator or profane person, as Esau, who for one morsel of meat sold his birthright"? (Eph. iv. 25—28, 29; Col. iii. 8; Heb. xii. 16.)

Would any evangelical minister now address those whom he supposed to be converted people as St. Peter addressed the "elect strangers," "Let none of you suffer as a murderer, or as a thief, or as an evil doer, or as a busybody in other men's matters"? (1 Peter iv. 15.)

From these considerations, then (amongst many others), I infer the utter groundlessness of the idea that there is any difference between the modern and the Apostolic Church of such a sort as to throw us back upon a way of speaking to the baptized contrary to that which the Apostles invariably adopted.

We have now examined, at greater or less length, all the epistles in which St. Paul writes to Churches, or bodies of Christians. Each of these letters bears its testimony to the fact of the wide-spread diffusion of the grace of the New Covenant throughout the Church. In every one the Apostle presupposes a *wide-spread*, rather than a *limited*, diffusion of the Spirit. The precepts and warnings contained in them can be applied in their entireness to Christians of this our day, only on the principle of Infant Baptismal Regeneration as held by the Catholic Church;

for on this principle, and on this alone, can the mass of
nominal Christians be held answerable for having received
grace.

And, indeed, this principle of the universal diffusion of
grace, and the consequent responsibility of the whole body
of Christians, is not only implied, but asserted over and
over again. Let us, even at the risk of incurring the
charge of repetition, mention a few places :—

"I say, through the grace given to me, *to every man that
is among you*, not to think of himself more highly than he
ought to think; but to think soberly, according as God
hath dealt *to every man* the measure of faith." "So we,
being *many*, are *one* body in Christ, and *every one* members
one of another." (Let the reader remember that this
Epistle is addressed to "all that are in Rome, beloved of
God, called saints."—Rom. xii. 3, 5.)

"Know ye not that ye are the temple of God?" "The
temple of God is holy, *which temple ye are.*" "Know ye
not that your bodies are the members of Christ?" "What,
know ye not that your bodies are the temple of the
Holy Ghost which is in you, which ye have of God?"
(1 Cor. iii. 16, 17; vi. 15, 19.)

"*Every man* hath his proper gift of God." (vii. 7.)

"The manifestation of the Spirit is given *to every man*
to profit withal." (xii. 7.) Also (13), "By one Spirit are
we ALL baptized into *one* body." "Now ye are the body
of Christ, and members in particular." (27.)

"We then, as workers together with Him, beseech you
also that ye receive not the grace of God in vain."
"Ye are the temple of the living God." (2 Cor. vi.
1, 16.)

"Ye are *all* the children of God by faith in Christ
Jesus. For *as many of you* as have been baptized into
Christ, have put on Christ." "Ye are *all* one in Christ

Jesus." (Galatians iii. 26—28.) "Jerusalem which is above
is free, which is our mother." (iv. 26.)

"Unto *every one* of us is given grace according to the
measure of the gift of Christ." (Eph. iv. 7.) "Grieve
not the holy Spirit of God, whereby *ye are sealed.*" (30.)

"God would make known what is the riches of the
glory of this mystery among the Gentiles; which is
Christ in you, the hope of glory: whom we preach,
warning every man, and teaching every man in all wisdom;
that we may present *every man* perfect in Christ Jesus."
(Col. i. 27, 28.)

"Ye are *all* the children of light, and the children of
the day : THEREFORE let us not sleep, as do others."
(1 Thess. v. 5, 6.)[1]

---

[1] Other instances are,—

"We *being many* are one body and one bread : for we are *all*
partakers of that one bread." (1 Cor. x. 17.)

"The head of *every man* is Christ." (xi. 3.)

"All these worketh that one and the selfsame Spirit, dividing to
every man severally as He will." (xii. 11.)

"For the edifying of the body of Christ : till *we all* come in the
unity of the faith," &c. (Eph. iv. 11, 13.) "Wherefore putting
away lying, speak *every man* truth with his neighbour : for we are
members one of another." (25.)

"Husbands, love your wives . . . for *we are members of His
body* . . . Let *every one of you in particular* so love his wife even
as himself." (v. 25, 30, 33.)

"Charged *every one of you*, as a father doth his children, that
ye would walk worthy of God, *who hath called you.*" (1 Thess. ii.
11, 12.)

"This is the will of God, even your sanctification . . . that
every one of you should know how to possess . . . For God hath
not called us unto uncleanness, but unto holiness . . . who hath
also given unto us His holy Spirit." (iv. 3, 4, 7, 8.)

"Of His own will begat He us with the word of truth, that we
should be a kind of first-fruits of His creatures. *Wherefore* [or

In strict accordance with all this we have St. John saying, "Of His fulness have *all* we received." (John i. 16.) We have our Lord saying (Matthew xxv. 15) that to "*every one*" is given talents according to his several ability, and so also He "gives to *every* man his work," (Mark xiii. 34,) and no man can do his work except he has a position in which, and means by which, to do it. And, lastly, in accordance with all this, we have St. Paul bidding the Ephesian elders to look to *all* the flock over which the Holy Ghost had made them overseers, to feed the Church of God—evidently implying that all the flock was the Church of God, and he cites his own example in that he had not ceased to warn *every one*. (Acts xx. 28.)

Such are the direct assertions, that all are in some measure partakers of the gift of God's Spirit and of His calling; and, as I have abundantly shown, what is here asserted in so many words is implied all through the teaching of the Apostles; and what is more, I cannot find one text contrary to such teaching. I cannot find one text which asserts that Baptism is *in any case* a dead, empty form. I cannot find one place which asserts that those to whom God has once given grace, will necessarily persevere in the use of it. Never, in any single instance, is any baptized Christian called upon to become regenerate. There is no intimation whatsoever of any invisible Church within the visible, to which grace

"ye know it," ἴστε], my beloved *brethren*, let *every man* be swift to hear, slow to speak, slow to wrath," &c. (James i. 18, 19.)

"Finally, be ye *all* of one mind, having compassion one of another . . . knowing that *ye are thereunto called*, that ye should inherit a blessing." (1 Pet. iii. 8, 9.)

Exception may perhaps be taken to the cogency of one or two of the above texts, but as a whole their testimony is overwhelming.

has been restricted. There are innumerable texts which imply that there were bad Christians as well as good amongst those to whom the Apostle wrote, but they are *invariably* spoken to as "falling away," or "receiving grace in vain," or "grieving the Spirit." In no one case is their fall ascribed to the withholding of grace on God's part; in *every case* to the abuse of it on their own.

Such was the Church, the kingdom of God, even in the Apostolic times. It was even in those days what our Lord, in His prophetic parables, described that it would be.

CHAPTER XII.

BAPTISMAL GRACE—THE PARABLES OF OUR LORD.

THE parables of our Lord will, on examination, be found
to contain features singularly in accordance with the great
Church principle of the universal diffusion of the grace
of the New Covenant in the Church, and of a particular
gift of the Spirit to each of its baptized members; and, I
may also add, singularly contrary to the doctrine of
the necessary perseverance of all who have been once
received into a state of grace.

Especially is this the case with those parables in which
our Lord expressly describes the "kingdom of God" in
its various aspects. By the "Parable of the Sower," for
instance, we are taught that, of three classes in which
the word of God takes root and appears above ground, in
one only does it come to perfection. In one of the three
the plant of grace withers, in another the word is choked.
(St. Matt. xiii. 6, 7.)

In the parable of the "Tares in the field," we are
warned that the appearance which the kingdom of God
will present, will be that of a field of wheat and tares
mingled together; and both, by the express direction of
the Householder, to grow together until the harvest,—
the tares not to be rooted up, lest the wheat should be
rooted up with them.

In the parable of the "Grain of mustard seed," we
have the Church of Jesus Christ growing from the

smallest of beginnings to be a tree overshadowing all
the nations of the earth. This is, of course, perfectly
incompatible with the idea of an invisible remnant being
the only Church.

I will give the teaching of the parable of the "Net cast
into the sea, and gathering of every kind," in the trenchant
words of Law, the author of the "Serious Call to a
Devout and Holy Life."

Bishop Hoadley, his Socinian opponent, appears to have
hazarded the assertion that the only true Church is the
Invisible Church. To which Law replies : "Our Saviour
himself tells us, that *The kingdom of heaven is like unto
a net that was cast into the sea, and gathered of every kind,
which when it was full they drew to shore, and sat down,
and gathered the good into vessels, but cast the bad away.*
And then says, *So shall it be at the end of the world.*

"This, my Lord, is a description of the state of Christ's
Church given us by Himself. Is there anything in this
description that should lead us to take it for an *invisible*
kingdom, that consists of one particular sort of people
invisibly united to Christ? Nay, is it not the whole
intent of the similitude to teach us the contrary, that His
kingdom is to consist of a mixture of good and bad
subjects till the end of the world? The kingdom of
Christ is said here to gather its members, as a net gathers
all kinds of fish ; it is chiefly compared to it in this
respect, because it gathers of *all kinds ;* which I suppose
is a sufficient declaration, that this kingdom consists of
subjects good and bad, as that the net that gathers of
every kind of fish takes good and bad fish.

" Let us suppose that the Church of Christ was this
invisible number of people united to Christ by such internal invisible graces : is it possible that a kingdom
consisting of this one sort of people, *invisibly good,* should

be like a net that gathers of every kind of fish? If it was to be compared to a net, it ought to be compared to such a net as gathers only of one kind, viz. good fish, and then it might represent to us a Church that has but one sort of members.

"But since Christ, who certainly understood the nature of His own kingdom, has declared that it is like a net that gathers of *every kind of fish ;* it is as absurd to say that it consists of only one kind of persons (viz. the invisibly good), as to say that the net which gathers of every kind has only of one kind in it. Further, *when it was full, they drew it to shore, and gathered the good into vessels, but cast the bad away ; so shall it be at the end of the world.* Now as it was the bad as well as the good fish which filled the net, and the Church is compared to the net in this respect ; so it is evident that bad men as well as good are subjects of this kingdom. And *I* presume they are members of that kingdom which they fill up, as surely as the fish must be in the net before they can fill it. All these circumstances plainly declare that the Church or kingdom of Christ shall consist of a mixture of good and bad people to the end of the world.

"Again, Christ declares *that the kingdom of heaven is like to a certain king which made a marriage for his son,* and sent his servants out into the highways, who *gathered together all as many as they found, both good and bad, and the wedding was furnished with guests."* (Matt. xxii. 2.)

"Nothing can be more evident than that the chief intent of this parable is to show that the Church of Christ is to be a mixture of good and bad to the end of the world. It is like a feast where good and bad guests are entertained ; but can it be like such a *feast* if only the *invisibly* virtuous are members of it? If the subjects of this kingdom are of one invisible kind, how can they bear

any resemblance to a feast made up of all kinds of guests?
Nay, what could be thought of more unlike to this kingdom, if it was such a kingdom as you have represented
it? . . . It may justly be expected, my Lord, that you
should show us some grounds for this distinction (between
the universal visible and the universal invisible Church).
Where does our blessed Lord give us so much as the least
hint that He has founded two universal Churches on
earth? Did He describe His Church by halves when He
likened it to a net full of all kinds of fish? Has He
anywhere let us know that He has another universal
kingdom on earth besides this, which, in the variety of
its members, is like a net full of all kinds of good and
bad fish?"[1]

So far this clear and powerful writer. A greater than
he, however, viz. Bishop Pearson, has given the same
judgment in a few decisive words in his "Exposition of
the Creed" (Article *Holy Catholic Church*):—

"Not that there are two Churches of Christ, one in
which good and bad are mingled together, another in
which they are good alone : one in which the saints are
imperfectly holy, another in which they are perfectly
such : but one and the same Church, in relation to
different times, admitteth, or not admitteth, the per-
mixtion of the wicked, or the imperfection of the godly."

But to proceed with other parables.

In that of the "Unmerciful Servant" (Matt. xviii. 23—
35), the kingdom of heaven is likened to a state of things
in which one who has asked and *obtained* forgiveness ("I
forgave thee all that debt, because thou desiredst me") is
finally cast away, because he does not forgive his brother.

---

[1] Reply to the Bishop of Bangor's Answer to the Representation
of the Committee of Convocation. 2nd Edit. p. 9.

If words mean anything, this parable teaches that men may fall from the grace of forgiveness, and be finally unforgiven.

In the parables of " the Talents " (Matt. xxv. 14—30) and of "the Pounds" (Luke xix. 11—27) we have the kingdom of heaven likened unto servants, to whom are entrusted by the Master, as to *His own servants* (Matt. xxv. 14), gifts of grace ; and, in each case, some of those who receive these gifts from His hands receive these gifts in vain. And these servants must be taken to represent His Church and all its members ; for in neither case is there any account of servants who receive nothing ; and St. Paul, in a chapter especially devoted to the gifts of grace in the Church, says, "The manifestation of the Spirit is given to *every man* to profit withal." (1 Cor. xii. 7.) And again : " To *every one of us* is given grace according to the measure of the gift of Christ." (Ephes. iv. 7.)

The parable of the "Barren Fig-tree" teaches us that a man may be in God's vineyard, *i.e.* in His Church, and be tended by Him, and be the subject also of the especial intercession of the Dresser of the vineyard ; and God may look for fruit from such an one—may come for years together seeking fruit from him, which God could not do unless He had given the man grace to bear fruit; and yet the man may be cut down at the last.

The parable of the "Prodigal Son "—however it may primarily refer to the elder or Jewish, and younger or Gentile body—unquestionably must be applied to the members of the Church of Christ as it exists in this our day. And it is so applied by all who would win souls to God. Yet it cannot be so applied as a whole, taking some of its most important statements into account, except on the assumption that those who are called to repentance

are *God's sons*, and must *return* to their *Father's house.*
The two sons represent two bodies of men in the Church
—the elder one betokens those who, after the example of
Samuel and John the Baptist, grow up and continue in God's
grace ; the younger represents those who fall from the grace
of the covenant and are afterwards converted and restored.

Both the prodigal and his brother are "*sons.*" Both
are originally in *their Father's house,* i.e. in the Church of
Jesus Christ. The son who leaves his home is yet a
"*son.*" It is that which makes his sin the deeper, and
his repentance the more bitter. When he returns, his
Father meets him as *His lost son*, and says respecting him,
"This my son was dead, and is alive again."

"My son." We have here the covenant relationship
established in time past, the "goodness" in which he
ought to have "*continued.*" (Rom. xi. 22 ; John xv.
1—6.)

"Was dead." Here we have the fall from grace into a
state of death. ("She that liveth in pleasure is dead
while she liveth." 1 Tim. v. 6.)

"And is alive again." Here we have the conversion of
him who was, and continued to be from the first, "*a son ;*"
but the privileges of whose sonship were suspended till
he returned to the bosom of his Father.

This parable illustrates how completely the most unreserved preaching of Baptismal Regeneration and the most
earnest calls to conversion are in accord with one another.
If you urge repentance and conversion on a sinner living
at a distance from God, it must be on the strength of his
past adoption into God's family, *if you are to take the
parable of the prodigal son as your guide ;* just as Isaiah
beseeches the children of Israel to return to God because
they were *His children* and *His people,* "I have
nourished and brought up *children*, and they have re-

belled against Me. The ox knoweth his owner, and the ass his master's crib; but Israel doth not know, *My people doth not consider.*" (Isaiah i. 2.)

In fact, I doubt whether the place can be named throughout the whole of the Old Testament, in which God calls on the children of Israel to repent and turn to Him, except on some ground of covenant mercy bestowed on one and all of them.

The comparison of our Lord's disciples and followers to "*salt*," coupled with the intimation that the salt may lose its savour and be good for nothing but to be cast forth, is directly opposed to the opinion of the necessary perseverance in grace of all to whom God has once vouchsafed grace. (Matt. v. 13 ; Luke xiv. 34, 35.)

The reception of grace cannot be more strongly implied than by a man's being compared to *salt*, the thing which preserves other things from corruption. The loss of grace is implied equally strongly by the very salt itself being corrupted and become good for nothing.

Another parable (or perhaps we should call it "parabolic similitude") yet remains second to none, both in its theological and practical importance,—"The Vine and the Branches." (John xv. 1—10.)

I will give the bearing of this on the subject in hand in the words of Bishop Beveridge, in a Sermon on the text, John xv. 7 : "If ye abide in Me, and My words abide in you, ye shall ask what ye will, and it shall be done unto you."

"There are two general heads of mankind—the first Adam, and the second, that is, Jesus Christ; who also was, in the most proper sense of the word, Adam— man in general—in that the whole nature of man was in Him, as it was in the first Adam. And so the Apostle calls Him, where, speaking of Adam and Christ, he saith,

'And so it is written, The first man Adam was made a
living soul ; the last Adam was made a quickening spirit.'
The last Adam, Christ, was made a spirit that maketh or
causeth life, as the first was the cause of death.   'For as
in Adam all die, even so in Christ shall all be made alive.'
In the first all died ; the second died for all, so that all
may live in Him again ; and so they will at the last day.
And all that will *may* be quickened by Him with newness
of life, and restored to the same happy state from which
they fell in the first Adam.   And so many will, according
to that [saying] of the Apostle, 'As by one man's disobedience many were made sinners, so by the obedience
of one shall many be made righteous.'

"This may seem a great mystery, that they who fell in
one man should rise again in another.   But the Apostle
unfolds it, where he saith, 'The first man is of the earth,
earthy ; the second man is the Lord from heaven.'   The
first man, in general, in whom all the rest were contained,
and therefore fell with him and in him, he was formed
out of the ground, and so was a mere man, and no more.
But the second man came down from heaven, and was the
Lord, the Lord of Hosts, the Almighty God there, before
He came from thence, yea, from all eternity.   He was the
Lord from heaven, and came from thence in a way suitable
to His divine glory, by being conceived of the Holy Ghost,
and born of a pure virgin, so as to become man, and yet
be God too in the same person.   And being thus God as
well as man, He was every way qualified to repair the loss
that mankind sustained by the fall of the first Adam, and
to restore them to their first estate as perfectly as if they
had never fallen from it. . . . . 'If ye abide in Me.'   He
doth not say, 'If ye be in Me,' but 'If ye abide in Me.'
For, speaking to His disciples, He supposeth them to be in
Him upon that account, because they were His disciples.

And He speaks to such only : for none can abide in Him, unless they first be in Him ; that is, unless they be taken out of the stock of the first Adam, and grafted into Him, the second. Thus He Himself explains it in this place, by comparing Himself to a vine, and His disciples to the branches in that vine : 'I,' saith He, 'am the vine, ye are the branches ;' implying that His disciples are in Him, as a branch is in the vine, so as to receive sap and nourishment from it. The same thing is elsewhere explained by their being members of His body, the Church ; for the Church, or congregation of all His faithful people, is called His 'body.' Of this body, He himself is the 'Head ;' and His disciples are all and every one, in his place and station, 'members of this body,' and so are acted on and governed by that Holy Spirit that proceedeth from Him, the Head ; which could not be, unless they were in Him as a branch is in the vine, or a member in the body of a man. But how can we, who are by nature of the stock of the first Adam, be taken out from thence, and made the members of the second, or, which is the same, His disciples ? This He himself hath taken care of, by ordaining a Sacrament for this end and purpose, saying to His Apostles, and in them to all the ministers of His Church, 'Go ye therefore, and make all nations disciples, by baptizing them,' &c. ; as the original words plainly import. Hence they who are baptized according to the form instituted by Christ Himself for that purpose, are said to be baptized into Him. And the Apostle saith, 'As many of you as have been baptized into Christ, have put on Christ.' But they who are baptized into Christ must needs be in Him ; and they who are in Him have laid aside their relation to Adam, and have put on Christ, so as to belong now to Him, as His flock, His disciples, His peculiar people.

"But it is not enough thus to be in Christ, but we must abide in Him. 'If ye abide in Me,' saith He, *implying that some may be in Him and yet not abide in Him.* Such are they who once were baptized, and so made members of His body, but are afterwards cut off by His Church, or by themselves : such as renounce their Baptism, or leave off to profess His doctrine and religion ; and such as only profess it, but do not take care to believe and live according to it."—Sermon xxxvii.

CHAPTER XIII.

THE VISIBLE CHURCH.

THE visible Church is the only one either mentioned, or contemplated, in the Scriptures. In the places where we should most expect it, as I have shown, there is not the least hint whatsoever given of any *invisible* body to which God has restricted His grace. It is a figment of man's invention, in order to get over a difficulty which the Apostolic writers meet in another way. The difficulty is that man should receive such a thing as the grace of God in vain. Modern Calvinism revolts at this, and insists upon having two Churches—one, the visible, consisting of the *many* who partake of outward sacraments ; the other, the invisible, consisting of the *few* who really partake of secret grace, and to all of whom God has vouchsafed perseverance to life eternal.

The Scripture writers, on the contrary, know nothing of this distinction. They recognise in every page that Christians can, do, and will fall from God, and receive His grace in vain. When they contemplate the case of a bad Christian, they *always assume him to have fallen from grace.* They never assume him to be excluded by God from some inner circle of grace. This is a matter of fact which cannot be gainsaid.

The Church of England, adhering closely to Scripture, in her Thirty-nine Articles recognises but one Church. In

M

her nineteenth article she calls the "visible" Church the
"Cœtus fidelium": "fidelis" being, of course, the translation of the Greek πιστὸς, or believer, taken in its wide and
ancient acceptation, as opposed to infidel or heathen,—
and not in its narrow and modern sense, as opposed to
nominal Christian.[1]

In the twenty-sixth article she asserts, respecting the
same visible Church, that in it "the evil be ever mingled
with the good." Not one word is there of "the good"
being an invisible Church by themselves.

And when we look to the strict meaning of the word
"Church," we see the absurdity of calling true Christians
an invisible *Church*.

They are not a "Church," because there is no possible
way of gathering them together. If we are to believe
St. Paul (1 Cor. xii.), the Church is a body, and, as such,
an organization; now true Christians are not yet an
organized body. They are scattered throughout the
Church in all parts of the world. They are separated
from one another, and every attempt to make them act in
concert breaks down. There is no password, no shibboleth,
whereby they can *infallibly* recognise one another.

Continually do we find that those who pray with fluency
and speak with unction either turn out rank hypocrites,
or by their uncharitableness and evil surmising make us
doubtful of their state in the sight of God. Continually
do we find that the most unpromising put to shame the

_____

[1] They who make "fidelis," or "faithful man," here to mean "true
Christian," make the nineteenth article stultify itself, and contradict
the twenty-sixth ; for if the *visible* Church consists of "fideles" in
the sense of true Christians *only*, what room is there for the invisible ?—what can it possibly consist of ? and the twenty-sixth
expressly asserts that in the visible Church the "evil are ever
mingled with the good."

apparently advanced, and the dull and cold condemn the fervid and spiritual.

Even a God-inspired prophet could not tell who were his brethren. He thought he was alone, and God assured him that he was but one of seven thousand.

And not only is there no invisible Church considered as a Church, but there never will be. The time of the Church's final purgation will be the time of the "MANIFESTATION of the sons of God." The righteous will then SHINE FORTH as the sun in the kingdom of their Father. The Church will be purged of hypocrites, and the righteous only will remain in it, but it will still be a *visible* Church.

It is of the very essence of a Church to be visible, gathered together, assembled, organized.

It is really as absurd to talk about the invisible Church if you really attach to it any idea of a Church, or build any doctrine upon its separate existence, as it is to talk of an invisible appearance, an unorganized organization, an unassembled assembly, a scattered gathering together. I believe, as strongly as any man can do, that the whole visible Church is for the sake of the true elect, but these true elect ones are not yet a Church, and any attempt for doctrinal purposes to treat them as at present a separate body is to go counter to the intention of God in having established a visible kingdom of grace, and instituted visible signs and tokens whereby we may know that we and our fellow Christians are in this kingdom and partakers of its grace.[1]

---

[1] I am aware, of course, that the term "Invisible Church" is applied to the Church of righteous souls in the unseen state; but this is not the sense in which it is used by those whose opinions I am now controverting.

CHAPTER XIV.

CERTAIN OBJECTIONS CONSIDERED.

WE now proceed to consider several passages frequently brought forward to prove that none can have received grace and adoption except those who are now living to it.

One of these texts is Rom. viii. 14: "As many as are led by the Spirit of God, they are the sons of God."

From this place it is argued that none who are not consciously living to their God and Saviour either are, or ever have been, adopted into His family.

Any Concordance would inform him who so reasons that there are *four* distinct senses in which the term "sons" or "children of God" is used in Scripture.

In the first and lowest sense, all men are children of God by *creation*. Thus we read, "Have we not *all* one Father; hath not one God created us?" and St. Luke, writing for Gentiles, carries up our Lord's genealogy to *Adam* as the *son* of God: "Who was the son of Enos, who was the son of Seth, who was the son of Adam, who was the son of God."

It is also to be remarked, that in the only missionary sermon of St. Paul to the heathen recorded in Scripture, that to the Athenians, he appeals to this very sonship. He quotes one of their own poets, as bearing testimony to this great truth. He includes himself with the idolatrous Athenians in this common sonship. "Forasmuch then as WE are the offspring of God, *we* ought not to think that the Godhead is like unto gold," &c. (Acts xvii. 29.)

The reader will notice that this preaching of the Apostle is exactly in accordance with his teaching in his Epistles, in making *some* blessing conferred in past time the ground and motive of present turning from sin to God.

But this, of course, is the first and lowest sense, and it was one in which if, when the Gospel was preached to the heathen, they stopped short, it was at the peril of their souls. They were by *creation*, it is true, the offspring of God, but still *not* in covenant; for St. Paul says of such, "At that time ye were without Christ, being aliens from the commonwealth of Israel, and strangers from the covenants of promise, having no hope, and without God in the world." (Ephes. ii. 12.)

Then, in the next place, the members of the Jewish, and, after them, the Christian Church, are the children of God by *adoption*.

"Israel is My son, My firstborn" (Exod. iv. 22); "I have nourished and brought up children" (Isa. i. 2); "Ye are all the children of God by the faith in Christ Jesus. For as many of you as have been baptized into Christ have put on Christ." (Gal. iii. 26, 27.)

Here, then, is a most important practical sense in which the Israelites and the Galatian Christians were children of God. But surely it could be said neither of the one nor of the other that they were "*led by the Spirit;*" for God says by Isaiah to the Israelites, "I have nourished and brought up children, *and they have rebelled against Me;*" and by St. Paul to the Galatian Christians, "O foolish Galatians, who hath bewitched you, that ye should not obey the truth?" (Gal. iii. 1.)

But this adoption is not the highest "sonship." It is intended to lead to a closer and higher relationship. And so we have a third sonship: "Love your enemies, bless them that curse you, do good to them that hate you, and

pray for them that despitefully use you and persecute you ;
that ye may be the children of your Father which is in
heaven : for He maketh His sun to rise on the evil and
on the good, and sendeth rain on the just and on the
unjust." (St. Matt. v. 44, 45.)

Here is a third and higher sense in which men are
children of God by bearing His image. Now, in this
sense, those are the children of God who are "led by the
Spirit ; " for the Spirit leads a man into perfect conformity
with God's will and character.

But to say that men who are not following the leading of
God's Spirit, and who love not their enemies, and who bless not
those that curse them, have never been grafted into Christ,
and so made God's children by adoption, is too palpable
a perversion of Scripture to be entertained for a moment.

In the fourth, and last, and best sense, men will be
children of God when they are raised up at the last day
in their incorruptible bodies. "They which shall be
accounted worthy to obtain that world, and the resurrection from the dead, neither marry, nor are given in marriage : neither can they die any more : for they are equal
unto the angels ; and are the *children of God*, being the
children of the resurrection." (Luke xx. 35, 36.)

And again, in the midst of a vision of the resurrection
state, " He that overcometh shall inherit all things ; and
I will be his God, and he shall be My son." (Rev. xxi. 7.)

All these various degrees of sonship are intended to lead
to one another. A man is born that he may be brought
into the covenant of grace, and so be made a member of
Christ and the child of God : he is made this in order that
he may be a son of God by bearing His image in all things ;
and he bears God's image here in order that he may be
raised up hereafter at the General Resurrection a glorified
son of God.

We have seen how the Apostle recognised the lowest of these degrees, and we know not what injury they do to Christ's Church who ignore any of these steps, who wilfully put out of sight any claim which God has upon a soul's allegiance.

In accordance with this we find, in many other passages of Scripture, various degrees of God's goodness and grace recognised; all expressed by the same name, and yet having different meanings, and the lower evidently intended to lead to the higher grade.

Thus the term "Kingdom of God" or "Kingdom of heaven" is in the New Testament applied to three things. There is, first, the "Kingdom of heaven" described in the parable of the "draw net," and other parables, in Matthew xiii. as a mixed state of things, containing both good and bad. This is, of course, the Church. Then there is the "Kingdom of God" in the heart, as "righteousness, and peace, and joy in the Holy Ghost." (Rom. xiv. 17.) To this the Church, or kingdom of grace, is intended to lead; and it would effectually do so, if the baptized would but apprehend that for which Christ has apprehended them in the net of Divine grace; and there is, lastly, the kingdom of God which will be revealed at Christ's coming. (2 Tim. iv. 1.)

Similarly Christians, who are in one sense (*i.e.* sacramentally) *dead* to sin in Christ, are yet called upon, within the compass of a few verses, to *die* to sin by denying it. "We are buried with Him by Baptism unto death." "Reckon yourselves *dead* to sin." "Let not *sin* therefore *reign*." (Rom. vi. 1, 11, 12.)

Again, the same figure occurs in Coloss. iii. 3, 5: "Ye are *dead*;" "*Mortify therefore* your members which are upon the earth; fornication," &c.

Again, the Corinthians (1 Cor. v. 7) *are* "*unleavened*;" therefore they are called upon to *become* "*unleavened*."

We now come to another text, extensively appealed to as limiting the efficacy of Baptism to those who afterwards live to God.

In 2 Cor. v. 17, we have the words : " If any *man be* in Christ, *he is* a new creature : old things are passed away ; behold, all things are become new."

From this it is argued that unless a man be savingly converted,—unless the old sins of his natural state be *completely* eradicated, and unless he have altogether new desires, feelings, and affections, he neither is, *nor ever has been*, a member of Christ. The answer to this is, of course, that a man must not only be grafted into Christ, but must *abide* in Him.

We have the whole doctrine of grafting into Christ, and union with Him and its results, in our Lord's similitude of the " Vine and its branches ;" and in that similitude HE recognises the awful truth that a man may have been brought unto Him, and yet be barren of the fruits of holiness and goodness here, and be finally lost hereafter. " Every branch *in Me* that beareth not fruit, God taketh away ;" and again, " If a man abide not *in Me*, he is cast forth as a branch, and is withered ; and men gather them, and cast them into the fire, and they are burned." (John xv.)

Sin of every kind has a tendency to separate a man from Christ, and cut him off from the fellowship of Christ's body.

This would be a sufficient answer to the inference above mentioned, but I cannot dismiss this passage from consideration without drawing attention to a fact which the circumstance of our living in a Christian country prevents us from duly realizing, viz. how true, in a sense, this text is of *all* the baptized.

When the Apostle says, " Old things are passed away ; behold, all things are become new," to *whom* does he

speak? Surely, every chapter of these two Epistles bears
testimony to the fact that the things of the old nature—
old lusts, old habits, even old idolatries—had not passed
away in the case of many in the Church to whom he
wrote; and yet we have seen how unreservedly and unmistakeably he addresses *all* as members of Christ. We
must look, then, for an interpretation of these words in
harmony with his other words. The Apostle is *here* not
contrasting some Christians with others, as being some in
Christ and some not, but he is speaking of what, in a
measure, belongs to *all* Christians, nominal and real, as
contrasted with the heathen.

We who are living in a nominally Christian state of
things, bad though it be, cannot easily realize the difference between our state and that purely heathen one
from which we have been delivered. The following
occurred to myself, in the presence of a large number of
others :—

Some years ago I had the privilege of meeting a leading
Missionary (C. M. S., now a Colonial Bishop) from the
diocese of Madras. I made some inquiries respecting the
Travancore native Christians, a body in communion with
some branch of the Greek Church, which had been settled
on the Coromandel Coast from the fourth or fifth century.
My desire was to know whether it would be possible to
employ them in our work there for the evangelization of
India. I was told that from the present condition of those
Churches there was no hope whatever of such a result, the
members of the communion with which he had come in
contact being in a helpless, degraded state, having little
more than the Christian name, and their very bishops
ordaining boys of a few years old to obtain the trifling
ordination fee. He gave me to understand that all efforts
to raise them had been utterly fruitless, that they were far

more superstitious than the Roman Catholics, and that the chief part of their Christianity consisted in the use of amulets or charms with the names of Christian saints written upon them.[1] " But," continued he, " notwithstanding all this, you are not to suppose for a moment that they are the same as the heathen around them. I assure you that between these Christians, low though their state be, and the idolatrous Hindoos, there is a gulf that seems impassable."

Another Missionary (C. M. S.) from a different part of India, and unacquainted with the preceding, actually uses this text as illustrating the difference between the heathen and the Christian state, in the following extract from a letter :—" You can form no idea with what consummate wisdom the principles of Hindooism have been made to entwine themselves into everything ; indeed, it becomes almost a *natural fact*, as well as a spiritual truth, in India, that ' if any man be in Christ, he is a new creature.' " [2]

---

[1] The reader will observe that I am not adopting this account of the state of these Christians as my own.

[2] In the above exposition I have assumed the correctness of the Authorized Version of this passage. It is questionable, however, whether the words, " If any man *be* in Christ, *he is* a new creature," be a correct translation of the Greek words, ὥστε εἴ τις ἐν Χριστῷ καινὴ κτίσις. In the Authorized Version, the sentence is divided into two clauses ; and to effect this the substantive verb has to be supplied in each, as the words in italics will show the unlearned reader. The oldest Latin translation renders the Greek without any addition, " If there be any new creature in Christ." In our Bibles there is a marginal reading, " If any man be in Christ, let.him be a new creature."

After long and careful consideration of this passage and its context, I am convinced that the only way of rendering it, so as to adhere closely to the natural meaning of the Greek, and also to preserve to it some connexion with the line of argument of the whole passage, is by taking τις as agreeing with κτίσις and rendering it as in

The case of Simon Magus (Acts viii. 9—24) is much relied upon by those who impugn Church doctrine. It is

the Vulgate : "If there be any, in Christ, new creature (or creation), [then] ancient things (ἀρχαῖα, not *old things*, which would require παλαιά) passed away (παρῆλθεν) ; behold, all things are become new."

In this case, of course, we avoid taking such liberties with the text as putting a stop after Χριστῷ, of supplying two substantive verbs, and of making the two words καινὴ κτίσις a sentence of itself, having neither its own subject or copula expressed ; "[he is] a new creation." We simply take the words "ἐν Χριστῷ" adverbially, according to one of the most common forms in Greek Syntax.

It is objected that this is contrary to New Testament usage, though, of course, well known in classical Greek. There are, however, some instances of it in the New Testament, as for instance τινὲς δὲ ἀπὸ τῆς Ἀσίας Ἰουδαῖοι (Acts xxiv. 18), and εἶπέν τις ἐξ αὐτῶν ἴδιος αὐτῶν προφήτης (Tit. i. 12), also Acts xv. 5, 24 ; Rom. i. 11.

The passage thus rendered is, "If there be any new creation (order of things, or dispensation) in Christ, ancient things passed away : behold, all things are become new : and all things are of God, who hath reconciled," &c.

This rendering enables us to establish the connexion of the passage with what goes before it, which the ordinary rendering does not.

St. Paul is evidently throughout this Epistle painfully conscious of the fact that certain false teachers were endeavouring to undermine his influence with his Corinthian converts. These persons he evidently alludes to in verse 12 as "glorying in appearance and not in heart." They even accused him of insanity. To this he answers (verse 13) : "Whether we be beside ourselves, it is to God, or whether we be sober it is for your cause. For the love of Christ constraineth us ; because we thus judge, that if one died for all, then all died ; and that He died for all that they who live [*i.e.* all the living] should not henceforth live unto themselves, but unto Him that died for them, and rose again."

Seeing, then, that Christ has thus redeemed all men, all must be accounted to be spiritually equal. There was no distinction of Jew or Gentile, as their false teachers would fain establish. And so "henceforth," the Apostle says, "know we no man after the

alleged that we have in him the example of a man who
received Baptism, and yet was afterwards pronounced by

flesh." He evidently has here before his eyes those who, in the
words of another Epistle (Gal. vi. 12, 13), desired to glory in men's
flesh, and against whom he opposed (Phil. iii. 3) the true mark of
Christianity that "it has no confidence in the flesh." "Yea," he
says, "even if we have known Christ after the flesh" (*i.e.* he
supposes the case of his having been an Apostle or companion of
Christ, who knew Him in the days of His flesh as a fellow Jew),
"now henceforth know we Him (after the flesh as a Jew) no more,"
for we now regard Him as having a common relationship to the
whole human race as their Second Adam, in whom all died
(federally) to rise again. "So," he proceeds, "if there be in this
new man—this Second Adam, any κτίσις—any new state of things,
then ancient things, *i.e.* the old way of access to God, the old seal of
circumcision, the old Levitical ministry did, as ἀρχαῖα, pass away,
behold all things are become new. We have now access through
a new and living way, Christ's blood is the blood of a new Covenant." Thus Chrysostom: "But behold a new soul (for it was
cleansed), and a new body, and a new worship, and promises new,
and covenant, and life and table and dress, and all things new
absolutely. For instead of the Jerusalem below we have received
that mother city which is above; and instead of a material temple,
have seen a spiritual temple; instead of tables of stone, fleshly
ones; instead of circumcision, baptism; instead of the manna, the
Lord's body; instead of water from a rock, blood from His side;
instead of Moses or Aaron's rod, the Cross; instead of the promised
land, the kingdom of heaven; instead of a thousand priests, one
High Priest; instead of a lamb without reason, a Spiritual Lamb.
With these and such like things in his thought, he said, 'All
things are new.' But *all* these *things are of God* by Christ, and
His free gift."—CHRYSOSTOM *in loco*.

The reader will observe how well the word ἀρχαῖα corresponds
with all this. If St. Paul had had chiefly in his eye the old Adam
in each individual Christian, he would undoubtedly have used the
word παλαιὸς as he does in Ephes. iv. 22.

Of course it is true that if any man be in Christ in the sense of
abiding in Him, such an one is internally and spiritually a new
creature or creation—for as the Saviour himself says, "He that

an Apostle to be " in the gall of bitterness and the bond of iniquity."

Now, why is this case adduced? If it is brought forward as a reason against Infant Baptismal Regeneration, to enable men to deny that each infant is, at its Baptism, received in very deed into that kingdom of grace which the Saviour emphatically declares to belong to children, then I utterly deny the inference. There is no analogy, no parallel whatsoever, between the case of Simon Magus and that of *any* infant, under *any* circumstances, brought to Christian Baptism. Those who think that there is, have great reason indeed to " take heed lest they despise *one* of these little ones."

If the case of Simon Magus is adduced as a reason against pronouncing that all adults, when baptized, beneficially receive the Sacrament, it is brought to disprove an assertion which I never heard of anybody making. The case of Simon is a difficult one, not at all with reference to the efficacy of his baptism, but with respect to the nature and efficacy of his *faith ;* for St. Luke mentions, not only that he " *was baptized,*" but that he " *believed.*"

---

abideth in Me, and I in him, the same bringeth forth much fruit ;" but this place (2 Cor. v. 17) rather looks to the external, outward objective creation of Christ, Who has brought into existence a new kingdom or new universe, in which all things are new. It is exceedingly curious to observe how this passage has been appealed to by two opposite parties to serve their purposes. Those writers who profess Baptismal Regeneration have said, "If any man be in Christ, he is a new creature. Baptism grafts men into Christ, therefore the baptized are in some sense new creatures." Their opponents have argued the very contrary from this same passage. "If any man be in Christ, he is a new creature. The vast majority of the baptized are not internally and spiritually new creatures, therefore they have never been in Christ." I may add that New Testament writers usually employ κτίσις to denote the creation or order of things considered as a whole.

("Simon himself believed also," v. 13.) He showed certainly some fruits of genuine faith, for it is expressly
asserted that he "clave stedfastly to Philip" ($\mathring{\eta}\nu$ $\pi\rho\sigma\sigma$-
$\kappa\alpha\rho\tau\epsilon\rho\tilde{\omega}\nu$). The word is the same which is used to express the steadfastness of the Pentecostal Christians (Acts
ii. 42). He could not have done this unless he had given
up for the time his magical arts. He received also with
apparent meekness the severe reproof of the Apostle, and
desired his prayers. The difficulties of his case bear
rather upon the saving nature of "faith" than of
Baptism.

It is altogether impossible to decide whether he, at the
time, received Baptism unworthily, or whether he lapsed
after Baptism, and so was one of those who, in the words
of St. Paul, "draw back unto perdition;" or, in those of
St. Jude, are "twice dead;" or, in the words of St.
Peter himself, "having escaped the pollution of the world
through the knowledge of our Lord and Saviour Jesus
Christ, are again entangled therein and overcome."

It may be well here to say a word or two respecting the
unworthy reception of Baptism by an adult. I cannot see
any difficulty in it which is not satisfactorily cleared up
by the Scripture similitude of the "graft." (Rom. xi.
17—24.) Baptism, *no matter what the state of heart of the
recipient*, at once brings the baptized into contact (if I
may use the expression) with the highest powers of the
unseen world. In some infinitely mysterious way the
human graft there and then comes into contact with the
new stock of humanity—the Second Adam.

If there be faith in the person baptized, he, at once,
begins to partake of the root and fatness of the Divine
olive-tree, which, *if he yields his will to* it (Rom. xi. 22—
24; John xv. 1—8), subdues to itself the whole inner
man (1 John iii. 6—9). If he has not faith, the saving

efficacy of the grace of Christ enters not into him ; *nevertheless he is, all the same, brought into contact with the True Vine,* BUT TO HIS CONDEMNATION.[1] His unbelief is the obstacle to the grace of the Saviour flowing into him. Christ would, but cannot, heal him, because of his unbelief (Mark vi. 5, 6). Till that is removed, the goodness of the Divine Olive cannot renew him. If God, after such sin, still vouchsafes to grant him repentance unto life, then the grafting takes beneficial effect. The grafting, I say, which he has already undergone, *for he has not to be grafted in anew.* He has not to be baptized over again, no matter what the circumstances of unbelief and impenitency which attended his original baptism ; for that would imply that a thing done *in* the name and by the authority of the ever-blessed Trinity had been an empty form.[2] In fact, the whole mystery and meaning of Baptism as an initial union with the Second Adam, is wrapped up in the simple fact of its being administered but once. Now if the inward and spiritual grace of it be identical with conversion, or any other moral change, call it what you will, the oftener a man is baptized the better. If it simply conveys that ordinary gift of the

---

[1] "I say that both good and bad may have, may give, and may receive the Sacrament of Baptism ; the good, indeed, usefully and unto health, but the bad hurtfully and penally, since that (sacrament) is equally perfect in each ; and its equal integrity in all is not affected by how much worse the man may be who has it among the evil, as neither by how much better the man may be who has it among the good."—ST. AUGUSTINE, *De Bapt. contra Don.* vi. 2.

[2] "Nothing more execrable or detestable can be said or thought, than that when the form of Baptism is imparted to infants, it is unreal or fallacious, in that remission of sins is spoken of and appears to be given, and yet is not at all effected."—ST. AUGUSTINE, *De Peccatorum Meritis et Remissione*, lib. i. c. 34. (Quoted in "Christian Remembrancer," vol. xxxii. p. 216.)

Spirit which accompanies preaching, why should it not be
repeated? for surely we' daily require the ordinary influence of the Spirit.   If Baptism be a Sacrament, no matter
what the circumstances under which it is received, to be
administered to a man *only once,* it must at once do its
work, and do it *once for all.*   And that work can only be
the bringing a man, either to his present salvation or
to his utter condemnation, into the one family, the
gathering him into the one fold, the grafting him into the
One Stock, the joining him to the one mystical body.[1]
The reader will observe that I find the above illustration
of a "graft" ready to my hand in Scripture : and if, in
making use of it, I have employed material images, such
as "root," "fatness," &c., they are only those which are
also employed by the Apostle in Romans xi.   In the sense
in which he uses them, so do I.

The case of Cornelius and his fellow-converts (Acts x.
44—48) receiving the gifts of God's Spirit before Baptism, is sometimes adduced to show that the Holy Spirit's
influences are not confined to Baptism.   Most certainly
(along with every passage in the Old Testament, where
the Holy Spirit's influence is mentioned) it does show
this, but it does not prove the thing which the objector
wants it to prove, that the *particular* gift which the Holy
Spirit conveys in Baptism can (ordinarily) be conveyed
at.any other time.   On the contrary, it rather proves

[1] "That Baptism we receive which is but one, because it cannot
be received often.   For how should we practise iteration of Baptism, and yet teach that we are by Baptism born anew, that by
Baptism we are admitted into the heavenly society of saints, that
those things be really and effectually done by Baptism which are
no more possible to be often done, than a man can naturally be
often born, or civilly be often adopted into one stock or family?"
—HOOKER, *Eccles. Polity,* Book v. chap. lxii. sec. 4

that the Baptismal gift is distinct from every other,
and that no other can supersede it; for those persons
who had received the gift of tongues required yet to be
baptized. This is the view which Bishop Beveridge takes
of this passage : " And the same Apostle, when, upon his
first preaching to the Gentiles, the Holy Ghost fell
on them, so that they immediately spake with tongues,
although some might have thought, there had been no
need of baptizing them, who had already received the
Holy Ghost ; yet he considering that this gift of the Holy
Ghost *was only to enable them to speak with tongues, not to
regenerate them,* he inferred from thence that they ought
the rather to be baptized ; 'Can any man,' said he, 'forbid
water ? ' &c." (Sermon xxxv.)

So also Archbishop Whately :

" Those who seek to go as far as they can towards doing
away all connexion of spiritual benefit with Baptism, and
reducing it to a mere sign of admission into a *community
possessing no spiritual endowments at all,* sometimes appeal
to the case of Cornelius and his friends, on whom 'the
Holy Ghost fell,' before they were baptized. But they
seem to forget that this was the miraculous gift of tongues,
of prophecy, &c. which never was, nor was ever supposed
to be, 'the inward spiritual grace' of Baptism. It was
never conferred at Baptism [see Acts viii. 16], but was
always bestowed, except in this one case, (in which there
was an obvious reason for the exception,) through the
laying on of hands of an Apostle." [1]

The "obvious reason" to which the Archbishop refers
is, no doubt, the importance of the occasion. The admission of Cornelius as a Gentile was, as it were, the beginning of a new dispensation. It was the first discovery of
the "mystery hid from ages and generations." (Coloss.

---

[1] Scripture Doctrine concerning Sacraments, p. 45.

N

i. 26, 27 ; Ephes. iii. 5, 6.) As such, it excited all the
prejudices of the Jewish converts to such an extent, that
St. Peter himself was sharply called to account for what
he had done. He referred, as his vindication, to this
miraculous outpouring of the Spirit, and compared it to
that which he and his fellow Apostles had experienced
on the day of Pentecost. (Acts xi. 15—17.) It was to
dispel these prejudices, in His ancient people, and to
induce them to embrace the new converts as brethren in
Christ, that God poured forth upon them the miraculous
gifts of the Spirit, as He had done on the Apostles at the
first. God could not have done this in order to disparage
His own ordinance, or to show His undoubted sovereignty,
by separating the inward grace from an outward sign, to
which He himself had attached that very inward grace.
One would really imagine from the way in which some
persons catch at this and any other place in which they
fancy they discover Regeneration independent of Baptism,
that "The Laver of Regeneration" was some invention or
suggestion of man, which God had condescended to adopt,
and which, as being a thing of man, He was ever setting
aside, rather than an ordinance which His own Son has
bound upon us, by His last parting words to His disciples.
· Every adult who receives Baptism beneficially, must
have experienced some work of the Holy Spirit previously
to enable him to believe in and accept Jesus Christ at all
(1 Cor. xii. 3): but not till he is baptized is he grafted
into the body of Christ.

'My sheep hear my voice, and I know them, and they
follow Me : and I give unto them eternal life ; and they
shall never perish, neither shall any man pluck them out
of My hand." (John x. 27, 28.)
From this place men argue that because many of the

baptized do not follow Christ, and, as far as we can see, die in their sins, and so lose eternal life, therefore they have never been grafted into Christ in their Baptism.

To answer this, we have only to ask, Whom does our Lord mean in this place by His sheep? Does He mean by "His sheep" the same persons whom He calls in chapter xv. the branches of Himself the Vine? If He does, then we must understand by the "sheep" the members of His Church, and we must of necessity consider as implied (though it be not expressed) in the parable of the "Shepherd and His sheep," that awful limitation which our Lord expressly and emphatically mentions in the parable of the "Vine and the branches"—that they only, whether "sheep" or "branches," will eventually be saved who abide in Him.

If our Lord represents, as He unquestionably does, the final salvation of the branches as conditional on their abiding in the Vine; and if the "branches" of the one parable are identical with "the sheep" of the other, then of necessity the salvation of the sheep also is conditional, on their abiding in the fold of Christ's goodness.

If the persons alluded to in each similitude are the same, common sense requires us to attach to the one similitude the limitation we find in the other. And that it is but fair and right to understand the condition of "abiding in the fold" to be implied, though it be not expressed, is evident from this also—that we have another parable, showing forth the love of Christ to His people, under the same figure of a "shepherd" and "sheep." This is the parable of the "lost sheep;" and this parable contemplates the case of sheep not abiding in the fold, but going astray, and not eventually being reclaimed by the Good Shepherd, though He goes to seek them. "How think ye? if a man have an hundred sheep, and one of them be gone astray, doth he

N 2

not leave the ninety and nine, and goeth into the mountains, and seeketh that which is gone astray? *And if so
be that he find it*," &c. (Matt. xviii. 12.) Now when I
see that in the similitude of the Vine and branches (which
implies a more intimate relationship than that of sheep to
a shepherd) the condition that the branches abide in the
vine is expressly mentioned; and when I find that in
another parable, in which our Lord employs the very same
image of a shepherd and his sheep, a degree of uncer-
tainty that the straying sheep will be found, is also
expressed,—I utterly refuse to interpret the text in question in so unconditional and absolute a sense as to nullify
the principle on which the hortatory teaching of all the
rest of Scripture depends. The hortatory teaching of the
whole of the rest of Scripture is based on the principle
that God desires the salvation of all whom His providence
has brought within His ordained means of grace, and so
all that have the sign of the covenant are held answerable
for its grace.

The above is a sufficient answer to the impugners of
Church truth; but let not the reader suppose that I
deny the predestinarian meaning of this text. I hope
and trust that it has that very predestinarian sense which
some draw from it,—that it does mean that Christ has
sheep to whom He has vouchsafed perseverance to life
eternal, and who will certainly abide in Him, and never
perish. I cannot, however, conceal. from myself the fact
that, whilst a small number of texts seem to imply that
God has granted final perseverance to some, there are a
far greater number which assert in terms which can neither
be mistaken nor explained away, that there is no degree of
grace from which men cannot, and will not, fall.[1]

---

[1] See the two lists of Scriptures on this subject in the chapter on
Election.

"Few, that is, eight souls were saved by water. The like figure whereunto even Baptism doth also now save us (not the putting away of the filth of the flesh, but the answer of a good conscience toward God), by the resurrection of Jesus Christ." (1 Peter iii. 20, 21.) This place is to be noticed, as the Apostle here asserts in the plainest terms the grace of Baptism ; it *now* saves us, being the antitype of those waters of the flood which saved the Church in the ark, whilst they drowned the ungodly world.

But the Apostle having made so strong an assertion, qualifies it, as indeed we should naturally expect, by the limitation, "Not the putting away of the filth of the flesh, but the answer of a good conscience toward God."

One would imagine that there could be but one view taken of the Apostle's assertion in connexion with its limitation. Such of course would be, that Baptism without sincere faith cannot profit. A Dissenting Commentary I have now before me, exactly expresses the Apostle's meaning : "The water of Baptism saves no man, *but as it is the means* of his getting his heart purified by the Holy Spirit." A living Church writer of eminence expresses the same in different words : " In order that it may be a saving ordinance, the conscience of the recipient must respond to the mercy of God." Archbishop Leighton gives more fully the same view : " That Baptism hath a power is clear, in that it is so expressly said, it doth save us : what kind of power is equally clear from the way it is here expressed : not by a natural force of the element ; though adapted and sacramentally used, it can only wash away the filth of the body ; its *physical efficacy reaches no further*, but it is in the hand of the Spirit of God, as other sacraments are, and as the Word itself is, to purify the conscience, and convey grace and salvation to the soul, by the reference it hath to, *and union with*, that which it represents." [1]

But though the Apostle introduces a limiting clause, it is contrary to all honest interpretation to press this so as to destroy his explicit declaration of the saving power of Baptism. Some fanatics in Calvin's time appear to have done this, in answer to whom he vindicates the true meaning of the Apostle, in the following words on this place: "But the fanatics, such as Schuencfeldius, absurdly pervert this testimony, while they seek to take away from Sacraments all their power and effect. For Peter did not mean here to teach that Christ's institution is vain and inefficacious, *but only to exclude hypocrites from the hope of salvation*, who, as far as they can, deprave and corrupt Baptism. Moreover, when we speak of Sacraments, two things are to be considered, the sign and the thing itself. In Baptism the sign is water, but the thing is the washing of the soul by the blood of Christ, and the mortifying of the flesh. The institution of Christ includes these two things. Now that the sign appears often inefficacious and fruitless, this happens through the abuse of men, which does not take away the nature of the Sacrament. *Let us then learn not to tear away the thing signified from the sign.*"

I must now, though most unwillingly, say a word or two respecting a gloss upon this passage put forth, some years ago, by a clergyman of the highest eminence in his party; as it illustrates so remarkably the treatment which Scripture receives, and the shifts to which even good men are obliged to have recourse in order to explain away the

---

[1] Substantially the same interpretation is given by Bishops Hall, Beveridge, Jeremy Taylor, Bethell; also by Augustine, Melancthon, Beza, Barrow, Matthew Henry, Pool, Wesley, Macknight, and Alford. Common sense can tolerate no other view.

force of Scripture allusions to the Sacraments. In the letter or tract I allude to,[1] which is principally occupied with the examination of this passage, the Apostle's words are explained as if he meant *to deny* all connexion between the outward sign and the inward grace.

The Apostle is made to say in effect, "Baptism doth also now save us, but by Baptism I do not mean water Baptism—I do not mean the outward rite at all, but I mean a sincere and enlightened conscience."[2] Of course the first thing which strikes one is, that if the Apostle meant that the outward rite of Baptism was in no way instrumental to salvation, why should he go out of his way to use the *word* "Baptism"? A good conscience cannot, by the most violent straining of figurative language, be called a "Baptism." It may be, and ought to be, the effect of Baptism, but is as distinct from it as possible ; much less can the "answer of a good conscience" be called "Baptism." Then, in the next place, if the Apostle, when he says that Baptism saves, means that a good conscience saves, no matter whether accompanied by Baptism or not, why should he bring forward the salvation in Baptism as the antitype (ἀντίτυπον) to a salvation in an ark wherein eight souls were *saved by water ?*

He must be hard pressed by this and other Scriptures, who, in order to nullify the connexion of Baptism with salvation, would have us believe,—first, that without any assignable reason the Apostle says one thing, and then corrects himself, as meaning another thing of a different

---

[1] Dr. McNeile's "Baptism doth Save."

[2] This is also the interpretation of Faustus Socinus in his work "De Baptismo Aquæ," cap. xii. p. 105. "From which words it is clear that Peter by the word 'Baptism' did not mean the water Baptism of which we speak, but another sort of Baptism altogether.'

class altogether, and then that the Apostle brings the
salvation of certain persons by water, as a type of an
internal state of heart no one feature of which is connected—even in the way of remote typical, or figurative
resemblance—with water or its application.

I adduce this instance as a sample, certainly an extreme
one, of the way in which the plainest Scripture statements
are treated as if they were no part of God's word.

I shall now give another extract from this letter as my
own vindication for having, in many places in this treatise,
asserted or implied that a large party in the Church ignore
any grace connected with the Sacraments.

"Appearing in itself to be useless, and resting on no
moral claim in the nature of things for our adoption, the
dutiful use of it [Baptism] proclaims submission to the
supremacy of Him, on whose *authority* it rests as its
ultima ratio. And thus, the willing and intelligent Baptism in water of an instructed adult, was a practical proof,
as well as a significant act, of his inward submission to
God. It certified him to the Church around as a man
whom God had graciously baptized into Christ, and whose
sin was washed away in the blood of Christ."

Again, in the next page. "He (St. Paul) was a chosen
vessel of God, to bear His name before the Gentiles, and
kings, and the children of Israel. To this end, he must
be accredited to the Church around him, have their confidence, and work with and by means of them. It became,
therefore, indispensable that he should not only be washed
from his sins in the sight of God by the Baptism made
without hands, but also in the sight of the Church by the
Baptism made with hands. Hence the exhortation of
Ananias to him, 'Why tarriest thou? Arise, and be baptized, and wash away thy sins, calling on the name of
the Lord.' 'The God of our fathers hath chosen thee.

You are His : avow yourself such without delay. You are
His soldier, secretly but really enlisted : enroll yourself in
the ranks openly, according to His general orders. You are
a pardoned sinner before God : proclaim it before men.'"[1]

Let the reader, having perused this, now turn to the
extracts I have given in Appendix B from Luther and
Cranmer. Let him particularly notice that, whereas
Luther and Cranmer account Baptism to be, under all
circumstances, an act of God, the writer of the above
considers it to be, under all circumstances, an act of the
MAN BAPTIZED—simply a practical proof, as well as a significant act, of his inward submission to God. Now, if
this be the meaning and intent of Baptism, inasmuch as
no one soul can really know the sincerity of another, it
seems to me that Baptism, by the hand of any minister
whatsoever, is a pure mockery, for no man can really vouch
for the sincerity of his fellow-man. And so, to carry out
fully this idea, not only must the Baptism of infants be at
once abandoned, but that of adults, by any hands *except
their own*.

If Baptism be an avowal of sincerity, inasmuch as each
individual is the sole judge of his own sincerity, each man
ought to baptize himself.

From the preceding extracts, one would imagine that
the leading view of Baptism which we find in the New
Testament is that it is a profession of faith ; whereas, in no
one single place in the New Testament is Baptism said to
be a profession of faith, or an avowal of faithfulness.

I repeat again, the place cannot be named where it is
said to be a profession. The place cannot be named where
it is not connected with spiritual grace, supposed to be

---

[1] " Baptism doth Save."—A Letter to the Bishop of Exeter, by
the Rev. Dr. McNeile. 3rd Edit. p. 24.

bestowed in it.   There is, of course, a profession of faith to be made before a man can be baptized ; but this takes place before the Baptism, and the Baptism itself is always the act of another, in the name of Him who commissioned him.

Faustus Socinus, in a comment upon the words of Ananias to the Apostle, in the work before quoted,[1] has an explanation of the meaning and intent of Baptism identical with that of the writer whose words I have transcribed. "Nothing else can be meant by the washing away of sins by Baptismal water, than that it is declared by the Baptism that the man's sins are already done away, and so this is, as it were, *publicly sealed*.   Wherefore, although it be granted that Ananias, when he bid St. Paul to be baptized and put away his sins, understood that through the external ablution his sins were washed away, yet it will not immediately follow, that through that Baptism the sins themselves were put away, but only that the washing of them away was *openly proclaimed* and sealed."

[1] "De Baptismo Aquæ," cap. vii.

CHAPTER XV.

EXAMINATION OF PASSAGES IN THE EPISTLES OF ST. JOHN AND ST. PETER.

SOME passages from the First Epistle General of St. John, bearing upon the doctrine of the New Birth, now claim our attention.

(1.) Chapter iii. verse 9. " Whosoever is born of God doth not commit sin ; for His seed remaineth in him : and he cannot sin, because he is born of God."

(2.) Chapter iv. verse 7. "Beloved, let us love one another: for love is of God; and every one that loveth is born of God, and knoweth God."

(3.) Chapter v. verse 1. " Whosoever believeth that Jesus is the Christ is born of God."

(4.) Chapter v. verse 4. " Whatsoever is born of God overcometh the world."

From these verses it is argued, that because the great body of baptized persons commit sin, or fall into sin, and love not one another, and are overcome by the world, therefore they have never been born into Christ's body in Baptism.

Such a meaning cannot be legitimately drawn from them.

The various explanations given of these passages, and the multiplied notes upon them, show that they are places of no ordinary difficulty. But wherein does the difficulty lie? Certainly not in reconciling them with the doctrine of Baptismal grafting into Christ, but with the words of

St. John in the same Epistle and with the words of St. James and St. Paul.[1]

They are utterly irreconcilable with the theory of the identity of regeneration and conversion.

Let us, at first, confine our attention to two of these places : the first, " Whosoever is born of God doth not commit sin ;" and the third, " Whosoever believeth that Jesus is the Christ is born of God."

If these two assertions are to be taken in their literal exactness, without any qualifying statement whatsoever, we have two almost irreconcilable marks of the new birth.

In the latter (" Whosoever believeth that Jesus is the Christ is born of God "), the definition is so comprehensive that it will include every nominal Christian; for the difference between a nominal Christian and an infidel is,

---

[1] St. John appears to assert the impossibility of the regenerate man committing sin. "He cannot sin, because he is born of God."

St. Peter, on the contrary, distinctly contemplates the possibility of the regenerate man sinning, for the persons whom he addresses as "born again, not of corruptible seed, but of incorruptible," he yet bids, on this very account, to "lay aside all malice, and all guile, and hypocrisies, and envies, and all evil speaking." (1 Peter i. 23; ii. 1.)

Similarly St. James. "Of His own will begat He us with the word of truth, that we should be a kind of first-fruits of His creatures. Wherefore, my beloved brethren, let *every man* be swift to hear, slow to speak, slow to wrath. . . . Wherefore lay apart all *filthiness* and *superfluity of naughtiness*," &c. (James i. 18, 19, 21.)

Similarly St. Paul. " Buried with Him in Baptism, wherein also ye are risen with Him . . . . If ye then be risen with Christ, ... mortify therefore your members which are upon the earth ; fornication, uncleanness," &c. (Col. ii. 12 ; iii. 1, 5.)

Here then is one Apostle asserting that the regenerate cannot sin, and the other three warning them against deadly sins, because of their liability to fall into them.

that the one believes and the other denies Jesus to be "the Christ."

In the former text ("Whosoever is born of God doth not commit sin"), on the contrary, the evidence of the new birth is spoken of in such a way that it would seem to exclude every Christian : even St. John, who says, "If we say that we have no sin, we deceive ourselves, and the truth is not in us ;" and St. James, "In many things we offend all."

To reconcile these two statements with the teaching which makes regeneration to be identical with conversion, two opposite methods have to be adopted. The latter statement has to be intensified in its meaning, so as to exclude as many merely professing Christians as possible ; the former has to be qualified in *its* meaning, so as to *in*clude as many (supposed) true Christians as possible.

The latter ("Whosoever believeth that Jesus is the Christ is born of God") is thus intensified in two well-known commentaries.[1] One, Pool's "Annotations,"— "'Whosoever believeth that Jesus is the Christ.' This is not meant of a mere professed, or of a slight and superficial, but of a *lively, efficacious, unitive, soul-transforming, and obediential* faith in Jesus as the Christ."

Again, in a commentary extracted out of Henry and Scott (Rel. Tract Soc.),—"Every one who has truly believed Jesus to be the promised Messiah, who has *received, honoured, and obeyed Him*, according to the Scriptures, is born of God," &c.

Here, then, is a text which, *at first sight*, appears as comprehensive as possible, which has to be accommodated to a theory by being seriously qualified in *one* direction.

Then take the other place, "Whosoever is born of God doth not commit sin." Now, inasmuch as vast numbers

---

[1] I have taken them as fair examples of popular interpretations.

of persons, who have exhibited and are exhibiting many signs of true and real conversion, do commit sin, this text has to be seriously qualified by another, a weakening or diluting process. Whosoever doth not commit sin "with a high hand," "wilfully," "habitually," "does not sin with allowance and satisfaction," and so on.

I do not think that two passages, written by the same hand, in the same letter, should be submitted to such diverse processes.

The latter one is especially dangerous. It has been said that the Apostle must mean, "cannot commit gross sin," or "sin with a high hand;" but is not the Apostle himself careful to exclude such a meaning, when he says, "ALL unrighteousness is sin;" and "Little children, let *no* man deceive you; he that doeth righteousness is righteous?"[1]

Again, neither will the explanation, *wilful* sin, answer the purpose; for the thing which makes sin to be sinful is that it is committed with the consent of the will: if it is not so, the deed is involuntary, and the man is not accountable.

Again, some have said that we must insert the word "habitually;" but this is most unwarrantable, for a single act of sin is still sin, even though it be preceded by, or followed by, no acts of the same sort.

If we would reconcile the statements of St. John with one another, with those of his brother Apostles, and with the actual state of things, we must take both these places as they stand.

[1] "'CANNOT SIN.' No explaining away of this declaration must be attempted, as is done by Cornelius à Lapide, who understands it of deadly sin; by Augustine [it will be seen, however, that Augustine elsewhere gives the truer and deeper comment] and Bede, who confine the ἁμαρτάνειν to the violation of brotherly love; or as Grotius, 'res de qua agitur aliena est ab ejusmodi ingenio.'"— ALFORD on chap. iii. 9.

They are irreconcilable with the theory that regeneration is conversion; they are in the strictest harmony with the view of regeneration as a grafting in Christ, and so a partaking of His nature.

Regeneration is the implanted *germ* of a new nature, the infusion of a new leaven, a union with Christ, which may be the smallest possible thing—as small in the eye of man as the grain of mustard-seed—in its beginning, but then it is calculated and intended to subdue the whole inner man. It is a net thrown as widely as possible, in order that *all* those caught in it may become as holy as possible.

Its theory, so to speak, is the greatest possible holiness of the greatest possible number. To this end, God grafts every Christian into Christ; but then the aim, the intent, the purpose of this engrafting, is no stinted measure of goodness, but the total abnegation of all sin, and the filling of the soul with all goodness.[1] When, then, St. John says, "Whosoever believeth that Jesus is the Christ is born of God," he supposes the net thrown as widely as possible; he contemplates the germ of the new nature in every man "naming the name of Christ." But when he says, "Whosoever is born of God doth not commit sin," he contemplates the grace of Regeneration, not in its

---

[1] "The two (*i.e.* the new birth and a state of sin) are incompatible, and in so far as a man is found in the one, he is thereby separated from the other. In the child of God is the hatred of sin; in the child of the devil the love of it; and every act done in virtue of either state, or as belonging to either, is done purely on one side or purely on the other. If the child of God falls into sin, it is an act against nature, deadly to life, hardly endured, and bringing bitter repentance; it is as the taking of a poison, which, if it be not corrected by its antidote, will sap the very springs of life."— ALFORD on chap. iii. 6.

germ, but in its result,[1] in its full and complete development ; and so he adds the remarkable words, "*for his seed*
REMAINETH in him." "Whosoever is born of God doth
not commit sin ; for His seed remaineth in Him : and he
cannot sin, because he is born of God." The new birth
is not an isolated thing,—a thing to be considered by
itself,—but it is the beginning, and ONLY the beginning, of
a supernatural life.

This life is a life derived from Christ as the new Head,
the Second Adam of His Church ; that, just as the world
derives a weak, sinful nature from Adam, so the Church
derives a new, holy nature from Christ.

In every member of the Church, then, there are, *or have
been*, two natures, two spiritual principles, two lives,—one,
the first, which is the old, the carnal ; the other, the second,
which is the new, the spiritual.

At our entrance into God's kingdom, we received the
seed of this new nature. We were then grafted into
Christ, and the kingdom into which we were introduced
is a state of things adapted, in God's wisdom, for the
springing up, growth, and nourishment of the new nature.

But then, as in the natural, so in the spiritual, the seed
may not even germinate ; or it may germinate, and yet, in

---

[1] " Because His seed abideth (or remaineth) in him : *i. e.* because
that new principle of life, from which his new life has unfolded,
which was God's seed deposited in him, abides, growing there,
and precludes the development of the old sinful nature. So the
majority of the better expositors, defining somewhat differently,
when they come to explain in detail this germ of spiritual life."
Again : " The children of God, in whom the Divine seed of their
eternal life abides, have in reality a holy privilege ; as Steinhofer
says, they sin not, and they cannot sin, just in proportion as the
new Divine life, unconditionally opposed to all sin, and manifesting
itself in God-like righteousness, is present and abides in them."—
ALFORD on chap. iii. 9, 10.

any particular case, be prevented by evil influences from coming to perfection.

And though men are made partakers of a new nature, the old is not destroyed ; it yet remains to regain the complete and final mastery over some, and to try and prove others, just as the remnant of the Canaanites remained in the Promised Land to prove the Israelites ; and yet, as it was through the Israelites' sin and want of faith that their enemies remained in the land, so it is through the Christian's want of faith, and to his peril, that the old nature remains in him. Now, the expression in 1 John iii. 9, " Whosoever is born of God doth not commit sin," exactly answers to all chis ; for it has regard to the aim, the tendency, the ultimate result of the new birth.

Almost any commentator will tell those of my readers who cannot consult the original, that the tense used by St. John in the expression, " is born of God," is not our (English) present, but another, the Greek perfect, a tense by which an action is supposed to be continued from a past to the present time. Thus it must (to preserve the sense of the original) be paraphrased : " Whosoever is born of God and continues so—whosoever *abides* in Christ —whosoever continues in the state into which he was re-born." It looks, then, to Christ as the Vine, and the members of His Church as the branches ; and with this exactly tallies the last two verses of the preceding chapter : " And now, little children, ABIDE in Him ; " (can we doubt the reference ?) " that, when He shall appear, we may have confidence, and not be ashamed of Him at His coming. If ye know that He [the Head, the Vine-stem] is righteous, ye know that *every one* that doeth righteousness is born of Him." (γεγέννηται, has been and continues to be born of Him).[1]

[1] Pool, whom I before quoted, in a note principally taken from Hammond, seems to recognise this only way of interpreting this

This is St. Augustine's exposition of these words : "He that is born of God sinneth not ; for were this nativity by itself alone in us, no man would sin ; and when it shall be alone, no man will sin. But now we as yet drag on that

saying :—"Only it is here to be noted that the phrase 'born of God' is not so to be taken as to denote only the act of this change, the first impression of this virtue on the patient, the single transient act of regeneration or reformation, and that *as in* the preter tense not a past, but rather a continued course, a permanent state (is indicated), so a regenerate man and a child of God are all one, and signify him that lives a pious and godly life, *and continues to do so.*"

"The Greek perfect is especially to be held firm in our exegesis. The Apostle does not say οὐ δύναται ἁμαρτάνειν, ὅτι ἐκ τοῦ Θεοῦ, ἐγεννήθη. This would testify to a past fact, once for all occurring without any reference to its present permanence. But he has said ὅτι ἐκ τ. Θ. γεγέννηται, because he has abiding in him that his birth from God . . . . The abiding force of this Divine generation in a man excludes sin ['qui eam indolem retinebit, non peccabit,' as Grotius (says) thus far right]: where sin enters that force does not abide. The γεγεννῆσθαι is in danger of becoming a γεννηθῆναι, a fact in the past, instead of a fact in the present, a lost life instead of a living one."—ALFORD on chap. iii. 9. Again—" 'Hath not seen Him, neither known Him.' First, observe the tense in which the verbs stand, that they are not aorists, but perfects ; and that some confusion is introduced in English by our perfect not corresponding to the Greek one, but rather partaking of the aoristic sense, giving the impression, 'hath *never* seen Him nor known Him,' *whereas* the Greek perfect denotes an abiding present effect resting on an event in the past. So much is this so, that ἔγνωκα and many other perfects lose altogether their reference to the past event, and point simply to the abiding present effect of it. ἔγνωκα is the present effect of a past act of cognition—'I know.' In the Greek perfect the present predominates ; in the English perfect (and in the German still more) the *past.* Hence, in very many cases, the best version-rendering of the Greek perfect is by the English present. And so here, without for a moment letting go the true significance of the tense, I should render, if making a version, 'seeth Him not, neither knoweth Him.'"—ALFORD on chap. iii. 6.

corrupt nature in which we were born, although, according to that in which we are new born, if we walk aright, from day to day, we are renewed inwardly." (St. Augustine, " Contra Mendacium.")

Again : "According to that, that we are born of God, we abide in Him who appeared to take away our sins, even in Christ, and we sin not,—this is that whereby the inner man is renewed from day to day. But according to that, that we are born of that man by whom sin came into the world, and death by sin, and so death passed upon all men, we are not without sin ; for we are not yet freed from his infirmity, until, by the *daily* renovation whereby we are born of God, our whole infirmity, arising from our birth in the first man, and which engages us in sin, be healed. And in consequence of the remains of this abiding in the inner man, though it day by day decreases in the advancing Christian, ' if we say we have no sin, we deceive ourselves, and the truth is not in us.' Wherefore, so far as we adhere to God by faith, hope, and love, and imitate Him, we have no sin, and are the sons of God. But so far as, in consequence of the frailty of the flesh, as yet unchanged by death, unpurified by a resurrection, evil and base motives arise within us, we sin. The one state is the first-fruits of the new man, the other is the remains of the old." (Augustine, " De Perfectione Justitiæ.")

The same principle of interpretation applies to the other two marks of the New Birth, viz. "loving one another," and " overcoming the world."

Another consideration, if duly weighed, puts it beyond all controversy that the Apostle St. John, in these Epistles, did not intend to cast any doubt on the reality of that engrafting into Christ of all those to whom he wrote, which St. Paul asserts of all the Christians to whom he wrote. This is the use which the Apostle makes of the

word "abide" (μένω) throughout this Epistle. His anxiety
is, not that those to whom he wrote should see as to
whether they ever *had been* in Christ, but as to whether
they *continued*, or *abode* in Him.

Let the reader observe the following places, and judge
for himself whether they are most in accordance with
Catholic or Calvinistic teaching. "He that saith he
abideth in Him, *ought himself also so to walk*, even as He
walked." (1 John ii. 6.) "Let that therefore *abide* in you
which ye have heard from the beginning. If that which
ye have heard from the beginning *remain* in you, ye also
shall continue in the Father and in the Son." (ii. 24.)
"But the anointing which ye have received of Him *abideth*
in you." (27.) "And now, little children, *abide* in Him."
(28.) "Whosoever *abideth* in Him sinneth not." (iii. 6.)
"Whosoever is born of God doth not commit sin; *for
His seed remaineth* in him." (9.) "He that loveth not
his brother *abideth* in death." (14.) (How can any be
"brethren," unless they have all, once at least, been included in the same fellowship?) "Ye know that no murderer hath eternal life *abiding in him.*" (15.) "He that
keepeth His commandments *dwelleth* [abideth, μένει] in
Him, and He in him. And hereby we know that He
abideth in us, by the Spirit which He hath given us." (24.)

He *that abideth* in the doctrine of Christ, he hath both
the Father and the Son." (2 John 9.)

I do not see how the above passages can be interpreted
in accordance with the rest of the Epistle, except on the
principle implied in the words of St. Augustine I have
before quoted.

One word, however, respecting the apparent omission of
reference to Baptism.[1]

---

[1] Dean Alford, in his remarks on chap. v. 5—7, explains the
"water" there referred to as the water of Baptism, and I do not

It may be said, that because St. John does not mention
Baptism when he says, "Whosoever believeth that Jesus
is the Christ is born of God," he intends to disconnect all
ideas of the New Birth with it.

Now, when I consider that the same St. John in his
Gospel records our Lord's words to Nicodemus, "Except
a man be born of water and of the Spirit," and that he
was among the number of those who heard the parting
words, "He that believeth and is baptized shall be
saved," I feel assured that such a thing never could cross
his mind as that a person professing to believe in God's
only-begotten Son, should refuse the right of initiation
into Him. I do not think that he could realize such a
thing to be possible. He would ask, " Can that be even
the seed of belief which could so treat the last solemn
injunction of the 'Word made flesh '?"

And now let me say something respecting the practical
application of John's doctrine, "He that is born of God

see how we can explain it otherwise, if we pay due regard to the
fact of the three witnesses, "the Spirit, the water, and the blood,"
being ever-present and *abiding* testimonies.

His words are, "This, their one testimony, is given by the
purification in the water of Baptism into His name, John iii. 5 ;
by the continual cleansing from all sin which we enjoy in and by
His atoning blood ; by the inward witness of His Spirit, which He
hath given us."

Again, on verses 10, 11 :—"Easily enough here we can syntheti-
cally put together, and conjecture of what testimony it is that he
is speaking : the Spirit by whom we are born again to eternal life,
the water of Baptism by which the new birth is brought to pass in
us by the power of the Holy Ghost (John iii. 5 ; Titus iii. 5), the
blood of Jesus by which we have reconciliation with God, and purification from our sins, and eternal life (John vi. 53)—these three
all contribute to and make up our faith in Christ, and so compose
that testimony which the Apostle designates in verse 11 by the
shorter term which comprehends them all."

doth not commit sin," "Every one that loveth is born of
God, and knoweth God." The most strenuous defenders
of Baptismal Regeneration, when occasion requires, use
either St. John's language, or language founded upon it.

Not only do such use it, but, as I shall show, they
are the only persons who use it in its integrity. Let the
reader mark well the following passages out of the Sermons
of one who has done as much to defend the High view of
Baptismal grace as any other living man :—" ' Whosoever
believeth that Jesus is the Christ is born of God.' This
is the first source of our life, our strength, our victory,
that we have strength not our own, but by a new and
spiritual birth of God—a birth whereby a new and
spiritual life above the world, apart from the world's life,
and unknown to the world, is imparted to the soul ; and
man, through grace, becomes the Son of God. Of this
birth the proofs are, the love of Christ, the love of one
another as members of Christ, the love of God in
keeping His commandments. Love is the proof of our
birth of God, because God is love. The son hath a likeness of the Father. He, then, who is a child of God,
must have a likeness to his Father. How could he be a
Son of God who had not *that* in him which God is,—love ?
He, then, who is born of God must have the love of God ;
he who loveth the Father must love Him, the Son, who is
begotten of Him ; he who loveth the Son must love them
also who are members of Him, the children of God in
Christ."

This passage is an extract from a sermon by Dr. Pusey.
The reader will observe how unreservedly he speaks of the
spiritual, obedient, loving Christian being the regenerate
man, the true child of God. And yet in the same sermon
towards the conclusion he speaks as unreservedly of the
seed of this grace being implanted in Baptism. "So

mostly it is with the grace of God. God lodges it in the soul. He places in Baptism a principle of life within us, which, if we allow it to work, as we grow on will fill our every power, penetrate our whole souls, transform this heavy mass of our earthliness into its own Divine nature, make us 'friends of God, fellow-citizens of the angels, lords of the world, rulers of ourselves.'" (Pusey's Parochial Sermons, vol. ii. pp. 345, 350.)

It will be clear from these two extracts from the same sermon how they who hold the doctrines of Baptismal Regeneration most unreservedly can yet speak of the true Christian as the only regenerate man, or child of God.

The real point in dispute is this. To what are we to attribute the fact that a man duly baptized lives the life of one who knows not God? The Calvinist virtually says that it is because God has withheld grace from the man. The Churchman, on the contrary, says that it is because the man has opposed or sinned away God's grace. Rather than suppose that God has withheld His grace the Churchman will always (no matter how great the difficulty about the assumption) assume that the man in question has fallen from grace, or has, through his own fault, not retained a seed, or has not continued in the goodness of God, or has forgotten that he was purged from his old sins (Gal. v. 4 ; 1 John iii. 9—15 ; Rom. xi. 22). And as we have shown throughout this book, he has the most solid Scripture grounds for making such an assumption.

And, again, I believe that none but those who hold the Church view can adopt the language of St. John in these passages in its integrity. They who identify Regeneration with Conversion and sever it from Baptism, almost invariably lay down marks of conversion which, when examined, are found to differ essentially from the marks laid down by the Apostle. The term "conversion" is

now virtually restricted to a change of views and feelings
with reference to the work of Christ, whereas the New
Birth, as described by St. John, is absolute freedom from
sin, and the love of our brethren.

Again, we cannot imagine a greater contrast than that
between St. John's view of spiritual illumination and the
views of spiritual illumination which are now current
amongst us; for St. John says, " He that loveth his brother
abideth in the light; . . . but he that hateth his brother
is in darkness, and walketh in darkness, and knoweth
not whither he goeth, because that darkness hath blinded
his eyes." (1 John ii. 10, 11.)

There remains now only one reference to the New Birth
unconsidered—that in 1 Pet. i. 23 : "Being born again,
not of corruptible seed, but of incorruptible, by the word
of God, which liveth and abideth for ever."

This is also a place which has been ignorantly quoted to
the disparagement of the efficacy of the initial Sacrament.

It has been argued that St. Peter, and St. James also
in a similar passage in his Epistle (James i. 18), by omitting
to mention the Sacrament, teach us to consider the written
word, rather than Baptism, as the instrument of God to
bring about Regeneration.

A moment's reference to the original will disprove this.
Neither in this, nor in any other place of Scripture, are
we said to be born *of* the word of God, but BY the word.
We are born OF God, ἐκ Θεοῦ; of water and the Spirit, ἐξ
ὕδατος καὶ πνεύματος : never ἐκ λόγου, of the word, but
διὰ λόγου, through or by the word.

The Bible (meaning, of course, not simply the book,
but the truths derived from it and expounded by the
teacher or preacher) is as necessary an instrument to
produce the New Birth as the Sacrament itself; for if it
were not for the word of God, we should know nothing

either of God or of His will. When a person hears the word of God, is convinced of sin by it, and comes to be baptized, then he is born again, διὰ λόγου ἐξ ὕδατος καὶ πνεύματος, through the word, of water and of the Spirit.

The very Baptism with which he is baptized is, as it were, the creature of God's word; and this word itself is the manifestation of His will. Baptism, I say, is but the creature of God's word; for it was instituted by the word of God's Son, and its perpetual efficacy is upheld and assured by the word of His promise.[1] All that is needful to be believed and taught about it is contained in His written word; the whole analogy of which word would lead us to give Baptism to infants, and to believe that by it they are engrafted into Christ.

The word "incorruptible" in the above passage is also ignorantly pressed into the argument. Because the seed

---

[1] " First of all, the Holy Ghost provoketh and stirreth up men to preach God's Word. Then He moveth men's hearts to faith, and calleth them to Baptism; and then, by faith and Baptism, He worketh so that He maketh them as new men again."—CRANMER, quoted in Lawrence, " Doctrine of Church of England on Baptism," p. 37.

So also Luther :—" Moreover, when we speak of the Word of the Gospel, we also include the Sacraments; for they have the promise of the Holy Spirit annexed, as well as of remission of sins."—LUTHER on Joel iii. 28.

" As regards the dogmatical use which some make of this passage (James i. 18), wishing to show that regeneration is brought about by the word as distinguished from the Sacrament of Baptism (Titus iii. 5—7), we may remark, that seeing the λόγος ἀληθείας designates the Gospel as a whole, without any respect to such distinction, nothing regarding it can be gathered from this passage. The word of the Lord constitutes, we know, the force of the Sacrament also, 'accedit verbum ad elementum, et fit Sacramentum.' And is it meant to be inferred that the readers of this Epistle were not baptized ?"—Note in ALFORD on James i. 18.

is called *incorruptible*, it is argued that the grace conferred cannot be lost; and because great numbers of the baptized do not persevere, therefore they were never "born again" in Baptism. To which I answer, Is the "*seed*" mentioned by St. Peter the same as the seed alluded to in our Lord's parable of the sower? The seed is there said to be "the word of God," and yet, however incorruptible the *seed* may be, the *plant* which springs from it may not be equally so; "because it has no root, it may *wither away;*" or, as St. Luke has it, "As soon as it sprung up it *withered away*, because it lacked moisture." (Luke viii. 6.)

The seed has to be retained. It has, in the words of St. John, to abide in the man, and upon this all depends. "*Let* that therefore abide in you which ye have heard from the beginning. *If* that which ye have heard from the beginning abide in you, ye also shall continue in the Father and in the Son."

One consideration connected with these two passages (1 Pet. i. 23; James i. 18) must now be noticed. It has been urged that the Apostles allude to a birth by the preached word alone at the moment of genuine conversion as distinguished from any birth in Baptism; but if so, how is it that they represent, or at least imply, that this new birth has already taken place in all those to whom they write? Multitudes of sayings throughout these Epistles are decisive respecting the fact that many to whom the Apostles wrote were not spiritually-minded Christians, some not even moral ones.

And yet St. Peter evidently looks upon the "new birth" as a thing which had taken place in the case of all to whom he wrote, and he grounds upon it an exhortation to "lay aside all malice, and all guile, and hypocrisies, and envies, and all evil speaking" (ii. 1), and beseeches these "new born ones" to abstain from fleshly lusts, and even goes so far as to say, "Let none of you suffer as a murderer, or as a thief, or as an evil-doer, or as a busybody in other men's matters" (iv. 15). Similarly St. James. He evidently considered that God had "of His own will" begotten Christians generally, and those particularly to whom he wrote his Epistle; for he grounds on the fact of their having been born again certain practical exhortations. "Wherefore lay apart all filthiness," &c. "Be ye doers of the word, and not hearers only." I ask the reader to peruse carefully these two Epistles, and mark the nature of the warnings delivered in them, and what sort of a Christian character they imply in those who could require them, and then say how it is conceivable that the writers should never once call upon such persons, as some among them evidently were, to be born again, unless they believed that they had all been born again in the rite their Master had instituted for this very purpose.

I have now, I think, shown sufficiently clearly the position which the Saviour has, in His infinite wisdom, assigned to the Sacrament of Baptism, as the means by which He unites men to Himself in the fellowship of His mystical Body, and makes them partakers of His nature, and I have also exhibited the harmony and undesigned coincidence of all Scripture with this view of sacramental union with Himself.

A number of minor objections may be urged from isolated texts, under which those who are determined to ignore sacramental grace run and shelter themselves; in the same way as the Socinian ignores both the express words and the general tenor of Scripture. He reads, in one class of texts, "The *man* Christ Jesus," or, "My Father is greater than I;" and so he refuses to submit to the teaching of another class, such as "The Word was

God," or "I and my Father are one." The Socinian, if he really received God's word as the word of his Creator and Judge, would search and see in what way these places could *both* be accepted in their fulness, as they are equally the words of the living God ; and he would find in the Catholic doctrine of the Trinity and Incarnation the perfect realization of both.

And so the man of God, who desires to be truly conformed to God's will, and to receive all His word in the love of it, must assuredly give its place to that sacramental teaching to which we have drawn attention.

No matter how it disarranges his previous system, he must make room for it, or his views of truth are so far imperfect,—not taking into real account *all* that God has revealed.

CHAPTER XVI.

OBJECTIONS ARISING FROM THE DOCTRINES OF PREDESTINA-
TION AND JUSTIFICATION.

THE sacramental vein of doctrine pervading, as I have
shown, all Scripture, has been in this last age of the
Church completely ignored, because of its supposed irre-
concilability with two other Scripture truths,—

The truth of God's eternal Election,

And the doctrine of Justification by Faith.

Let us see with what reason.

First, it is supposed to be inconsistent with God's
having elected certain men to eternal life.

That there is a doctrine of Election which a Christian
must realize is most certain. Of that there can be no
doubt. But then many further questions arise with
reference to this Election, as, To what does God elect
men? Does He so elect men to His benefits, whatsoever
these are, that those elected *must* necessarily respond to
His Election? He certainly did not so elect the Jews;
for He elected them to blessings to which they in no
respect responded.

And to what does He elect Christians? Does He elect
them to outward privileges, or to inward grace? if to
inward grace, to what degrees of it? Does He elect all
who receive from Him *any* inward spiritual grace to final
glory? or does He elect men to spiritual grace which

they may resist and lose—to grace, that is, short of final perseverance to eternal life ?[1]

Into these questions I shall not enter, because I am not writing a formal treatise on this subject. My object now is to show that one doctrine cannot nullify another; but that, cost what it may, both must be held, realized, prayed over, lived to, together.

If the doctrine of Election (what the Election is I am not now entering upon) is to be found anywhere in Scripture, it is to be found in the Epistle of St. Paul to the Romans, in the words of our Lord in St. John's Gospel, and in the Epistles of St. Peter and St. Jude.

I shall now (carefully abstaining from the use of technical expressions connected with controversies on this subject) assume that we are desirous of believing and laying to heart all that God says, and see whether we can do so when God speaks both of Election and Baptism.

If the doctrine of Election is anywhere in Scripture, it is to be found in the eighth, ninth, tenth, and eleventh chapters of the Epistle to the Romans. But what doctrine of Election? Certainly not one inconsistent with holding

[1] Augustine, for instance, the first of the Fathers who taught systematically the doctrine of election, held that men might be elected by God to various degrees of spiritual grace, and yet not have perseverance vouchsafed to them. His words are, "Of two *pious* persons why to one is granted final perseverance, to another it is not granted, is to be resolved into the still more inscrutable purpose of God." (De Dono Perseverantiæ, c. viii. ix.) Again, "Wonderful indeed! most wonderful! that God should to some of *His own sons, those whom He has regenerated in Christ,* and to whom He has given faith, hope, and love, *not give perseverance,* while He imparts forgiveness, grace, and sonship to the sons of strangers."

For further information on this point the reader is directed to Bishop Harold Browne's "Exposition of the Thirty-nine Articles," Art. xvi. pp. 366, 367, sixth edition.

all the baptized dead to sin in Baptism : for the sixth chapter is an integral part of the Epistle to the Romans : and in it we have the most decided assertion possible that all the baptized are "buried with Christ by Baptism into death, that like as He" (Christ) "was raised from the dead by the glory of the Father, so we also" (*i.e.* all the baptized) "should walk in newness of life."

Again, to all the Roman Christians, without exception, the Apostle says, "Reckon yourselves dead indeed unto sin, but alive unto God, through Jesus Christ our Lord ;" and for this practical end,—"Let not sin *therefore* reign in your mortal bodies, that ye should obey it in the lusts thereof."

Here, then, is a doctrine of Baptism of the highest practical character, and the most universal practical application ; for, as I said, it makes all the baptized answerable for grace.

From the eighth to the eleventh chapters we have a doctrine of Election. Does this doctrine modify or limit the application of the doctrine of Baptism contained in the sixth chapter ? Not a word of any such thing.

On the contrary, at the conclusion of this deep argument on Election, the Apostle pauses, as it were, and makes a practical application of what he is saying, grounded on the doctrine of union with Christ, and that union not indissoluble,—not, when once made, made for ever, but strictly coincident with accountability.

"Behold, therefore, the goodness and severity of God : on them that fell, severity ; but toward thee, goodness, IF THOU CONTINUE IN HIS GOODNESS ; otherwise thou also shalt be cut off." (Rom. xi. 22.)

Observe here how the Apostle singles out and addresses the individual Roman, the member of a Church whose "faith was spoken of throughout the whole world." "If thou continue in His goodness; otherwise thou shalt be cut off."

Here we have our Lord's teaching respecting the vine and the branches,—" Every branch in Me that beareth not fruit, God taketh away." "If a man abide not in Me, he is cast forth as a branch, and is withered," &c.

Reader, I would most solemnly ask you, are these words of St. Paul consistent with *your* doctrine of Election?

Would not the hearers of a (so-called) Calvinist preacher be startled and offended beyond measure to hear such words from him towards the conclusion of a discourse on God's electing love?

And yet the inspired Apostle scruples not to insert such a warning in the conclusion of *his* discourse upon this deep truth.

The teaching of the sixth chapter of this Epistle shows how such a warning presupposes and requires that doctrine of baptismal grafting into Christ's body which I have been insisting on throughout this treatise.

Again, in St. John's Gospel, the Saviour says, " Ye have not chosen Me, but I have chosen you, and ordained you, that ye should bring forth fruit, and that your fruit should remain."

And yet in this same Gospel we have—" Abide in Me, and I in you." " Every branch in Me that beareth not fruit God taketh away." "If a man abide not in Me, he is cast forth as a branch, and is withered; and men gather them and cast them into the fire, and they are burned."

Reader, is your doctrine of Election consistent with believing and confessing both these things? If not, it is not your Saviour's.

Again, take the words of the inspired St. Peter. In his First Epistle we have his converts addressed as " elect according to the foreknowledge of God the Father, through sanctification of the Spirit, unto obedience and sprinkling of the blood of Jesus Christ;" and yet, in his Second Epistle, he deems it consistent to say to these same converts—those, too, who "had obtained like precious faith with him"—"Wherefore the rather, brethren, give diligence to make your calling and election sure : for if ye do these things, ye shall never fall : for so an entrance shall be ministered unto you abundantly into the everlasting kingdom of our Lord and Saviour Jesus Christ." (2 Peter i. 10, 11.)

The Church doctrine of Baptism is in strict accordance with, nay, requires, both these ; for it implies an initial sanctifying gift of the Spirit on all the baptized, *in order to*, but not necessarily *followed by*, their obedience ; and it implies also that God should have, in His purposes of mercy, chosen them to this spiritual gift, and by His providence brought it about that they should receive it. Reader, does your doctrine of Election enable you to realize both these things? and can you hold it, and also heartily hold the last three verses of the second chapter of this Epistle? Can you contemplate, as the Apostle did, men escaping the world "through the knowledge of the Lord and Saviour Jesus Christ," and being "again entangled therein and overcome," and "the latter end worse with them than the beginning"? (2 Peter ii. 20.)

Again ; St. Jude writes to those who are "sanctified by God the Father, and preserved in Christ Jesus, and called;" and yet he feels it necessary to warn these persons, in such a state of grace, by the example of others, in a parallel state of grace, who fell from it and were lost in consequence :—

"I will therefore put you in remembrance, though ye once knew this, how that the Lord, having *saved* the

P

people out of the land of Egypt, afterward destroyed
them that believed not. And the angels that kept not
their first estate, but left their own habitation, He hath
reserved in everlasting chains under darkness unto the
judgment of the great day." (Jude 5, 6.)

Reader, is your doctrine of Election consistent with the
sanctified—the (hitherto) *preserved*—the *called*, receiving
such a warning, and having two such examples brought
before them ?

But at the beginning of this part of my argument I
said that only in this last age of the Church have men,
who claim to be heard as expounders of God's word,
ignored sacramental grace, because of its supposed inconsistency with the doctrine of Election.[1]   At the time of
the persecution, in the reign of Queen Mary, we read that
Bradford, when in prison, submitted to Cranmer, Ridley,
and Latimer, a scheme for committing the leading English
Reformers to a more decided confession of what he conceived to be the true doctrine of Predestination and
Election.   He received from Ridley this memorable
answer :—" Sir, in those matters I am so fearful, that I
dare not speak farther, yea, almost none otherwise, than
the very text doth, as it were, lead me by the hand."
And yet this Bradford, holding thus decidedly the absolute
(Calvinistic) doctrine of Predestination, scruples not to
write upon Baptism thus (Works, Parker Soc. p. 89):
" As by Baptism we are engrafted into Christ, so by the
Supper we are fed with Christ."   And in the next page :
" As, therefore, in Baptism is given unto us the Holy
Ghost and pardon of our sins, which yet lie not lurking
in the water ; so, in the Lord's Supper, is given unto us
the communion of Christ's body and blood ; that is, grace,
forgiveness of sins," &c.

[1] See Appendix C.

I quote this man's words as furnishing an example of the way in which the most decided predestinarians of that age expressed themselves upon the Sacraments.

And, in fact, Calvin, when formally writing on the Sacraments, frequently makes use of equally decisive language; thus, in a place I have before quoted (Institutes, IV. ch. xvi.): "Paul comprehends the whole Church when he says that it was cleansed by the washing of water. In like manner, from his expression in another place, that by Baptism we are engrafted into the body of Christ (1 Cor. xii. 13), we infer that infants, whom he enumerates among His members, are to be baptized in order that they may not be dissevered from His body." [1]

But, in the second place, men think it their duty to ignore sacramental grace, because of its supposed incom-

---

[1] The reader who desires to pursue this part of the subject further, will find the whole bearing of the doctrine of Predestination on that of Baptismal Regeneration most ably discussed in an article in the *Christian Remembrancer* for January 1850, entitled "Recent Arguments on Baptismal Regeneration." The writer distinctly shows, in the first place, that St. Augustine never allowed his Predestinarian views to interfere with the most unqualified assertion of the Regeneration of Infants in Baptism. He also shows that the Schoolmen, Peter Lombard, Aquinas, Anselm, and Bernard, who were all fully committed to the Sacramental teaching of the Church of their times, and in fact extended and intensified that teaching, yet held the doctrines of Election and Final Perseverance, and propounded them in far stronger terms than those of the seventeenth article. And, lastly, the reviewer shows by numerous extracts, that the most rigid Calvinistic divines of the reign of Elizabeth expressed themselves on Baptismal grace in a very different way from what our present Calvinists do.

The reader will find some of the statements of Augustine, Bernard, and Aquinas on Election, placed side by side with their statements respecting Baptismal Regeneration, in Appendix C at the end of this book.

patibility with justification by faith only. The very same line of argument which I have taken with reference to the doctrine of Election is a complete answer to this also.

If the doctrine of Justification by Faith is to be found anywhere in Scripture, it is to be found in the fourth and the former part of the fifth chapter of St. Paul's Epistle to the Romans; and yet, in the latter part of the fifth chapter, the same Holy Spirit who inspired the rest of this Epistle gives us the doctrine of the "two Adams;" and in the sixth, the burial and resurrection of all the baptized with Christ, the Second Adam, in Baptism.

If the way of salvation, and the terms of admission into the kingdom of heaven, are to be found anywhere, they are to be found in the words of Christ the Saviour and King; and yet the very same Saviour who says respecting Himself, "Whosoever believeth in Him, shall not perish," says, in the same discourse, "Except a man be born of water and of the Spirit, he cannot enter into the kingdom of God:" and in His very last words on earth, joins "believing" and "being baptized" as both necessary to salvation.

Again; if ever man was justified by faith, it was St. Paul: and yet, when he was converted, it was said to him by one commissioned by his Saviour, "Arise, and be baptized, and wash away thy sins."

Whatever, then, your doctrine of Justification, if it be not in perfect consistence with the "new birth of water and the Spirit being the entrance into Christ's kingdom;" with being "baptized for the remission of sins;" with Baptism being a means of salvation in *its* place as well as faith in *its* place; with Christ "sanctifying His Church with the washing of water;" with the "doctrine of baptism" being a first "principle of the doctrine of Christ"

(John iii. 5 ; Acts ii. 38 ; Mark xvi. 16 ; Eph. v. 26 ; Heb. vi. 2) ; if it be not in perfect consistence with these statements, assuredly it is not based on all Scripture ; assuredly a part of its foundation is on the sand of your notions, not on the rock of the unerring word. It may be very consistent with itself, and in strict accordance with what those, whose powers of religious slander you fear, call "clear views of Divine grace ; " but all this is gained at the expense of its agreement with the words of your Saviour, and the testimony of the Spirit.

If ever man held justification by faith, it was Martin Luther ; and if there be any book in which he embodied what he held, it is his Commentary on the Galatians ; and yet, on Gal. iii. 27, he thus expresses himself : " Therefore the righteousness of the law, or of our own works, is not given, but Christ becomes our garment. This place is to be carefully noted, as it stands opposed to the fanatics who extenuate the majesty of Baptism, and speak of it wickedly and impiously. Paul, on the contrary, adorns Baptism with magnificent titles, calling it the 'washing of regeneration, and renewing of the Holy Ghost;' and here says that all the baptized 'have put on Christ.' "[1]

And again ; Calvin speaks of it thus : " We ought to consider that, at whatever time we are baptized, we are washed and purified once for the whole of life. Wherefore, as often as we fall, we must recall the remembrance of our Baptism, and thus fortify our minds, so as to feel certain and secure of the remission of sins : for though when once administered it seems to have passed, it is not abolished by subsequent sins. For the purity of Christ was therein offered to us, is always in force, and is not

---

[1] See further extracts from Luther, in Appendix B.

destroyed by any stain; it wipes and washes away all our defilements." (Institutes, Book IV. ch. xv. 3.)

Cranmer, in the Homily of Salvation or Justification, has—"Our office is, not to pass the time of this present life unfruitfully and idly, after that we are baptized or justified." [1]   Again, in his answer to Gardiner, which was published in 1550, and received his last corrections just before his martyrdom: "And where you (Gardiner) say that in Baptism we receive the Spirit of Christ, and in the Sacrament of His body and blood we receive His very flesh and blood, this your saying is no small derogation to Baptism, wherein we receive not only the Spirit of Christ, but also Christ Himself, whole body and soul, manhood and Godhead, unto everlasting life, as well as in the Holy Communion. For St. Paul saith, 'As many as be baptized into Christ have put on Christ.' Nevertheless, this is done in divers respects; for in Baptism it is done in respect of regeneration, and in the Holy Communion in respect of nourishment and augmentation." (Cranmer's Works on the Lord's Supper, Parker Soc. p. 25; see also pp. 34, 45, 64, 92.) [2]

Again; Latimer, who was burnt at the stake for his protest against Romanism, has—"What is so common as water? every foul ditch is full of it; yet we wash our remission of our sins by Baptism; for like as He was found

---

[1] Again, in the same Homily, Part II. (to the doctrinal statements of which I need not say that the Clergy of the Church of England are committed by the Eleventh Article) :—"Therefore we must trust only in God's mercy, and that sacrifice which our High Priest and Saviour Jesus Christ, the Son of God, once offered for us upon the cross, to obtain thereby God's grace and remission, as well of our original sin in Baptism, as of all actual sin committed by us after our Baptism, if we truly repent and turn unfeignedly to Him again."

[2] See further extracts from Cranmer, in Appendix B.

in rags, so we must find him by Baptism. There we begin;
we are washed with water; and then the words are added;
for we are baptized in the name of the Father, the Son,
and the Holy Ghost, whereby the Baptism receiveth his
strength." (Bp. Latimer's Remains, Parker Soc. p. 127.)

Again; Ridley, who was also burnt for his profession of
the principles of tne Reformation, speaks of the "water
in Baptism being sacramentally changed into the fountain
of Regeneration." And again: "The water in Baptism
hath grace promised, and by that promise the Holy Spirit
is given; not that grace is included in water, but that
grace cometh by water." (Ridley's Works, Parker Soc.
pp. 12, 240.)

But to show further how perfectly futile is the objection
raised against sacramental doctrine, because of its supposed
incompatibility with justification by faith, let us consider
for a moment, "why salvation is by faith?" Simply that
it may be by grace. (Rom. iv. 16.) Why is faith said to
justify? Not because there is any merit in faith, but because it looks simply to *Christ*. Faith is that in the soul
which apprehends God's mercy in Christ; it is the eye of
the soul which looks to Christ.

Therefore it justifies, or is said to justify, because it leads
to Christ the Justifier; and in the Sacraments, Christ the
Justifier gives Himself to the souls that turn to Him and
seek Him.

And, in fact, Baptism has more of *free* grace in it than
faith has; for faith, though the gift of God, is yet an act of
our own hearts, whereas Baptism is God's act altogether.
And if this be so with the conscious adult, how much
more with the unconscious infant![1]

---

[1] "If the covenant of faith can belong to infants, then it is certain they can have the benefit of faith before they have the grace;

No act of grace, on God's part, can be imagined more unconnected with man's deservings than the conveyance of Christ's nature to an unconscious infant. No merit, not even of faith, can be pleaded.

And this leads us to a deep moral reason for the sacramental part of Christ's religion.

We are exposed to temptations, not only from our carnal, but also from our intellectual and spiritual nature.

We are tempted, for instance, to spiritual pride.

If salvation were simply and entirely through an act of our spirits apprehending God, the Great Spirit, and what He has done for us in His Son, the very intellectual and spiritual nature of our salvation might puff us up ; and, by fostering spiritual pride—that most hateful of sins in God's sight — infinitely deteriorate our whole moral being.

And such an effect we find but too often produced. We find, in a marvellous way, spiritual pride of the most offensive kind, blighting the Christian character of thousands in whom there are the clearest views of salvation by grace through faith.

What, then, can more tend to humble and cast out such pride than the sacramental truths of Scripture—that our salvation is dependent not exclusively upon our superior nature laying hold of God's truth, but upon outward acts, so mean and insignificant in themselves as washing with a little water, and the tasting of a morsel of bread and a drop of wine? God, by having chosen two things, so mean and weak in themselves, to be the outward channels of His grace, has, in very deed, cast down imaginations.

that is, God will do them benefit before they can do Him service : and that is no new thing in religion, that God should love us first." — JEREMY TAYLOR : *Liberty of Prophesying*, vol. v. p. 564. Eden's Edit.

He has, in very deed, shown how He can make "things that are not to confound things that are," that neither flesh nor spirit should glory in His presence.

And again ; we are permitted to see another deep moral reason for holding sacramental grace ; which reason we may put as follows :—

Nothing has done more to destroy the true life of Christianity than the attempt to make it a sort of philosophical system.

The tendency of much of modern popular Theology is to exhibit Christianity as a sort of science, having its causes and effects—moral and mental, of course, but still causes and effects—connected according to certain known laws. The causes are, the exhibition of certain influential motives—such as the love of God shown in the plan of redemption ; the (natural) effects of these are the drawing of the heart and affections Godward, the implantation of a new principle, &c.

Now, all this is true ; but being *only* part of the truth, when held *alone*, it is held wrongly, and therefore mischievously. For the doctrine of the Sacraments at once and for ever makes Christianity (humanly speaking) unphilosophical. It introduces a disturbing element, because a supernatural one ; for it teaches us that there are in Christianity two ordinances which produce a religious effect not according to any laws of cause and effect with which *we* are acquainted. The Sacrament of Baptism grafts a person into Christ, not because there is anything in Baptism itself calculated to do so, but because of the will of God and promise of Christ to be with His Church to the end of the world.

When a man heartily accepts the doctrine of Baptism as it is laid down in Holy Scripture, he must hold *all* Christianity to be supernatural. He believes that he is,

in some inscrutable way, partaker of the nature of One
who is now at the right hand of God; he believes also
that his fellow-Christians are not merely his fellow-
Christians because they hold the same body of truth
which he holds—as the members of a political party may
be united by holding the same opinions—but he believes
that both they and he have been grafted supernaturally
into the Second Adam.

CHAPTER XVII.

BAPTISMAL GRACE, AS BEARING ON THE PREACHING OF CONVERSION.[1]

ANOTHER stumbling-block in the way of the full realization of Baptismal Regeneration, in the case of many pious and well-meaning Christians, has been a fear lest its

[1] In this chapter and in chapter iii. I use the word "conversion" in its popular acceptation, as synonymous with true repentance and a change of heart. Let it, however, be distinctly understood, that the word used for the needful change throughout the New Testament is not "conversion," but "repentance" ($\mu\epsilon\tau\acute{a}\nu o\iota a$).

The word "conversion" occurs but once in the New Testament, in Acts xv. 3—"declaring the conversion of the Gentiles." It is, consequently, never applied to designate the repentance of a baptized sinner. The necessary change in a sinful Christian is always called repentance (Rom. ii. 4; 2 Cor. vii. 9, 10; 2 Tim. ii. 25; Heb. vi. 1, 6; xii. 17; 2 Pet. iii. 9): and no marvel; for repentance is by far the deeper word of the two, if we look to its derivation. It always signifies an internal change, whereas the verb translated once or twice by convert ($\epsilon\pi\iota\sigma\tau\rho\acute{\epsilon}\phi\epsilon\iota\nu$) merely signifies turning—turning round or turning back in the middle of a walk. It primarily refers to an external action, and it scarcely ever loses entirely its external signification. It is the word used when it is said of our Lord that He "turned him about in the press" (Mark v. 30). In James v. 19, 20, it is spoken respecting turning from the error of a *way* :—"If any do err (or wander) from the truth, and one convert," or "turn him"—still keeping up the external idea of a way, and turning in it. I do not, in writing the above, discard the conventional use of this word "conversion." In one place, Luke xxii. 32, it seems synonymous with repentance. I merely wish to show that "repentance" is of the two by far the deeper, truer, and more Scriptural term.

reception should hinder the mass of baptized Christians from seeking true conversion to God.

It is presumed that the careless and worldly will rest satisfied with their Baptismal engrafting; and make it "a screen to hide from themselves the necessity of the complete actual change of mind and disposition necessary to them." If such do so, we can only say that they do it in wilful ignorance of the doctrine, and in wilful despite of the grace and intent of Holy Baptism;—for what is the doctrine and grace of it? "We are buried with Christ by Baptism into death, that . . . we *should* walk in newness of life." How can you express the great needful change more thoroughly than by the expression, "walking in newness of life"? And St. Paul here insists that each one's Baptism is a thing which, by its very nature, makes "walking in newness of life" incumbent upon each baptized man.

Again; true conversion is surely synonymous with "yielding ourselves unto God, as those that are alive from the dead, and our members as instruments of righteousness to God." And this, as I have shown (pp. 92—98), is made by the Apostle dependent on the Christian's Baptismal death and resurrection. (Rom. vi.)

Again; if the soul's conversion to God, and walking with Him, are described anywhere, they are in Colossians iii.; and all the heavenly precepts of this chapter (as I have shown above, p. 102) are also dependent on the reception of union with Christ in Baptism. So that, in point of fact, reception of Baptismal grace is an additional motive for turning to, abiding in, and walking with God. An additional motive, did I say? It is, in fact, *the* motive; for it reaches all. The true doctrine of Baptism teaches us that God has an interest in, and has given grace to, the whole visible Church.

Not some few, partakers of a secret election, but all who have been dedicated to God in Baptism, have been brought into the body of the Crucified, that, through the power and grace of His Cross, they may walk as God's children.

With reference to the idea, that any number of the baptized are deceiving themselves by thinking that Baptism is a passport to heaven, or that it does away with the necessity of any further change in the vast majority of nominal Christians, I can only say that in the course of a ministry which I have exercised in six places, in which I have myself visited from house to house, and ascertained, as far as practicable, the spiritual condition of the inmates, *I have never yet met with one such case. The proportion of professing Christians under such a delusion is, I am certain, perfectly inappreciable.* I have now before me a work, entitled "Fireside Preaching," written by a man taking very opposite views of Baptismal grace to myself, and written apparently to recommend searching house-to-house visiting. In the preface to it, I find the following corroboration of my own experience in this matter : "I have never, in a somewhat extensive experience, met with a poor person *who placed any reliance upon his Baptism.* No! when solemnly appealed to, the unconverted *invariably* shake their head, and confess, with painful consciousness of the truth of what they are uttering, ' I am not born again.' "

I believe that in thousands of parishes there is the most widespread and destructive unbelief in any spiritual grace whatsoever conveyed, under any circumstances, in the Sacrament of Baptism. There is a vague idea among the professing members of the Church, that it is right and proper that a child should be baptized ; but they have no notion whatsoever (at least that they can express) of any grace or responsibility connected with it. I say this most confidently; for, for years past, I have been in the habit, whenever I baptized, of questioning the parents and god-parents upon the subject.

But though I have never met with a case of a person who thus abused the doctrine of Baptism, I have met with multitudes—and those, I am afraid, but the index of a still larger number—who abused the opposite doctrine, to the destruction of their souls. I have met with multitudes who allowed themselves to remain in a state of impenitence, on the plea that they never had had sufficient grace, if any at all, given to them; that conversion is entirely the work of God, and that they themselves can do nothing to forward it, and that they must wait His time. I say that this is the master-delusion among the unconverted poor. In a whole district which I could name, comprising many counties, saturated with what is called "Gospel preaching," the answer given to earnest exhortations to repentance is, "When God wants me, He will call me." Of course, all idea of the holiness of the human body is out of the question.

I do not see how any preacher, who has ever had the doctrine of Baptism revealed to him by God's Spirit, can possibly ignore the reception of Baptismal grace in those professing Christians to whom he is preaching conversion and repentance. How does God, by the mouth of all His prophets, call His ancient people to repentance? "I have nourished and brought up children, and they have re-belled against Me." "Israel doth not know, My people doth not consider." The reader will see, by referring to the passages from the Old Testament which I have brought forward in Appendix A, that God *invariably* called His ancient people to turn to Him (*i.e.* to be converted), by reminding them of their interest in Him, and covenant relationship to Him.

If we go to the New Testament, we shall find that the texts on which the strongest appeals to bring about conversion can be grounded, are such as presuppose an initial reception of grace and adoption ; such are—" We then, as workers together with Him, beseech you also that ye receive not the grace of God in vain ;" or, " I will arise and go to my Father, and will say to Him, Father, I have sinned against heaven, and before Thee, and am no more worthy to be called Thy son ;" or, " Know ye not that your bodies are the temples of the Holy Ghost which is in you, which ye have of God ; and ye are not your own, but ye are bought with a price ? therefore, glorify God in your bodies, and in your spirits, which are God's."

If any preacher would enforce such texts as, " Put off the old man," " Be renewed in the spirit of your minds," " Put on the new man," he will find that he can only do so on the assumption that they are addressed to members of Christ's body—*i.e.* if he would enforce them in accordance with their context ; as a reference to the chapter in which they occur (Ephes. iv.) will show him in a moment.

Is a preacher endeavouring to draw souls to his Master, by pleading Christ's own invitation, " Come unto Me, all ye that labour and are heavy laden ?" it would be some help to him, in dispelling unbelief, or rebuking backwardness, if he " earnestly believed " that Christ had already received, as infants, those whom He now called,—that once He had in very deed embraced all of them in the arms of His mercy, and had made that very kingdom theirs, the good things of which they must yet come and claim at His hands.

And I cannot see how any preacher, who holds Baptismal Regeneration as set forth in Scripture, can possibly forbear to preach the need of conversion, or repentance, to that multitude of baptized persons who are now sinning away their souls. How can a man look at the spiritual and moral state of the baptized,—believe them to be in very deed dedicated to God,—believe also that God has in very deed ratified that dedication by a real gift of grace, —and yet not call upon them to turn to God, and flee to the cross? If the wrath of God be in store for any, it is in store for the " *sinners in Zion*,"—for those who " grieve," " vex," and " quench" the Spirit.

The wider a man believes the diffusion of grace in the Church to be, the more earnestly will he call upon men not to receive it in vain : that is, if *he himself yet abides in Christ ;* for a man may take up the holding of Baptismal Regeneration, as another takes up the denial of it, as a party cry.[1] Of the two, it appears to me that the

---

[1] Inexpressible harm has been done to the doctrine of grace in Holy Baptism by its having been preached by unspiritual men, in unrighteousness, or oftener in presumptuous ignorance and contempt of the true grounds on which the Church requires it (and every other truth) to be maintained and defended. Men who, on the most solemn occasion in their lives, professed before God and His Church that " they are persuaded that the Holy Scriptures contain sufficiently all doctrine required of necessity for eternal salvation," and that they " are determined by God's grace, out of the said Scriptures, to instruct the people committed to their charge ;" have come down to parishes and preached this doctrine of Baptism without the smallest attempt to reconcile the holding of it with other doctrines, equally with it, parts of God's truth. They have proved and maintained it solely on Prayer-book grounds, giving themselves no further trouble than citing one or two passages of the Baptismal Service. I suppose this has been because the Prayer-book references are more ready to hand ; but it has been fatal to the general reception of a truth, calculated above all others to preserve holiness in the Church.

Well would it have been if those who assume to be the more dutiful sons of the Church had, in this respect, " heard the Church," and been at some trouble to set forth the Scripture arguments for this doctrine, and to meet on their own grounds the preju-

man who holds Baptismal grace, without calling upon the great mass of Christians to turn to God through His Son, is infinitely more inconsistent than the other.

The higher the grace of Baptism, the greater the contrast between it and the lives of the baptized, and consequently the more urgent need to win them back by any man who would deliver his own soul. There will, of course, be this essential difference, that the Churchman never can broach the *time* of conversion as that of the first reception of grace. By so doing, he would cut away the ground from under himself.

" Baptismal Regeneration" and " Conversion" are the natural complements to one another in the scheme of Divine grace. If the preacher preaches Baptismal Regeneration without setting forth the daily conscious putting off of the old man, and the putting on of the new,——without urging the necessity of each individual Christian coming to Christ for himself, when he becomes conscious of good and evil,——then, of course, the effect is deadening.[1]

If conversion be preached to Christian congregations, as if they were so many heathen,——if all grace of Baptism be ignored, or the grace attached to it be pronounced real

dices of sincere though mistaken Christians. Then men would not have dared to call that unscriptural or unspiritual which every book of Scripture bears witness to, viz. that God gives to all whom He brings under His covenant, grace to fulfil its obligations.

[1] There are three consecutive Sermons (xxxv. xxxvi. xxxvii.) of Bishop Beveridge, well worthy of the attention of those who preach, as well as those who deny, Baptismal Regeneration. In Sermons xxxv. and xxxvii., from which I have given copious extracts in Appendix B and at page 157, the Baptismal Regeneration of Infants is most clearly and strongly maintained. In the intermediate Sermon (xxxvi.) the conscious coming to Christ is equally clearly set forth as necessary to salvation.

Q

only in the case of those who afterwards profit by some change, not in the least degree connected with Baptism,—then Satan, seeing the way thus cleared for him, will insinuate (as he does in the ears of hundreds of thousands, who hear what is called "the Gospel" preached) that God does not really wish for their holiness; they are as the heathen, why should they not enjoy themselves as the heathen?

And, as far as I can see, this latter error is far more widespread and more destructive than the former; I believe that for one soul slain by the perversion of sacramental teaching, there are thousands lost by the grossest perversion of the doctrine of conversion. We can scarcely have any idea of the extent of false teaching connected with conversion—I mean such a preaching of it as leads the unconverted to suppose that they have, as yet, nothing to do with God; and so that it is not their fault if they are now alienated from God, inasmuch as they can do nothing to forward or retard their repentance. If God designs it for them, He will choose His own time; and they must wait till then.

And they who have been most earnest in preaching conversion, and most honoured by God in turning sinners to repentance, have, when it came in their way, acknowledged, most fully and unreservedly, the grace of Baptism.

I do not think two men can be named more instrumental in reviving the doctrine of conversion than Wesley in the last, and Simeon in the present, century; and yet see how they hold to Christ's words.

Wesley, in a treatise on Baptism (and when a man writes a treatise on a subject, you must look into such a work for his matured and carefully weighed opinions), thus expresses himself (Works, vol. x. p. 148, 4th edition) :—

"By Baptism we are admitted into the Church, and, consequently, made members of Christ its Head. The Jews were admitted into the Church by circumcision, so are the Christians by Baptism. For, 'as many as are baptized into Christ,' in His name 'have' thereby 'put on Christ' (Gal. iii. 27); that is, are mystically united to Christ, and made one with Him. For 'by one Spirit we are all baptized into one body' (1 Cor. xii. 13); namely, the Church, the body of Christ (Ephes. iv. 12). From which spiritual vital union with Him proceeds the influence of His grace upon those that are baptized; as, from our union with the Church, a share in all its privileges, and in all the promises Christ has made to it."

"By Baptism we who were by nature children of wrath, are made the children of God. And this regeneration, which our Church in so many places ascribes to Baptism, is more than barely being admitted into the Church, though commonly connected therewith; being grafted into the body of Christ's Church, we are made the children of God by adoption and grace. This is grounded on the plain words of our Lord, 'Except a man be born again of water and the Spirit, he cannot enter into the kingdom of God.'"

So also Simeon, in a passage often quoted :—

"There are two things to be noticed in reference to this subject,—the *term* regeneration, and the *thing*. The term occurs but twice in the Scriptures; in one place it refers to Baptism, and is distinguished from the receiving of the Holy Ghost; *which, however, is represented as attendant upon it*: and in the other, it has a totally distinct meaning, unconnected with the subject. Now the term they (*i.e.* the Reformers) use as the Scripture uses it, and the thing they require as strongly as any person can require it.

"Again; if we appeal, as we ought to do, to the Holy Scriptures, they certainly do, in a very remarkable way,

Q 2

accord with the expressions in our Liturgy (Baptismal).
St. Paul says—'By one Spirit are we *all* baptized into
one body, whether we be Jews or Gentiles, whether we be
bond or free ; and have been ALL made to drink into one
Spirit.' And this he says of all the visible members of
Christ's body (1 Cor. xii. 13—27). Again ; speaking of
the whole nation of Israel, infants as well as adults—
'They were all baptized unto Moses in the cloud and in
the sea ; and did ALL eat the same spiritual meat ; and
did all drink the same spiritual drink : for they drank of
that spiritual rock that followed them : and that Rock
was Christ.' (1 Cor. x. 1—4.)

"Yet, behold, in the very next verse he tells us that
with many of them God was displeased, and overthrew
them in the wilderness. In another place he speaks yet
more strongly still—'As many of you,' says he, 'as are
baptized unto Christ have put on Christ.' Here we see
what is meant by the same expression as that before mentioned, of the Israelites being baptized unto Moses (the
preposition εἰς is used in both places) : it includes all that
had been initiated into his religion by the rite of Baptism ;
and of them universally does the Apostle say, '*they have
put on Christ.*' Now, I ask, have not the persons who
scruple the use of that prayer in the Baptismal Service
equal reason to scruple the use of these different expressions ?

" Again, St. Peter says—' Repent and be baptized, every
one of you, for the *remission of sins*' (Acts ii. 38) : and in
another place—' Baptism doth now save us :' and speaking elsewhere of baptized persons who are unfruitful in the
knowledge of our Lord Jesus Christ, he says—'He hath
forgotten that he was purged from his old sins ' (2 Peter
i. 9). Does not this very strongly countenance the idea
which our Reformers entertained, that the remission of

our sins, and the regeneration of our souls, are attendant
on the baptismal rite?" (Works, vol. ii. p. 259.)

As I said respecting some former passages, I do not for
one moment quote either of these men as authorities; but
simply to show how those whom the religious world has
ever looked upon as the most successful teachers of
"conversion," have yet, when it came in their way, been
neither afraid nor ashamed to bring forward, in its integrity, what God in Scripture says respecting the grace
of Baptism.[1]

---

[1] A large number of minor objections the reader will find fully
answered in a tract entitled, "The Sacrament of Responsibility;
or, Testimony of Scripture to the Teaching of the Church in Holy
Baptism." London : Bell and Daldy.

CHAPTER XVIII.

THE EFFECTS OF BAPTISMAL GRACE, AND THE PRACTICAL RESULTS OF HOLDING THE TRUTH RESPECTING IT.

Two considerations yet remain :—

I. The effects of Regeneration itself.

II. The practical results of holding the truth respecting it.

I. The effects of Regeneration.

It is one thing to have been, in Baptism, made a partaker of the nature of the Second Adam ; another, to have the knowledge and belief of this truth influencing our hearts and lives.

What is the effect of this heavenly and spiritual grace and strength which has been constantly flowing into the stream of our corrupt nature since the day of Pentecost?

Unquestionably, to raise up in the Church a standard of holiness, and to diffuse throughout it an amount of holiness such as the elder Church never knew.

Under the old dispensation men might repent and serve God, but they could not have the gift of Regeneration. Regeneration could not be bestowed till the new nature was provided in the person of Jesus Christ, and means ordained for its diffusion by the descent of the Spirit and the setting up of the Church.[1] In the New Dispensation,

---

[1] "The Christian New Birth was not till after Christ's birth, as men were not new-born till Christ was born (John i. 12) ; as their regeneration did not go before, but only followed His generation:

in which Regeneration was first given, there has been in
the family of God both a far higher standard of godliness
and a far wider diffusion of it. I say this, fully bearing
in mind the corruptions of the Church both in doctrine
and practice.

Take the greatest names of the Old and the New Testament, and compare their lives, so far as we have any record
of them.

The Old Testament saints, Abraham, Isaac, Jacob, David;
and the New, St. Peter, St. Paul, St. John, St. Stephen.

Though Abraham was the father even of the faithful in
Christ, and David the man after God's own heart, can any
one doubt but that the faith of the two blessed Apostles,
Peter and Paul, purified their hearts to an infinitely
greater extent than Abraham's faith purified his heart,
or David's his ?

And yet Abraham's faith saw Christ afar off; and
David's faith describes His sufferings as if he had stood
at the foot of the cross.

It was not the faith only which made the difference, for
the faith of both looked to Christ; but what the faith
acted upon and nourished, even the new nature which the
Patriarchs had not, and the Apostles had. In respect of
this, it is that the least in the kingdom of heaven is greater
than the greatest of those who desired to see it.

We read continually, as has been well said, of the elder
saints being allowed in things that would have removed
them altogether from the rank of saints under the Gospel.
God, not having given to them the new nature, did not

so the word could not be used in this its highest, most mysterious
sense, till that great mystery of the birth of the Son of God into
our world had actually taken place."—ARCHBISHOP TRENCH : *New
Test. Synonyms*, third edition, p. 70.

lay upon them the burdens which the new nature alone can sustain.

Then take some of the names mentioned with honour *for their faith*, in the eleventh of Hebrews—Gideon, Jephthah, Samson; compare their faith, and its effects on their lives—we will not say with that of Apostles, or Fathers of the Church, such as Ignatius, Irenæus, Augustine; but compare them with some of our English saints, such as Leighton, or Ken, or Beveridge, or Martyn, or that noble band who in our days have gone to preach the Gospel, one after another, in the most deadly climate in Africa, knowing full well that the average term of life of those who preceded them was not a year.

Consider that the character of Christian saints is not to be judged of by one or two brilliant acts of heroism in God's service, but from the fact that the whole record of their lives is a record of one unceasing warfare against the smallest remainder of sin—one unremitting struggle to be perfect in holiness and the love of God. Consider that the annals of corrupt ages and of fallen Churches are not destitute of men who, in the midst of an atmosphere of superstition, and amidst numberless mistakes of doctrine, have yet made it the one business of their lives to convert their fellow-creatures, and to be perfect in the love of Christ themselves.

And then compare the amount of godliness diffused through the whole Church in each case.

Look at the respective spiritual states of the Israelites at the commencement of the elder Church, and the Christians at the commencement of the younger.

God, through Moses, upbraiding the one as stiff-necked, and swearing that none of that evil generation should enter into His rest; and the same God inspiring His Apostle to write to a body of men in Thessalonica, to whom the profession of Christ had brought not one temporal benefit, but only the bitterest persecution—" We are bound to thank God always for you, brethren, as it is meet, because that your faith groweth exceedingly, and the charity of every one of you all towards each other aboundeth." (2 Thess. i. 3.)

Consider what a wide gulf between the spiritual states of those to whom they are respectively addressed, we have revealed to us by the whole tenor of the Books of Moses, and by that of the Epistles of St. Paul.

To the circumcised Jew, Moses offers, if he will keep God's law, "blessings in the city and in the field; blessings in the fruit of his body, the fruit of his ground, the fruit of his cattle, the increase of his kine, the flocks of his sheep, his basket and his store."

To the baptized Christian, on the contrary, St. James begins—" My brethren, count it all joy when ye fall into divers temptations; knowing this, that the trying of your faith worketh patience; but let patience have her perfect work, that ye may be perfect and entire, wanting nothing." And St. Paul—"And not only so, but we glory in tribulations also; knowing that tribulation worketh patience, and patience experience, and experience hope, and hope maketh not ashamed."

Here, then, is an inspired Prophet promising temporal rewards of obedience to the people of God in his time; and inspired Apostles pronouncing the people of God in their time blessed, because they were partakers of the lot of their Divine Master in tribulation and suffering. Why this difference? Because the one had a new nature, and the other not; and this new nature was the life-giving one of a suffering Messiah, which was to be perfected in His followers by *their* partaking of the same sufferings by which He was perfected.

The effect of Regeneration then is, as we should have supposed from the exalted nature of Him of Whom the regenerate are members, a far wider diffusion of a far higher goodness amongst God's people. Nor is all this in the least degree invalidated by after declensions in the Church, by the abounding of iniquity, by the development of a great apostasy, and by the fact of many Christians being more wicked than Jews or heathen; for all these things our Lord foretold : and His Apostles continually warn men lest they sin away the grace of the New Covenant; and if they do so, it is, of course, only likely that they should fall into greater depths of sin, because of more violence done to God's Spirit. To Christians, whether as a body or as individuals, far more than to the Jews, the warning of our Lord's parable is applicable, that if the evil spirit does return to the empty house, the last state will be worse than the first.

Still it may be asked, "Is all this better state of things the fruit of Baptism only?" Certainly not.

Regeneration in Baptism, be it remembered, is only the seed, not its growth or development. To the growth or perfection of the plant many other things must contribute. The providence of God must, ordinarily speaking, bring to bear upon the recipient of His grace many things—such as the care of pious parents or spiritual pastors ; and there must be that divine pruning, or purging, often by sicknesses or calamities, by the distresses attending a hard lot in this world, or by persecution for righteousness' sake, borne meekly and forgivingly after Christ's example.

And there must also be the possession of the written word, as that by which the seed is internally nourished ; for it is the word of God, and the doctrines drawn from it, and the teaching grounded upon it, which, by the power of God's Spirit, fills the mind with thoughts of God and heavenly desires; and there must also be the constant and faithful use of the Sacrament of the Lord's Supper, by which the inner man is renewed and strengthened with Christ's very strength.   Take the Apostolic Church as an example.   Never has the Church, as a whole, borne such fruits of Regeneration as it did then; but never did these means for aiding the growth of the new life contribute as they did then.   Those were times of bitterest persecution, when the word of God dwelt in men richly, and Christians .had scarcely any other books to divide its influence over them.   Then there was the broadest possible line between the Church and the world, and the Holy Communion was daily or weekly received, not by the few, but by the many.   Everything then contributed to the growth of the regenerate life.   Because that by persecution men felt that from day to day their lives were in their hands, and their property ever liable to confiscation, they realized habitually that they had no continuing city here; and so it was more natural for such to live as strangers and pilgrims, looking by faith to Him Who is invisible.   Then were they constant at religious assemblies in which the word of God was read and expounded, and men encouraged one another by united prayers and thanksgivings; and universally did they regard the Eucharist as a mystical communion with their Saviour, and habitually did they partake of it.

If the fruits, then so universal, are now more stinted, is it not because of prosperity, of riches, of security, all which things have a natural tendency to deaden men to the realities of the unseen? or is it not because of the withholding or perversion of God's word, or because men habitually neglect, or do not believe that they truly partake of Christ in the nourishing and sustaining Sacrament?

II. But we must now consider, in the last place, the practical effects of holding the truth of our having been regenerated in Baptism.

It is, as I said, manifestly one thing to have had, through God's grace, a benefit conferred by such a rite as Baptism, and quite another thing to hold and realize the doctrinal truth that Baptism is the channel of this grace.

A man may have received this gift, and yet, through defective religious teaching be all his life seeking an interest in Christ when he has one already.

A man, too, may bring his child to the laver of Regeneration, and regard our Saviour's Sacrament merely as an edifying ceremony, and so receive it back in positive unbelief of any benefit having been conferred. We have already, in former parts of this treatise, necessarily anticipated much which will come under the head of practical application; for so exceedingly practical is the doctrine of Baptismal Regeneration, that in some of the leading passages bearing on it, such as Rom. vi., Col. ii. iii., we deduce the doctrine from the application to the heart and life.

Still it may be well, though at the risk of repetition, to advert separately to some of the motives for trust in God and holiness of life, furnished by Baptismal doctrine.

The first and most important result of believing sincerely what God has revealed respecting this Sacrament, will be to realize to every baptized man that all the precepts of Scripture are addressed to him; and, if he has turned or is turning to God, through Christ, that all the promises of Scripture belong to him.

From the beginning to the end of the Bible, it is taken for granted that those to whom it is addressed are, by an initial rite, in covenant relationship with God, and in a state of grace; and those who are thus addressed are not to doubt this, or to wait for something further, but at once to begin in earnest, or to continue in earnest, the working out of their salvation.

The Bible is not addressed to, nor intended for, the heathen. The first part of it was inspired for the circumcised Jew; the whole for the baptized Christian. In both cases, God first gathers out a family, and then He gives to this family His word to be their guide.

First, He took one nation in Abraham, as His family; then, from the first, He gave them Circumcision that they (individually) might know that they were in His family; then He gave them His word, addressed to them *as a circumcised nation.*

Then, afterwards, He enlarged this family; He gathered together into it His children scattered abroad; and when He did this, He added to His word, for He gave the New Testament, containing far richer promises and far more heart-searching precepts. But before giving the New Testament, with its far deeper principles, to His Church, He had taken care to give another covenant initial rite, whereby they who had these higher precepts might know that they were addressed to them, and that they had received grace, the grace of the New Covenant, to fulfil them. The precepts of the New Testament are universally addressed to those who are in some degree partakers of Christ the Second Adam. It is taken for granted that they have all been made so in Baptism. He, then, who realizes this, will, in reading his Bible, take everything as said to himself.

When, for instance, in the Book of Proverbs, he reads, "My son, give Me thine heart," he will not hesitate, and put such words from him, and say, "This does not yet belong to me; I must have more evidence that I am God's child." He will rather reverently say to God, "Take my heart; make my heart right with Thee. Thou hast given to me the adoption ; give me the love and holiness which mark Thy true sons."

And again, when he reads in the Prophets all the promises of God to His people—all the denunciations of God's wrath against the backslidings of His people—all the precepts or threatenings to Israel, to Judah, to Zion, to God's elect, His chosen, he will realize that all these belong, in a far deeper and more extended sense, to the visible Church of Jesus Christ. He will be assured that if Circumcision had enrolled the Jew into a company of men, of whom, and to whom, such things could be said, Baptism (unless God's purposes of grace are narrower than they were) has brought him into a body to which pertain benefits of which the Jewish were but the shadow. Every promise, then, to . Zion, every threat against the backslidings of God's people, he will feel that he has a part in. He will be ceaselessly asking himself, not merely " Am I saving my soul ?" but "Am I fulfilling my position in the present Zion of God ?"

And if such will be his personal application to himself of the Old, how much more of the New Testament—more especially the Apostolical Epistles—those parts of it so peculiarly addressed to the Church, as the elect of God, the body of Christ ?

Whenever, then, he reads that Christians are, as members of Christ's body, to be holy, to keep their bodies under subjection, to yield themselves unto God as those that are alive from the dead, to bear one another's burdens, to be at peace with one another, as called in one body ; whenever, I say, the man who realizes the grace of the Christian covenant finds such precepts as these, he will take them as said directly to himself, because that in Baptism he was brought into this fellowship.

But, it may be said, can a baptized man do this without further light and help from God ?

Assuredly not. It requires the special aid of God's Spirit truly to take to ourselves, and savingly to profit by, the least of Christ's words, much more such wondrous words as those in which He has embodied sacramental truth. If a man be under the influence of teaching which makes him deem it superstitious or unscriptural to take some words of God in their plain acceptation, he will, of course, refuse to contemplate them—he will be double-minded in his secret prayers to God to reveal them to him in their integrity.

If the doctrine of Baptism be, as St. Paul asserts it to be, one of the first principles of the doctrine of Christ, assuredly it cannot be esteemed a secondary matter without the soul suffering grievous loss.

We find, for instance, men who have lived in the faithful recognition of much evangelical and moral truth, but in the tacit unbelief of the grace which Christ conveys through sacraments, actually praying to God, almost at the end of their Christian career, that He would give them an interest in Christ.

The true belief in the "one Baptism," I need not say, must have the effect of at once doing away with all those doubts, so destructive of a Christian's peace, as to whether he has an interest in Christ.

In illustration of the above, I cannot forbear giving to the reader the following passage from Melancthon :—

"The principal meaning and end of Baptism we gather from the promise, 'He that believeth and is baptized shall be saved ;' for Baptism is rightly called a sacrament, because it is annexed to this promise in order to testify that the promise of grace belongs, in very deed, to the man who is baptized. And hence we must think of this testimony, just as if God, by some new voice from heaven, bears witness that He Himself receives him [into favour].

And so, after the man baptized understands [Christian]
teaching, let him exercise this faith, let him believe that
he is in very deed accepted by God for Christ's sake, and
is being sanctified by the Holy Ghost.

"If we would make good use of Baptism in after life,
let it daily admonish us (thus). Behold, by this sign God
bears witness that thou hast been received into His favour.
His will is, that this testimony be not contemned. Wherefore believe that thou art truly accepted by him, and in
this faith call upon Him. Such is the daily use of
Baptism."—*Loci Theologici: De Baptismo.*[1]

I would now, in conclusion, call the reader's attention
to some most important practical instruction which he will
find in God's word, which by its very nature is such that
it can only be effectively, or with any sincerity, applied
to men's hearts and consciences by those who hold the
Baptismal engrafting into Christ of all in the Church.

In the Apostolical Epistles we find certain holy dispositions inculcated upon Christians, as those to which they
are pledged as members of Christ.

They are bid to cultivate certain graces, not because
these graces adorn a profession of religion, but because
God has brought them into a state of grace, viz. membership with Christ, in order that they may, through this
grace, produce these holy fruits.

Again : men are bid to crucify and abhor certain sins,
not because these sins disgrace the Christian character,
but because, by the commission of these sins, they rend
asunder, or defile, or cut themselves off from, Christ's
mystical body.

---

[1] A similar Evangelical application of Baptism will be found in
the remarkable work of Aonio Paleario, on the "Benefit of Christ's
Death," page 83, Religious Tract Society's Edit.; also in Latimer's
Sermons, xxxvii. pp. 133, 134, Parker Society.

To give instances. In Romans xii. 3—5, we have the Apostle exhorting the Roman Christians to humility. " I say, through the grace given unto me, to every man that is among you [let the reader remark how he addresses *all*], not to think of himself more highly than he ought to think; but to think soberly, according as God hath dealt *to every man* the measure of faith." And on what grounds does the Apostle urge this grace on these converts? Not because of the intrinsic beauty and worth of this first Christian virtue, nor because of the eternal honour and glory which will follow it, if it be a genuine fruit of the Spirit; though these would certainly be legitimate grounds on which to urge men to cultivate it, and in other places these grounds are urged; but the reason he assigns is, that all they to whom he wrote were "one body in Christ." "For as we have many members in one body and all members have not the same office: so we, being many, are one body in Christ, and every one members one of another."

Again; in 1 Cor. xii., we find the Apostle bidding the Corinthians to cultivate tender sympathy with one another, to be kind and considerate, to condescend to one another's infirmities, and honour those inferior to them even in spiritual attainments. And on what special ground does he urge all these things upon them? On the one ground that all to whom he wrote were members of Christ; for he begins his exhortation with—"By one Spirit are we all baptized into one body." He illustrates it by the mutual sympathy of the members of the human frame; and he concludes it with the words—"Now ye are the body of Christ, and members in particular."

A moment's consideration will serve to convince the reader that, if he is to apply to himself this particular instruction in righteousness, and endeavour to act upon it in his intercourse with his fellow-Christians, this can only

R

be by sincerely believing that both he himself, and the baptized Christians by whom he is surrounded, have all been grafted into this one body.

To whatsoever extent he looks upon the Baptism of the majority of those with whom his lot is cast, as a mere ceremony, in which the Holy Spirit did not really baptize them into Christ's body, just to that extent will he be unable to realize practically the Apostle's motive to Christian sympathy.

I do not, of course, mean to assert that this is the only Scripture motive for the cultivation and exercise of these graces. I do not doubt but that the love of his Saviour constrains many a Christian to exercise them, who, through defective religious teaching or prejudice, does not realize the doctrine of the Church being the body of Christ ; still we have here the Apostle urging a particular motive, over and above every other. And it is impossible to imagine that the Holy Spirit should have directed Apostles to urge any one motive, to any virtue or grace whatsoever, which may be safely dispensed with because others appear in the eye of man more efficacious.

But again (and I would invite the reader's most earnest attention to this last instance that I shall give), the Holy Spirit urges upon Christians purity of body and soul, by reminding them that their very bodies are the members of Christ. " Know ye not that your bodies are the members of Christ ? Shall I then take the members of Christ, and make them the members of an harlot ? God forbid." (1 Cor. vi. 15.) Let it be observed that the Apostle does not here say that sins of impurity are to be avoided because of their inconsistency with a *profession* of Christianity. Neither does he bid men shun such sins because of the degradation into which they sink both body and soul, and the wrath of God, which they will eventually draw down on the sinner.

But the Holy Spirit would have Christians abhor sins of impurity and lust because they have been grafted into Christ's body. (1 Cor. vi.) "Know ye not that your bodies are the members of Christ? Shall I then take the members of Christ, and make them the members of an harlot? God forbid. What? know ye not that your body is the temple of the Holy Ghost which is in you, which ye have of God, and ye are not your own? For ye are bought with a price : therefore glorify God in your body, and in your spirit, which are God's." (1 Cor. vi. 19, 20.)

It appears to me utterly impossible for any one who does not believe that all the baptized have at their Baptism been really grafted into Christ, to urge this Scripture motive to holiness upon them.

In a large series of Tracts against sins of impurity, published by the Religious Tract Society, this one motive to holiness, so strongly urged by the Apostle, is not once used.[1]

Let us take the case of a minister, or teacher, or parent, believing that unless a young person showed manifest signs of real conversion, he was on no account to be considered to have been regenerate and grafted into Christ's body in Baptism. Such a one would naturally think that the commission of such a sin as fornication was the surest pos-

[1] This apostolic motive to purity is entirely omitted from Mr. Ryle's tract "ARE YOU HOLY?" as is to be expected from the well-known opinions of its writer.

I am sorry to say, too, that it is almost altogether ignored in two or three most Christian and useful tracts, published by Wertheim, entitled "Honest Advice to Young Englishmen;" "Kind Words to the Young Women of England, on a Serious Subject;" "A Mother's Care for her Daughter's Safety." I say "almost;" for though 1 Cor. vi. 18, 20, is once referred to, it is not cited in full, as other texts are, nor is *any* exhortation grounded upon its doctrine. Notwithstanding this omission, however, I would most earnestly recommend these tracts to the notice, and their object to the prayers, of my brethren.

R 2

sible sign that the person in question was in no sense, and
never had been, a member of Christ; and so he would
hold such a mode of warning Christian people of the awful
evil of such sins to be either a useless or a dangerous
one. It would be, from his point of view, useless if the
person to be warned had ever been really regenerate; for
then higher motives, such as those arising from a sense of
justification, would keep him in an atmosphere far above
the reach of such evil influences; and if he had never
been (in the view of his instructor) regenerated, such an
appeal would be dangerous : for it would lead him to
imagine that he once had been grafted into Christ when
he never had been.

But supposing the young person's Baptism to have been
what St. Paul presumes it to be in all cases (Rom. vi. 3, 4;
Gal. iii. 27 ; 1 Cor. vi. 15 ; xii. 13, 17), a real engrafting
into Christ's body, what an awful responsibility upon
those who do not warn him against sins so fearfully pre-
valent, by bringing before him the full iniquity of such
sins ! The full iniquity of sins of impurity is, that they
defile Christ's body,—those members which are His, not
ours ; and none can urge this consideration on Christians
in danger of such sins, unless they believe that such
Christians have been in very deed made partakers of the
grace which Baptism was instituted to convey.

When one thinks of the devastation which these forms of
iniquity are working among baptized Christians, how can
ministers of Christ be free from men's blood, if such warnings do not form a part of their public teaching to their
baptized flocks ? And how can parents answer for their
children's souls, unless they teach them (as the Church
directs them in her Catechism) that they are members of
Christ, and so that their very bodies are to be reverenced
and held sacred as in union with His ?

But they are fearful lest baptized men should deem themselves members of Christ when they are not. Had St. Paul any such fear? His fear is, not that men should think that they are members of Christ when they are not, but lest they should fail to realize it when they all are.

"Still," Unbelief will rejoin, "may not this Church be a natural society, and this wondrous way of speaking of it oriental and figurative?" This cannot be, for the Apostle says, "We are members of His body, of His flesh, and of His bones" (Eph. v. 30); and, as if to show that they who would empty his words of all supernatural import, do it at their own peril, he adds, "This is a great mystery; but I speak concerning Christ and the Church."

Reader, does it seem too great a thing that men on earth should partake of a gift so awful? Consider, I beseech you, that Christian dispensation in which you are now living, how it began, how it is carried on, how it will terminate. It began with no less a miracle than the Incarnation; "the Word was made flesh;" it is carried on by One in your nature on the throne of the heaven of heavens; and at its close all men will rise again in their bodies.

You hold these things, and you believe in original sin and the mystery of its transmission from the first Adam. You know not, then, what part of your probation it may be to submit your whole inner man to the doctrine of the Second Adam, and of the means which He has consecrated for making His brethren one with Himself. In such a dispensation of grace, it is not for you to ask, "How can these things be?" Far other words befit a creature redeemed by God Incarnate. Say you rather, "Lord, to whom shall we go? Thou hast the words of eternal life." "Lord, I believe, help Thou mine unbelief."

CHAPTER XIX.

ON ELECTION AND FINAL PERSEVERANCE, AND THEIR BEARING ON BAPTISMAL REGENERATION.

HAVING in several places in the foregoing pages asserted that there is no grace from which Christians are not said in Scripture to be liable to fall, I think it will be well to give the reader the passages on which I ground this assertion, in order that he may judge for himself; and as some persons are, in the Scriptures (in equally plain terms), said to be elected to grace, and some apparently to perseverance in grace, I have given along with these places those which are usually adduced in support of the latter doctrines.

TEXTS ASSERTING ELECTION TO GRACE.

The Strength of Israel will not lie NOR REPENT: FOR HE IS NOT A MAN THAT HE SHOULD REPENT. (1 Sam. xv. 29.)

I SAID, I WILL NEVER BREAK MY COVENANT WITH YOU [i.e. to give you the whole land of Palestine], and ye shall make no league, &c. (Judges ii. 1, 2.)

I am the Lord, I CHANGE NOT; therefore, ye sons of Jacob are not consumed. (Malachi iii. 6.)

For the Lord will not forsake his people, for his great name's sake: because it hath pleased the Lord to make you his people. (1 Sam. xii. 22.)

TEXTS ASSERTING MAN'S LIABILITY TO FALL FROM GRACE.

THE LORD REPENTED that he had made Saul king over Israel. (1 Sam. xv. 35.)

WHEREFORE I ALSO SAID, I WILL NOT DRIVE THEM OUT FROM BEFORE YOU. (Judges ii. 3.)

As for you, your carcases, they shall fall in this wilderness. . . . YE SHALL KNOW MY BREACH OF PROMISE. (Numb. xiv. 32, 34.)
Wherefore the Lord God of Israel saith, I SAID INDEED that thy house and the house of thy father should walk before me for ever, BUT NOW THE LORD SAITH, BE IT FAR FROM ME. (1 Sam. ii. 30.)

But if ye shall still do wickedly, ye shall be consumed, both ye and your king. (1 Sam. xii. 25.)

" And of all my sons (for the Lord hath given me many sons,) he hath chosen Solomon my son to sit upon the throne of the kingdom of the Lord over Israel. And he said unto me, Solomon thy son, he shall build my house and my courts : for I HAVE CHOSEN HIM TO BE MY SON, AND I WILL BE HIS FATHER. (1 Chron. xxviii. 5, 6.)

Then the word of the Lord came unto me, saying, BEFORE I FORMED THEE IN THE BELLY I KNEW THEE ; and before thou camest forth out of the womb I sanctified thee, and I ORDAINED THEE A PROPHET UNTO THE NATIONS. (Jer. i. 4, 5.)

I have hallowed this house, which thou hast built, TO PUT MY NAME THERE FOR EVER. (1 Kings ix. 3.)

The steps of a *good* man are ordered by the Lord : and he delighteth in his way. THOUGH HE FALL, HE SHALL NOT BE UTTERLY CAST DOWN : FOR THE LORD UPHOLDETH HIM WITH HIS HAND. I have been young, and *now* am old ; yet have I not seen the righteous forsaken, nor his seed begging bread. *He is* ever merciful, and lendeth ; and his seed *is* blessed. Depart from evil, and do good ; and dwell for evermore. For the LORD loveth judgment, AND FORSAKETH NOT HIS SAINTS ; THEY ARE PRESERVED FOR EVER : but the seed of the wicked shall be cut off. The righteous shall inherit the land, and dwell therein for ever. The mouth of the righteous speaketh wisdom, and his tongue talketh of judgment. THE LAW OF HIS GOD IS IN HIS HEART ; NONE OF HIS STEPS SHALL SLIDE. (PS. xxxvii. 23—31.)

And the vessel that he made of clay was marred in the hands of the potter : SO HE MADE IT AGAIN ANOTHER VESSEL, AS SEEMED GOOD UNTO THE POTTER TO MAKE IT. O house of Israel, cannot I do with you as this potter ? (Jer. xviii. 4, 6.)

And thou, Solomon my son, know thou the God of thy father, and serve him . . . . for if thou seek him he will be found of thee, BUT IF THOU FORSAKE HIM HE WILL CAST THEE OFF FOR EVER. (1 Chron. xxviii. 9.)

BUT IF YE SHALL AT ALL TURN FROM FOLLOWING ME, ye or your children, then . . . this house, which I have hallowed for my name, I WILL CAST OUT OF MY SIGHT. (1 Kings ix. 6, 7.)

BUT WHEN THE RIGHTEOUS TURNETH AWAY FROM HIS RIGHTEOUSNESS, and committeth iniquity, *and* doeth according to all the abominations that the wicked *man* doeth, shall he live? ALL HIS RIGHTEOUSNESS THAT HE HATH DONE SHALL NOT BE MENTIONED : in his trespass that he hath trespassed, and in his sin that he hath sinned, IN THEM SHALL HE DIE. Yet ye say, The way of the Lord is not equal. Hear now, O house of Israel ; Is not my way equal? are not your ways unequal? When a righteous *man* TURNETH AWAY FROM HIS RIGHTEOUSNESS, and committeth iniquity, and DIETH IN THEM ; for his iniquity that he hath done shall he die. AGAIN, WHEN THE WICKED MAN TURNETH AWAY FROM HIS WICKEDNESS THAT HE HATH COMMITTED, AND DOETH THAT WHICH IS LAWFUL AND RIGHT, he shall save his soul alive. Because he considereth, and turneth away from all his transgressions that he hath committed, he shall surely live, he shall not die. (Ezek. xviii. 24—28.)

And at what instant I shall speak concerning a nation, and concerning a kingdom, to build and to plant it ; IF IT DO EVIL IN MY SIGHT, THAT IT OBEY NOT MY VOICE, THEN I WILL REPENT OF THE GOOD, WHEREWITH I SAID I WOULD BENEFIT THEM. (Jer. xviii. 9, 10.)

In that day, saith the Lord of hosts, will I take thee, O Zerubbabel, my servant, the son of Shealtiel, saith the LORD, AND WILL MAKE THEE AS A SIGNET : FOR I HAVE CHOSEN THEE, SAITH THE LORD OF HOSTS. (Hag. ii. 23.)

As I live, saith the Lord, though Coniah the son of Jehoiakim king of Judah were the SIGNET UPON MY RIGHT HAND, YET WOULD I PLUCK THEE THENCE. (Jer. xxii. 24.)

NEW TESTAMENT.

* MY SHEEP HEAR MY VOICE, AND I KNOW THEM, AND THEY FOLLOW ME : AND I GIVE UNTO THEM ETERNAL LIFE ; AND THEY SHALL NEVER PERISH, NEITHER SHALL ANY MAN PLUCK THEM OUT OF MY HAND. My Father, which gave *them* me, is greater than all; and no *man* is able to pluck *them* out of my Father's hand. (John x. 27—29.)

* Now before the feast of the passover, when Jesus knew that his hour was come that he should depart out of this world unto the Father, HAVING LOVED HIS OWN WHICH WERE IN THE WORLD, HE LOVED THEM UNTO THE END. (John xiii. 1.)

* YE HAVE NOT CHOSEN ME, BUT I HAVE CHOSEN YOU, AND ORDAINED YOU, THAT YE SHOULD GO AND BRING FORTH FRUIT, AND THAT YOUR FRUIT SHOULD REMAIN : that whatsoever ye shall ask of the Father in my name, he may give it you. (John xv. 16.)

* And we know that all things work together for good to them that love God, TO THEM WHO ARE THE CALLED ACCORDING TO HIS PURPOSE. FOR WHOM HE DID FOREKNOW, HE ALSO DID PREDESTINATE TO BE CONFORMED TO THE IMAGE OF HIS SON, THAT HE MIGHT BE THE FIRST-BORN AMONG MANY BRETHREN. MOREOVER WHOM HE DID PREDESTINATE, THEM HE ALSO CALLED : AND WHOM HE CALLED, THEM

How think ye ? IF A MAN HAVE AN HUNDRED SHEEP, AND ONE OF THEM BE GONE ASTRAY, doth he not leave the ninety and nine, and goeth into the mountains, and seeketh that which is gone astray ? AND IF SO BE THAT HE FIND IT, verily I say unto you, he rejoiceth more of that *sheep*, than of the ninety and nine which went not astray. (Mat. xviii. 12, 13.)

* I am the true vine, and my Father is the husbandman. EVERY BRANCH IN ME THAT BEARETH NOT FRUIT HE TAKETH AWAY : and every *branch* that beareth fruit, he purgeth it, that it may bring forth more fruit. IF A MAN ABIDE NOT IN ME, HE IS CAST FORTH AS A BRANCH, AND IS WITHERED ; and men gather them, and cast *them* into the fire, AND THEY ARE BURNED. As the Father hath loved me, so have I loved you : CONTINUE YE IN MY LOVE. IF YE KEEP MY COMMANDMENTS, YE SHALL ABIDE IN MY LOVE; even as I have kept my Father's commandments, and abide in his love. (John xv. 1, 2, 6, 9, 10.)†

* Well ; because of unbelief they were broken off, and THOU STANDEST BY FAITH. Be not highminded, but fear : for if God spared not the natural branches, TAKE HEED LEST HE ALSO SPARE NOT THEE. Behold therefore the goodness and severity of God : on them which fell, severity ; but toward thee, goodness, IF THOU CONTINUE IN HIS GOODNESS : otherwise thou also shalt be cut off. (Rom. xi. 20—22.)

---

* Let the reader particularly notice that the texts in the parallel columns which have an asterisk before them are spoken to the same persons. This applies in a measure to all the texts taken from the Apostolical Epistles, for all the Churches to whom these were addressed were in the same ecclesiastical and spiritual state.

† For comparison of John x. 27 with xv. 1—10 see above, page 178, in chapter xiii.

HE ALSO JUSTIFIED: AND WHOM HE JUSTIFIED, THEM HE ALSO GLORIFIED. What shall we then say to these things? If God *be* for us, who *can be* against us? (Rom. viii. 28—31.)

* Peter, an apostle of Jesus Christ, to the strangers scattered throughout Pontus, Galatia, Cappadocia, Asia, and Bithynia, ELECT ACCORDING TO THE FOREKNOWLEDGE OF GOD THE FATHER, THROUGH SANCTIFICATION OF THE SPIRIT, UNTO OBEDIENCE AND SPRINKLING OF THE BLOOD OF JESUS CHRIST: Grace unto you, and peace, be multiplied. Blessed *be* the God and Father of our Lord Jesus Christ, which according to his abundant mercy hath begotten us again unto a lively hope by the resurrection of Jesus Christ from the dead, to an inheritance incorruptible, and undefiled, and that fadeth not away, RESERVED IN HEAVEN FOR YOU, WHO ARE KEPT BY THE POWER OF GOD THROUGH FAITH UNTO SALVATION READY TO BE REVEALED IN THE LAST TIME. (1 Peter i. 1—5.)

* But he that lacketh these things is blind, and cannot see afar off, AND HATH FORGOTTEN THAT HE WAS PURGED FROM HIS OLD SINS. WHEREFORE THE RATHER, BRETHREN, GIVE DILIGENCE TO MAKE YOUR CALLING AND ELECTION SURE: FOR IF YE DO THESE THINGS, YE SHALL NEVER FALL: for so an entrance shall be ministered unto you abundantly into the everlasting kingdom of our Lord and Saviour Jesus Christ. (2 Peter i. 9—11.)

* Jude, the servant of Jesus Christ, and brother of James, TO THEM THAT ARE SANCTIFIED BY GOD THE FATHER, AND PRESERVED IN JESUS CHRIST, *and* called. (Jude 1.)

* I will therefore put you in remembrance, though ye once knew this, how the Lord, HAVING SAVED the people out of the land of Egypt, AFTERWARDS DESTROYED them that believed not. And the ANGELS WHICH KEPT NOT THEIR FIRST ESTATE, but left their own habitation, he hath reserved in everlasting chains under darkness unto the judgment of the great day. (Jude 5, 6.)

They went out from us, but they were not of us; FOR IF THEY HAD BEEN OF US, THEY WOULD (*no doubt*) HAVE CONTINUED WITH US: but *they went out,* that they might be made manifest that they were not all of us. (1 John ii. 19.)

These are spots in your feasts of charity, when they feast with you, feeding themselves without fear: clouds *they are* without water, carried about of winds; trees whose fruit withereth, without fruit, TWICE DEAD, plucked up by the roots. (Jude 12.)

FEAR NOT, LITTLE FLOCK; FOR IT IS YOUR FATHER'S GOOD PLEASURE TO GIVE YOU THE KINGDOM. Sell that ye have, and give alms; PROVIDE YOURSELVES bags which wax not old, A TREASURE IN THE HEAVENS THAT FAILETH NOT, where no thief approacheth, neither moth corrupteth. (Luke xii. 32, 33.)

Wherefore WE RECEIVING A KINGDOM WHICH CANNOT BE MOVED, LET US HAVE GRACE, whereby we may serve God acceptably with reverence and GODLY FEAR: FOR OUR GOD IS A CONSUMING FIRE. (Heb. xii. 28, 29.)

For there shall arise false Christs, and false prophets, and shall shew great signs and wonders: insomuch that, if (*it were*) POSSIBLE, THEY SHALL DECEIVE THE VERY ELECT. (Matt. xxiv. 24.)

Take heed therefore unto yourselves, and to ALL THE FLOCK, OVER THE WHICH THE HOLY GHOST HATH MADE YOU OVERSEERS, TO FEED THE CHURCH OF GOD, WHICH HE HATH PURCHASED WITH HIS OWN BLOOD. For I know this, that after my departing shall grievous wolves enter in among you, NOT SPARING THE FLOCK. Also OF YOUR OWN SELVES shall men arise, speaking perverse things, to draw away disciples after them. Therefore watch, and remember, that by the space of three years I ceased not to warn EVERY ONE night and day, with tears. (Acts xx. 28—31.)

This thou knowest, that ALL THEY WHICH ARE IN ASIA BE TURNED AWAY FROM ME; of whom are Phygellus and Hermogenes. (2 Tim. i. 15.)

["All they of Asia," that is, Proconsular Asia, including Ephesus, the Church in which city the Apostle addresses as "elect in Christ" and "predestinated."]

Being born again, NOT OF CORRUPTIBLE SEED, BUT OF INCORRUPTIBLE, by the word of God, which liveth and abideth for ever. For all flesh is as grass, and all the glory of man as the flower of grass. The grass withereth, and the flower thereof falleth away: but the word of the Lord endureth for ever. And this is the word which by the gospel is preached unto you. (1 Peter i. 23—25.)

Now the parable is this : THE SEED IS THE WORD OF GOD And some fell upon a rock ; and AS SOON AS IT WAS SPRUNG UP, IT WITHERED AWAY, because it lacked moisture. And some fell among thorns ; and the thorns sprang up with it, and choked it. (Luke viii. 11, 6, 7.)

For God hath not appointed us to wrath, BUT TO OBTAIN SALVATION BY OUR LORD JESUS CHRIST, who died for us, that, whether we wake or sleep, we should live together with him. (1 Thes. v. 9, 10.)

Let us labour therefore to enter into that rest, LEST ANY MAN FALL AFTER THE SAME EXAMPLE OF UNBELIEF. (Heb. iv. 11.)

* But we are bound to give thanks alway to God for you, brethren beloved of the LORD, because GOD HATH FROM THE BEGINNING CHOSEN YOU TO SALVATION THROUGH SANCTIFICATION OF THE SPIRIT AND BELIEF OF THE TRUTH : whereunto he called you by our gospel, to the obtaining of the glory of our Lord Jesus Christ. (2 Thess. ii. 13, 14.)

* QUENCH NOT THE SPIRIT. (1 Thess. v. 19.)

Now the Spirit speaketh expressly, that in the latter times some SHALL DEPART FROM THE FAITH, giving heed to seducing spirits, and doctrines of devils. Having damnation, because they have cast off THEIR FIRST FAITH. For SOME ARE ALREADY TURNED ASIDE AFTER SATAN. (1 Tim. iv. 1; v. 12—15.)

' The Lord is faithful, WHO SHALL STABLISH (στηρίξει) YOU, and keep you from evil. (2 Thess. iii. 3.)

They that are unlearned and unstable wrest, as they do also the other scriptures, to their own destruction. YE THEREFORE, BELOVED, seeing ye know these things before, BEWARE LEST YE ALSO, being led away with the error of the wicked, FALL FROM YOUR OWN STEADFASTNESS (τοῦ ἰδίου στηριγμοῦ). (2 Peter iii. 16, 17.)

And the very God of peace sanctify you wholly; and I pray God your whole spirit and soul and body be preserved blameless UNTO THE COMING OF OUR LORD JESUS CHRIST. FAITHFUL IS HE THAT CALLETH YOU, WHO ALSO WILL DO IT. (1 Thess. v. 23, 24.)

In the body of his flesh through death, to present you holy and unblameable and unreproveable in his sight: IF YE CONTINUE IN THE FAITH GROUNDED AND SETTLED, AND BE NOT MOVED AWAY FROM THE HOPE OF THE GOSPEL, which ye have heard, and which was preached to every creature which is under heaven; whereof I Paul am made a minister. (Col. i. 22, 23.)

Hath not the potter power over the clay, of the same lump to make one vessel unto honour, and another unto dishonour? What if God, willing to shew his wrath, and to make his power known, endured with much longsuffering the vessels of wrath fitted to destruction : AND THAT HE MIGHT MAKE KNOWN THE RICHES OF HIS GLORY ON THE VESSELS OF MERCY, WHICH HE HAD AFORE PREPARED UNTO GLORY, even us, whom he hath called, not of the Jews only, but also of the Gentiles? As he saith also in Osee, I will call them my people, which were not my people; and her beloved, which was not beloved. (Rom ix. 21—25.)

But in a great house there are not only vessels of gold and of silver, but also of wood and of earth; and some to honour, and some to dishonour. IF A MAN THEREFORE PURGE HIMSELF FROM THESE, HE SHALL BE A VESSEL UNTO HONOUR, sanctified, and meet for the master's use, and prepared unto every good work. (2 Tim. ii. 20, 21.)

Nevertheless the foundation of God standeth sure, having this seal, THE LORD KNOWETH THEM THAT ARE HIS. And, Let every one that nameth the name of Christ depart from iniquity. (2 Tim. ii. 19.)

These shall make war with the Lamb, and the Lamb shall overcome them : for he is Lord of lords, and King of kings : and they that are with 'him are called, and chosen, and FAITHFUL. (Rev. xvii. 14.)
[Not only called and chosen, but faithful—i.e. they endure to the end. "Be thou faithful unto death."]

* But we are bound to give thanks alway to God for you, brethren beloved of the Lord, because GOD HATH FROM THE BEGINNING CHOSEN YOU TO SALVATION THROUGH SANCTIFICATION OF THE SPIRIT AND BELIEF OF THE TRUTH: whereunto he called you by our gospel, to the obtaining of the glory of our Lord Jesus Christ. (2 Thess. ii. 13, 14.)

* WHEN HE SHALL COME TO BE GLORIFIED IN HIS SAINTS, and to be admired in all them that believe (because our testimony among you was believed) in that day. WHEREFORE ALSO WE PRAY ALWAYS FOR · YOU, THAT OUR GOD WOULD COUNT YOU WORTHY OF THIS CALLING, and fulfil all the good pleasure of his goodness, and the work of

faith with power: that the name of our Lord Jesus Christ may be glorified in you, and ye in him, according to the grace of our God and the Lord Jesus Christ. (2 Thess. i. 10—12.)

[Let the reader particularly notice that this place occurs in an epistle written to Christians, of whom the apostle says, "Knowing, brethren beloved, your election of God;" and respecting whom he gives thanks, "because God hath from the beginning chosen them to salvation through sanctification of the Spirit."

He deemed it right to pray for those thus "elect," that God would count them "worthy of this calling" of being glorified at Christ's coming.]

Wherein God, willing more abundantly to shew unto the heirs of promise the immutability of his counsel, CONFIRMED IT BY AN OATH: that by two immutable things, in which *it was* impossible for God to lie, WE MIGHT HAVE A STRONG CONSOLATION, who have fled for refuge to lay hold upon the hope set before us: which *hope* we have as an anchor of the soul, both sure and steadfast, and which entereth into that within the vail. (Heb. vi. 17—19.)

Wherefore, HOLY BRETHREN, PARTAKERS OF THE HEAVENLY CALLING, consider the Apostle and High Priest of our profession, Christ Jesus. Wherefore (as the Holy Ghost saith, To-day if ye will hear his voice, harden not your hearts, as in the provocation, in the day of temptation in the wilderness: when your fathers tempted me, proved me, and saw my works forty years. Wherefore I was grieved with that generation, and said, They do alway err in *their* heart; and they have not known my ways. So I SWARE IN MY WRATH, THEY SHALL NOT ENTER INTO MY REST). TAKE HEED, BRETHREN, LEST THERE BE IN ANY OF YOU AN EVIL HEART OF UNBELIEF, IN DEPARTING FROM THE LIVING GOD. But exhort one another daily, while it is called To-day; lest any of you be hardened through the deceitfulness of sin. For we are made partakers of Christ, IF WE HOLD THE BEGINNING OF OUR CONFIDENCE STEADFAST UNTO THE END. (Heb. iii. 1, 7—14.)

* For by one offering HE HATH PERFECTED FOR EVER THEM THAT ARE SANCTIFIED. *Whereof* the Holy Ghost also is a witness to us: for after that he hath said before, This *is* the covenant that I will make with them after those days, saith the Lord, I will put my laws into their hearts, and in their minds will I write them; and their sins and iniquities will I remember no more. (Heb. x. 14—17.)

* He that despised Moses' law died without mercy under two or three witnesses: of how much sorer punishment, suppose ye, shall he be thought worthy, WHO HATH TRODDEN UNDER FOOT THE SON OF GOD, AND HATH COUNTED THE BLOOD OF THE COVENANT, WHEREWITH HE WAS SANCTIFIED, AN UNHOLY THING, AND HATH DONE DESPITE UNTO THE SPIRIT OF GRACE? For we know him that hath said, Vengeance *belongeth* unto me, I will recompense, saith the Lord. And again, THE LORD SHALL JUDGE HIS

PEOPLE. *It is* a fearful thing to fall
into the hands of the living God.
(Heb. x. 28—31.)

Who shall separate us from the
love of Christ? *shall* tribulation, or
distress, or persecution, or famine, or
nakedness, or peril, or sword? As
it is written, For thy sake we are
killed all the day long; we are accounted as sheep for the slaughter.
Nay, in all these things we are more
than conquerors through him that
loved us. For I am persuaded, that
neither death, nor life, nor angels,
nor principalities, nor powers, nor
things present, nor things to come,
nor height, nor depth, nor any other
creature, shall be able to separate
us from the love of God, which is in
Christ Jesus our Lord. (Rom. viii.
35—39.

Who shall separate us from the
love of Christ? *shall* tribulation, or
distress, or persecution, or famine, or
nakedness, or peril, or sword? As it
is written, For thy sake we are killed
all the day long; we are accounted
as sheep for the slaughter. Nay, in
all these things we are more than conquerors through him that loved us.
For I am persuaded, that neither
death, nor life, nor angels, nor principalities, nor powers, nor things present, nor things to come, nor height,
nor depth, nor any other creature,
shall be able to separate us from the
love of God, which is in Christ Jesus
our Lord. (Rom. viii. 35—39.)

[NOTE.—I have inserted this passage
in both lists because of the fearfully
significant omission of one word from
the catalogue of things here said to be
unable to separate us from Christ.
That word is "sin." If sin can be
properly called "a creature," then
this passage is decisive on the final
perseverance of the apostle, and those
whom he means by "we," "us." If
the omission of the word is intentional,
the passage is equally strong in the
other direction.

St. Bernard, a strong predestinarian,
in commenting on this passage, notices
this omission. "He omits to add,
'nor our own selves,' because it must
be with our own free will that we can
alone forsake God. Excepting this
free will of ours, there is nothing,
absolutely nothing, for us to fear."]

And the Lord shall deliver me from
every evil work, and will preserve *me*
unto his heavenly kingdom : to whom
be glory for ever and ever. Amen.
(2 Tim. iv. 18.)

[NOTE.—I have inserted this text
because I find it usually brought
forward in lists of texts on final
perseverance.

If the reader considers that the
apostle wrote it on the eve of his martyrdom, when he had just written, "I
am now ready to be offered, and the
time of my departure is at hand. I
have fought a good fight, I have
finished my course, I have kept the
faith :" I think he will agree with me
that it is very perilous to quote it as
decisive in favour of the necessary

final perseverance of every one who has once begun the Christian race.]

In whom ye also *trusted*, after that ye heard the word of truth, the gospel of your salvation : in whom also after that ye believed, YE WERE SEALED WITH THAT HOLY SPIRIT OF PROMISE, WHICH IS THE EARNEST OF OUR INHERITANCE UNTIL THE REDEMPTION OF THE PURCHASED POSSESSION, unto the praise of his glory. (Ephes. i. 13, 14.)

Blessed *be* the God and Father of our Lord Jesus Christ, who hath blessed us with all SPIRITUAL BLESSINGS IN HEAVENLY PLACES IN CHRIST : ACCORDING AS HE HATH CHOSEN US IN HIM BEFORE THE FOUNDATION OF THE WORLD, that we should be holy and without blame before him in love : having PREDESTINATED US UNTO THE ADOPTION OF CHILDREN BY JESUS CHRIST TO HIMSELF, according to the good pleasure of his will, to the praise of the glory of his grace, wherein he hath made us accepted in the beloved. In whom we have redemption through his blood, the forgiveness of sins, according to the riches of his grace ; wherein he hath abounded toward us in all wisdom and prudence ; having made known unto us the mystery of his will, according to his good pleasure which he hath purposed in himself: that in the dispensation of the fulness of times he might gather together in one all things in Christ, both which are in heaven, and which are on earth ; *even* in him : IN WHOM ALSO WE HAVE OBTAINED AN INHERITANCE, BEING PREDESTINATED ACCORDING TO THE PURPOSE OF HIM WHO WORKETH ALL THINGS AFTER THE COUNSEL OF HIS OWN WILL: THAT WE SHOULD BE TO THE PRAISE OF HIS GLORY, WHO FIRST TRUSTED IN CHRIST. (Eph. i. 3—12.)

For *it is* impossible for those who were ONCE ENLIGHTENED, AND HAVE TASTED OF THE HEAVENLY GIFT, AND WERE MADE PARTAKERS OF THE HOLY GHOST, AND HAVE TASTED THE GOOD WORD OF GOD, AND THE POWERS OF THE WORLD TO COME, IF THEY SHALL FALL AWAY, to renew them again unto repentance ; seeing they crucify to themselves the Son of God afresh, and put *him* to an open shame. For THE EARTH WHICH DRINKETH IN THE RAIN THAT COMETH OFT UPON IT, and bringeth forth herbs meet for them by whom it is dressed, receiveth blessing from God : BUT THAT WHICH BEARETH THORNS AND BRIARS IS REJECTED, and *is* nigh unto cursing; whose end *is* to be burned. (Heb. vi. 4—8.)

Follow peace with all *men*, and holiness, without which no man shall see the Lord : LOOKING DILIGENTLY LEST ANY MAN FAIL OF THE GRACE OF GOD ; lest any root of bitterness springing up trouble *you*, and thereby many be defiled ; lest there *be* any fornicator or profane person, as Esau, WHO FOR ONE MORSEL OF MEAT SOLD HIS BIRTHRIGHT. For ye know how that afterward, when he would have inherited the blessing, he was rejected ; for he found no place of repentance, though he sought it carefully with tears. (Heb. xii. 14—17.) BUT YE ARE COME UNTO MOUNT SION, and unto the city of the living God, the heavenly Jerusalem, and to an innumerable company of angels to the general assembly and church of the firstborn, which are written in heaven, and to God the Judge of all, and to the spirits of just men made perfect, AND TO JESUS THE MEDIATOR OF THE NEW COVENANT, AND TO THE BLOOD OF SPRINKLING, THAT SPEAKETH BETTER THINGS THAN THAT OF ABEL. SEE THAT YE REFUSE NOT HIM THAT SPEAKETH. For if they escaped not who refused him that spake on earth, much more *shall not* we *escape*, if we turn away from him that *speaketh* from heaven. (Heb. xii. 22—25.)

But there were false prophets also among the people, even as there shall be false teachers among you, who privily shall bring in damnable heresies, even DENYING THE LORD THAT

BOUGHT THEM, and bring upon themselves swift destruction. And many shall follow their pernicious ways; by reason of whom the way of truth shall be evil spoken of. FOR IF GOD SPARED NOT THE ANGELS THAT SINNED, but cast *them* down to hell, and delivered *them* into chains of darkness, to be reserved unto judgment. (2 Pet. ii. 1, 2. 4.)

CAST NOT AWAY THEREFORE YOUR CONFIDENCE, which hath great recompence of reward. For ye have need of patience, that, after ye have done the will of God, ye might receive the promise. For yet a little while, and he that shall come will come, and will not tarry. NOW THE JUST SHALL LIVE BY FAITH : BUT IF [ANY MAN] DRAW BACK, MY SOUL SHALL HAVE NO PLEASURE IN HIM. (Heb. x. 35—38.)

[NOTE.—Much of the force of the original is lost by our translators having inserted the words "any man," in italics, in the last verse. In reality, the verse runs : " Now the just shall live by faith : but if he (*i. e.* ὁ δίκαιος, the justified man) draw back, my soul shall have no pleasure in him."]

Be not thou therefore ashamed of the testimony of our Lord, nor of me his prisoner : but be thou partaker of the afflictions of the gospel according to the power of God ; WHO HATH SAVED US, AND CALLED US WITH AN HOLY CALLING, NOT ACCORDING TO OUR WORKS, BUT ACCORDING TO HIS OWN PURPOSE AND GRACE, WHICH WAS GIVEN US IN CHRIST JESUS BEFORE THE WORLD BEGAN, but is now made manifest by the appearing of our Saviour Jesus Christ, who hath abolished death, and hath brought life and immortality to light through the gospel : whereunto I am appointed a preacher, and an apostle, and a teacher of the Gentiles. For the which cause I also suffer these things : nevertheless I am not ashamed : FOR I KNOW WHOM I HAVE BELIEVED, AND AM PERSUADED THAT HE IS ABLE TO KEEP THAT WHICH I HAVE COMMITTED UNTO HIM AGAINST THAT DAY. (2 Tim. i. 8—12.)

Take heed unto thyself, and unto the doctrine ; CONTINUE IN THEM : FOR IN DOING THIS THOU SHALT BOTH SAVE THYSELF, and them that hear thee. (1 Tim. iv. 16.)

HOLD FAST THE FORM OF SOUND WORDS, which thou hast heard of me, in faith and love which is in Christ Jesus. THAT GOOD THING WHICH WAS COMMITTED UNTO THEE KEEP by the Holy Ghost which dwelleth in us. This thou knowest, that ALL THEY WHICH ARE IN ASIA BE TURNED AWAY FROM ME ; of whom are Phygellus and Hermogenes. IF A MAN THEREFORE PURGE HIMSELF FROM THESE, HE SHALL BE A VESSEL UNTO HONOUR, sanctified, and meet for the master's use, *and* prepared unto every good work. FLEE ALSO YOUTHFUL LUSTS : but follow righteousness, faith, charity, peace, with them that call on the Lord out of a pure heart. But CONTINUE THOU in the things which thou hast learned and hast been assured of, knowing of whom thou hast learned *them*. (2 Tim. i. 13—15; ii. 21, 22; iii. 14.)

[Timothy was one of the first saints of the apostolic age, but in the epistles addressed to him there is not one word

[respecting his final triumph being absolutely assured to him, but many words to exhort him to hold fast, continue, &c. This may not imply any doubt of Timothy's perseverance, but it certainly does teach modern assertors of this doctrine a strong lesson.]

AND THE GLORY WHICH THOU GAVEST ME I HAVE GIVEN THEM; that they may be one, even as we are one: I in them, and thou in me, that they may be made perfect in one ; and that the world may know that thou hast sent me, AND HAST LOVED THEM, AS THOU HAST LOVED ME. Father, I will that they also, whom thou hast given me, be with me where I am ; that they may behold my glory, which thou hast given me : FOR THOU LOVEDST ME BEFORE THE FOUNDATION OF THE WORLD. (John xvii. 22—24.)

GOD HATH NOT CAST AWAY HIS PEOPLE WHICH HE FOREKNEW. Wot ye not what the scripture saith of Elias? how he maketh intercession to God against Israel, saying, Lord, they have killed thy prophets, and digged down thine altars ; and I am left alone, and they seek my life. But what saith the answer of God unto him? I have reserved to myself seven thousand men, who have not bowed the knee to *the image* of Baal. EVEN SO THEN AT THIS PRESENT TIME ALSO THERE IS A REMNANT ACCORDING TO THE ELECTION OF GRACE. (Rom. xi. 2—5.)

And this is the Father's will which hath sent me, THAT OF ALL WHICH HE HATH GIVEN ME I SHOULD LOSE NOTHING, but should raise it up again at the last day. And this is the will of him that sent me, that EVERY ONE WHICH SEETH THE SON, AND BELIEVETH ON HIM, MAY HAVE EVERLASTING LIFE : AND I WILL RAISE HIM UP AT THE LAST DAY. (John vi. 39, 40.)

Having eyes full of adultery, and that cannot cease from sin ; beguiling unstable souls : an heart they have exercised with covetous practices : cursed children : WHICH HAVE FORSAKEN THE RIGHT WAY, and are gone astray, following the way of Balaam *the son* of Bosor, who loved the wages of unrighteousness. For when they speak great swelling *words* of vanity, THEY ALLURE THROUGH THE LUSTS OF THE FLESH, *through much* wantonness, THOSE THAT WERE CLEAN ESCAPED FROM THEM who live in error. While they promise them liberty, they themselves are the servants of corruption : for of whom a man is overcome, of the same is he brought in bondage. For IF AFTER THEY HAVE ESCAPED THE POLLUTIONS OF THE WORLD THROUGH THE KNOWLEDGE OF THE LORD AND SAVIOUR JESUS CHRIST, THEY ARE AGAIN ENTANGLED THEREIN, AND OVERCOME, THE LATTER END IS WORSE WITH THEM THAN THE BEGINNING. For it had been better for them not to have known the way of righteousness, than, AFTER THEY HAVE KNOWN IT, TO TURN FROM THE holy commandment delivered unto them. But it is happened unto them according to the true proverb, The dog *is* turned to his own vomit again : and THE SOW THAT WAS WASHED to her wallowing in the mire. (2 Peter ii. 14, 15, 18—22.)

Ye are the salt of the earth : BUT IF THE SALT HAVE LOST HIS SAVOUR, wherewith shall it be salted? it is thenceforth good for nothing, but to BE CAST OUT, and to be trodden under foot of men. (Matt. v. 13.)
Salt *is* good : but IF THE SALT HAVE LOST HIS SAVOUR, wherewith shall it be seasoned? It is neither fit for the land, nor yet for the dunghill ; *but* MEN CAST IT OUT. He that hath ears to hear, let him hear. (Luke xiv. 34, 35.)

But the CHILDREN OF THE KINGDOM SHALL BE CAST OUT INTO OUTER

DARKNESS: there shall be weeping and
gnashing of teeth. (Matt. viii. 12.)

And ye shall be hated of all *men*
for my name's sake: but HE THAT
ENDURETH TO THE END SHALL BE
SAVED. (Matt. x. 22.)

Then his lord, after that he had
called him, said unto him, O thou
wicked servant, I FORGAVE THEE ALL
THAT DEBT, because thou desiredst
me: shouldest not thou also have had
compassion on thy fellow-servant, even
as I had pity on thee? And his lord
was wroth, and delivered him to the
tormentors, till he should pay all that
was due unto him. So LIKEWISE
SHALL MY HEAVENLY FATHER DO
ALSO UNTO YOU, IF YE FROM YOUR
HEARTS FORGIVE NOT EVERY ONE HIS
BROTHER THEIR TRESPASSES. (Matt.
xvii. 32—35.)

For *the kingdom of heaven is* as
a man travelling into a far country,
who called HIS OWN SERVANTS, and
delivered unto them his goods. And
unto one he gave five talents, to
another two, and to ANOTHER ONE;
to EVERY MAN according to his several
ability; and straightway took his
journey. . . And CAST YE THE UNPRO-
FITABLE SERVANT INTO OUTER DARK-
NESS: there shall be weeping and
gnashing of teeth. (Matt. xxv. 14,
15, 30.)

And the Lord said, WHO THEN IS
THAT FAITHFUL AND WISE STEWARD,
whom *his* lord shall make ruler over
his household, to give *them their* portion of meat in due season? BLESSED
IS THAT SERVANT, whom his lord when
he cometh shall find so doing. Of a
truth I say unto you, that he will
make him ruler over all that he hath.
BUT AND IF THAT SERVANT say in his
heart, My lord delayeth his coming;
and shall begin to beat the men-
servants and maidens, and to eat and
drink, and to be drunken; the lord
of that servant will come in a day
when he looketh not for *him*, and
at an hour when he is not aware,
AND WILL CUT HIM IN SUNDER, AND
WILL APPOINT HIM HIS PORTION
WITH THE UNBELIEVERS. (Luke xii.
42—46.)

S

Now when the congregation was broken up, many of the Jews and religious proselytes followed Paul and Barnabas; who, speaking to them, persuaded them to CONTINUE IN THE GRACE OF GOD. (Acts xiii. 43.)

Confirming the souls of the disciples, *and* exhorting them to CONTINUE IN THE FAITH, and that we must through much tribulation enter into the kingdom of God. (Acts xiv. 22.)

For this cause, when I could no longer forbear, I SENT TO KNOW YOUR FAITH, LEST BY SOME MEANS THE TEMPTER HAVE TEMPTED YOU, AND OUR LABOUR BE IN VAIN. For now we live, IF ye stand fast in the Lord. (1 Thess. iii. 5, 8.)

BEING CONFIDENT OF THIS VERY THING, THAT HE WHICH HATH BEGUN A GOOD WORK IN YOU WILL PERFORM IT UNTIL THE DAY OF JESUS CHRIST: even as it is meet for me to think this of you all. (Phil. i. 6, 7.)

[Do they who cite this text mean to assert that St. Paul predicates this perseverance of ALL his Philippian converts? for he distinctly says, "Even as it is meet for me to think this of you all." The apostle cannot mean this: for, in the first place, he bids them "work out their salvation with fear and trembling;" then he tells them that he counts not himself to have "attained," or to have "apprehended." He bids them in this respect (iii. 15, 16) be like-minded with himself; and, above all, he warns them how many walked, of whom he had told them often that "their end was destruction:" and these could not have been the heathen, as I have shown above (page 117).

Then, also, on this hypothesis, what an unaccountable difference there must have been between the Philippian and the Corinthian Churches. St. Paul's words of confidence respecting the Corinthians are as strong as those respecting the Philippians, when he says to the former, "Jesus Christ: WHO SHALL CONFIRM YOU TO THE END, that ye may be blameless in the day of our Lord Jesus Christ. GOD IS FAITHFUL, BY WHOM YE WERE CALLED unto the fellowship of His Son Jesus Christ our Lord" (1 Cor. i. 8, 9). And yet we see, by every chapter of this latter Epistle, that it was far indeed from his thoughts to assert the neces-

But if thy brother be grieved with *thy* meat, now walkest thou not charitably. DESTROY NOT HIM WITH THY MEAT, FOR WHOM CHRIST DIED. For meat DESTROY NOT THE WORK OF GOD. All things indeed *are* pure; but *it is* evil for that man who eateth with offence. (Rom. xiv. 15, 20.)

* And through thy knowledge shall the WEAK BROTHER PERISH, FOR WHOM CHRIST DIED? But when ye sin so against the brethren, and wound their weak conscience, YE SIN AGAINST CHRIST. (1 Cor. viii. 11, 12.)

KNOW YE NOT THAT YE ARE THE TEMPLE OF GOD, AND THAT THE SPIRIT OF GOD DWELLETH IN YOU? IF ANY MAN defile (or destroy, $\phi\theta\epsilon\iota\rho\epsilon\iota$) the temple of God, him will God destroy ($\phi\theta\epsilon\rho\epsilon\hat{\iota}$); for the temple of God is holy, WHICH TEMPLE YE ARE. (1 Cor. iii. 16, 17.)

But I keep under my body, and bring *it* into subjection: LEST THAT BY ANY MEANS, WHEN I HAVE PREACHED TO OTHERS, I MYSELF SHOULD BE A CASTAWAY. (1 Cor. ix. 27.)

We then, *as* workers together *with him*, BESEECH YOU ALSO THAT YE RECEIVE NOT THE GRACE OF GOD IN VAIN. (2 Cor. vi. 1.)

Christ is become of no effect unto you, whosoever of you are justified by the law; YE ARE FALLEN FROM GRACE. (Gal. v. 4.)

sary and predestined completion of
God's work in each of them.]

The elders which are among you I
exhort, who am also an elder, and a
witness of the sufferings of Christ,
AND ALSO A PARTAKER OF THE GLORY
THAT SHALL BE REVEALED. (1 Pet. v. 1.)

If by any means I might attain unto
the RESURRECTION OF THE DEAD. NOT
AS THOUGH I HAD ALREADY ATTAINED,
either were already perfect: but I follow after, if that I may apprehend
that for which also I am apprehended
of Christ Jesus. Brethren, I COUNT
NOT MYSELF TO HAVE APPREHENDED:
but *this* one thing *I do*, forgetting
those things which are behind, and
reaching forth unto those things which
are before. (Philip. iii. 11—13.)

And all that dwell upon the earth
shall worship him, WHOSE NAMES ARE
NOT WRITTEN IN THE BOOK OF LIFE OF
THE LAMB SLAIN FROM THE FOUNDA-
TION OF THE WORLD. (Rev. xiii. 8.)

He that overcometh, the same shall
be clothed in white raiment; AND I
WILL NOT BLOT OUT HIS NAME OUT OF
THE BOOK OF LIFE, but I will confess
his name before my Father, and before
his angels. He that hath an ear, let
him hear what the Spirit saith unto
the churches. (Rev. iii. 5, 6.)

HE THAT OVERCOMETH shall inherit
all things; and I will be his God, and
he shall be my son. (Rev. xxi. 7.)

And if any man shall take away
from the words of the book of this
prophecy, GOD SHALL TAKE AWAY HIS
PART OUT OF THE BOOK OF LIFE, AND
OUT OF THE HOLY CITY, and *from* the
things which are written in this book.
(Rev. xxii. 19.)
[How can a man's name be blotted
out of the book of life, unless it has
been once written in that book? The
Canon of the New Testament closes
with a warning against Calvinistic
perverseness.]

Let me now draw the reader's attention to the two
catalogues of texts, which I have put side by side, in the
preceding pages.

Let him notice, in the first place, that I have, in several
cases, given some context with the particular text. I am
quite aware that, by so doing, I have taken away the edge
from some highly-prized theological weapons; but that I

cannot help. Let us deal honestly with the word of God. He will certainly so order it, that weapons from his armoury, unfairly used, shall ultimately pierce the hands of those that use them.[1]

In the next place, let me say a word respecting the selection of texts in the first or left-hand column. As my intention in putting these two sets of passages in juxtaposition is to meet the unfair inferences against the Baptismal Regeneration of infants drawn from the first list, I have not trusted myself in my selection of passages in favour of final perseverance, but have taken them from works published by those who are avowedly supporters of Calvinistic views. I mention this because the well-informed reader will find in that column many places that are anything but conclusive in favour of the very view they are adduced to support.[2]

---

[1] I will give an instance of the way in which the context materially modifies a text. In a tract by Mr. Ryle, entitled "Never Perish," the text, "I will never leave thee, nor forsake thee," is quoted to uphold the idea of "Once in grace, always in grace." Let the reader refer to the verses before and after it, and he will see with what reason. "Let your conversation be without covetousness; and be content with such things as ye have: for He hath said, I will never leave thee, nor forsake thee. *So that we may boldly say, The Lord is my helper, and I will not fear what man shall do unto me.*" (Heb. xiii. 5, 6.) Let the reader also remember from what Epistle this is quoted, and some of the other passages in that Epistle, and he will see why I have not inserted it in the above lists. Similarly with Luke xii. 32, 33. The modern Calvinist says, "It is your Father's good pleasure to give you the kingdom; *therefore grace is indefectible.*" The Saviour says, "It is your Father's good pleasure to give you the kingdom. *Sell that ye have, and give alms.*" The contrast between the two applications would be ludicrous were it not for the awful nature of the subject. The whole context is upon covetousness.

[2] I have gone very carefully over a large number, given under the Seventeenth Article, in Dr. Wilson's "Thirty-nine Articles,

In the next place, let the reader be assured that I have not put these texts side by side to undermine the doctrine of Predestination to life. I desire to uphold and teach, in its place, that predestinarian view of Scripture truth by which alone we can be assured that, from such a world as this, Christ shall ultimately have His full number of saved souls to be His bride—the reward of His unspeakable humiliation.

But I cannot for a moment consent to allow this truth, secret to us till the great day, both in the mode in which God will bring it about, and the persons in whose favour He will bring it about; I cannot, I say, allow such a doctrine to upset a great practical fact, which every prophet in the Old Testament, and every apostle in the New, brings to bear upon every circumcised or baptized sinner within his reach, in order to keep him from sin—the fact that all who have received the sign of the covenant are answerable for its grace.

If the reader asks me how I reconcile these two sets of Scriptures, I say, I cannot. Their complete reconciliation lies in the mystery of the probation of God's intelligent creatures, whose probation is real, though God foreknows its issue, and has foreordained his acts accordingly.

Perhaps the nearest approximation to a logical holding of both is to be found in the doctrine of St. Augustine, that there is an inner election within the outer. An inner election, that is, of some to perseverance within the outer election of the Church to grace; that there is an election to many degrees of grace short of final perseverance and an election within that to final perseverance.[1]

---

illustrated by extracts from the Liturgy. Nowell, &c." The only passages which I have omitted, which are given by him, are two or three from the Prophets, unmistakeably referring to the yet future conversion of Israel.

[1] See Appendix C.

This is certainly the view to be deduced from some clear statements of that great saint.

Let me now ask the reader's attention to the second column.

I know no words strong enough to describe the hardihood of those who, with these texts in their Bibles, assert that grace is indefectible, or that a man once in grace is always in grace ; and yet this is actually asserted over and over again, in popular publications, by those who would make void the application to the present visible Church of the express Scripture statements respecting the effect of Baptism.

The grace cannot be named from which it is assumed that Christians cannot fall. It is implied, it is assumed, it is asserted in these Scriptures that men can and do fall from the grace of the application of Christ's blood (Heb. x. 29), from the grace of the Spirit of God in the heart (Heb. vi. 4), and from some degrees of faith, hope, and even love (Heb. x. 38). It is implied that a man may be forgiven, and yet delivered to the tormentors (Matt. xviii. 35) ; that he may be Christ's servant, and yet have his portion with the unbelievers (Luke xii. 46) ; that he may be "salt," and be "cast out" (Matt. v. 13) ; "in the vine," and yet "gathered to be burned" (John xv. 6) ; like the fallen angels, he may not keep his first estate (Jude 6) ; or he may "escape the pollution of the world through the knowledge of Christ," and yet have his "latter end worse than the beginning" (2 Pet. ii. 20).

By comparing together the assertions of Scripture in these two parallel columns the reader will see the wisdom of those who framed the Seventeenth Article of the Church of England.

In that Article we have, first of all, a statement,

moderate and guarded, yet clear and unmistakeable, to the effect that the ultimate safety of some souls, and so the certainty of Christ's reward, is assured to Him by God the Father, and so is not left to the chances of a world like ours.

At the commencement of this, in the first sentence, we have a statement that this counsel of God respecting particular souls is "*secret to us;*" and it may well be said to be secret, for there is (apparently) no present sign of grace whatsoever, which is an infallible index of ultimate perseverance.[1] There is no present grace of any Christian soul which will enable a man, either in his own case, or in that of others, to thrust himself upon the judgment-seat and forestall the award of the great day.

In the second part of the Article we have the use and abuse of this doctrine : that it is only for some ; that it must be preached and taught with the greatest care and reserve, or the preacher may drive men to "wretchlessness of most unclean living," and so go himself into eternity with the blood of souls on his head, through his indiscriminate flinging about of that which is "a most dangerous downfall" to the carnal many ; whilst it is a most healing cordial to the few who "feel in themselves the working of the Spirit of Christ mortifying the works of the flesh."

In the last clause of this Article we have a very plain intimation that a doctrine like this, secret in its certain and sure application, even in the case of those most advanced in grace—a doctrine, the reconciliation of which

---

[1] "They who are of this society have such marks and notes of distinction from all others as are not object unto our sense ; only unto God, who seeth their hearts and understandeth all their secret cogitations, to Him they are clear and manifest."—HOOKER, *Eccles. Pol.* iii. ch. ii. sec. 2.

with human responsibility is known only to God—is not for a moment to nullify that practical application of God's promises, and declaration of His will, which pervades all Scripture. Now, if there be one truth more certain than another in Holy Scripture, it is the truth that God's grace belongs to the whole visible Church, and is confirmed to that Church by *visible* sacraments.[1]

I would now ask the reader's attention to another inference to be drawn from this second catalogue of Scriptures, and that is, how utterly they refute the notion that the conveyance of real grace to the baptized is to be regarded as merely a high supposition ; that they are merely *assumed* to be regenerate, or in grace, or *assumed* to have had the Spirit. If this is the way in which the great things said of Baptism are to be reconciled with the present state of the baptized, then another way, altogether different from that which we find in Scripture, would have been taken by Prophets and Apostles in dealing with the irreligious. They would have been plainly told that Baptism, in their case, had been only a form ; that they must seek admission into the true Church ; that they never had been born again, and must seek adoption into God's family. But exactly the contrary is said to them. Bad Christians are *always* assumed to have fallen from grace. Imperfect Christians are urged not to receive it in vain, and not to quench the Spirit. Unstable Christians are reminded of those who, in past times, sinned themselves out of God's favour. *In no single instance is any baptized man called upon to be " born again."*

I cannot imagine how all this can be reconciled with the " hypothetical view" of the gift in Baptism, or with the rule of " high supposition," or of " charitable assumption."

---

[1] See above, pages 147, 148. Also chapters vi. vii. ix. x. ; and for Old Testament, chapter v. and Appendix A.

The Apostle St. Paul, for instance, in Rom. vi. 3, assumes the whole Roman Church to be united to Christ in Baptism. In Rom. xi. 22 he contemplates some one among them displeasing God by sin. Now, on the hypothetical principle, he would have said to this man, "When I wrote on Baptism, I assumed you to be in God's goodness; but, from your present sin, I find you never were." But the Apostle really says just the contrary. He speaks to this man on the principle that the grace in which he had included him was real; "continue in his goodness, otherwise thou shalt be cut off." Again, the Apostle writes to the whole Corinthian Church as "in Christ." He asserts, "By one Spirit are we all baptized into one body." But he knew too well that there were party divisions among them, and that some were again overtaken with the temptations of the wicked city in which their lot was cast. How does he meet the case of these sinners? Not by throwing doubts on the reality of their state of grace, but by *broadly reasserting it.* "Know ye not," he says to the party leaders among them, " that ye are the temple of God, and that the Spirit of God dwelleth in you? If any man defile (or destroy) the temple of God, him will God destroy; for the temple of God is holy, which temple ye are." (1 Cor. iii. 16, 17.) Similarly to the unclean among them: " Know ye not that your members are the members of Christ?"

Again, he writes to the Galatians : "As many of you as have been baptized into Christ have put on Christ." He then has to meet the unwelcome fact that some of them have apostatized from their standing in Christ and sought salvation through the Mosaic law; and how does he meet their error? Not by qualifying his former statement, but by again implying it, and asserting their fall from grace : "Christ has become of none effect unto you

whosoever of you are justified by the law ; ye are fallen
from grace." (Gal. v. 4.)

Let the reader go over this second list of passages, and
he will see that every one of them, without exception,
which warn the irreligious, or unstable, or unforgiving,
warn them on the principle that they fall from something
real—some real goodness, real grace, real forgiveness.

Whatever secret reconciliation there may be between
the doctrines represented by these two columns ; between
the grace of God's secret purpose and the grace of God's
outward visible seal ; certainly this hypothetical principle,
this high supposition, this charitable assumption view, is
not the reconciliation. I know no principle more dangerous. It makes the interpretation of all Scripture
uncertain in the highest degree. It opens the door for
men to nullify the most important statements in God's
word.

And now, with respect to certain places in the Old
Testament to which appeal in favour of this principle has
been made. I have carefully gone over (as the reader
will see by the texts in Appendix A) the whole of it,
with reference to this principle of interpretation, and
cannot find one single place in which the prophets address,
on this hypothetical ground, the sinners of the various
wicked generations to which God sent them.

Appeal has been made to such places as Isaiah lx. and
Jeremiah xxxi. and xxxii., on the ground that the glorious
things there predicted of the Jewish nation, that they
should "be *all* righteous, and inherit the land for ever,"
must be understood hypothetically, and as a high supposition ; for it is assumed that these chapters are only prophecies of the *present* state of the Christian Church,
in which all, of course, are not righteous, and that they can
have no further fulfilment. I deny this utterly. I believe

that these and similar prophecies have been as yet but partially fulfilled in this present state of grace ; and that for their complete fulfilment we must look to the time indicated by the Apostle in the eleventh chapter of his Epistle to the Romans. I cannot but believe that the full accomplishment of these prophecies lies in the future of that wondrous people, whom God, in all their dispersions, has yet kept so separate. There are so many strictly national matters in the particular prophecies referred to, so many indications of national distinction (though, of course, none in Christ) between the converted Israel and the other Christian nations which will be joined to them, that I cannot but think that they point to a literal restoration of God's ancient people.[1] But supposing that any one (because of such places as Col. iii. 11) is unwilling to accede to this view, still let him consider that the images of strictly material prosperity and glory, as coincident with, yet contradistinguished from, spiritual prosperity and glory, are so palpable in these prophecies, that no past or present state of Christendom can at all answer to them.

Difficulties there are connected with every interpretation, but *that* interpretation will present the most difficulty to the humble-minded which attaches any unreality to the promises of God, or to the sacraments of His grace.

[1] The mind of Bishop Butler evidently could not rest in a mere spiritual fulfilment of these prophecies.

" Thus, that the Jews have been so wonderfully preserved in their long and wide dispersion, which is indeed the direct fulfilling of some prophecies, *but is now mentioned only as looking forward to somewhat yet to come.* . . . . Things of this kind naturally *turn the thought of serious men towards the full completion of the prophetic history concerning the final restoration of that people;* concerning the establishment of the *everlasting kingdom among them,* the kingdom of the Messiah ; and the future state of the world under this sacred government. " (Analogy, Part II. chap. vii.)

CHAPTER XX.

RECAPITULATION OF THE ARGUMENT, AND CONCLUSION.

It may be well to present to the reader in as concise a form as possible the substance of the arguments used in the foregoing chapters.

The teaching of Scripture on the subject of Baptismal Regeneration may be summed up in the following five conclusions :—

I. Things pertaining to salvation are in twelve or thirteen places more or less directly connected with Baptism.[1]

II. All the Christians of the Apostolic Churches are assumed to have been brought into a state of grace at the time when they received Baptism.[2]

III. This state of salvation is not supposed to ensure infallibly the present holiness or eternal salvation of those once brought into it. On the contrary, the members of the Apostolic Church are always addressed in the Epistles as if they were in danger of falling into sin, and liable to be cast finally away.[3]

IV. Those who fall away are always assumed to fall from grace. They are never assumed to fall into sin because their Baptism was unaccompanied with grace.[4]

[1] Pp. 1—8.
[2] Pp. 83—149 ; particularly pp. 86, 87, 88, 95, 99, 105—108, 124, 125, 134.
[3] Pp. 83—148 ; particularly pp. 88—90, 96, 104, 125—128, 132, 136—138.
[4] Pp. 90, 91, 98, 102, 108, 124—126, 133, 138—140.

V. In no one case are baptized Christians called upon by any Apostle to become regenerate. They are called upon to repent, to turn to God, to cleanse their hands, to purify their hearts, but never to seek the New Birth.[1]

The teaching of Scripture upon two or three other points bears very directly upon all this.

1. When the Apostles assume that the whole baptized body are partakers of the grace of the New Covenant, they do but follow up and develop a mode of address adopted by God's ancient prophets in addressing the members of the Church of their days, for these prophets are represented throughout the whole of the Old Testament as assuming that all the circumcised members of that Church are partakers of the covenant which God made with Abraham.[2]

2. The teaching of those parables of our Lord which relate to His Church presupposes that all the professing members of that Church have received some grace, and is singularly inconsistent with the supposition that the grace of the Christian covenant is limited to a select few in the Church, and is absolutely irreconcilable with the doctrine of the indefectibility of grace.[3]

Again, extraordinary prominence is given in Scripture to the fact that God sent to prepare the way of His Son one who was commissioned to baptize in water for the remission of sins, and Christ's own reception of Baptism at the hands of this man is the first act of His public life which God has caused to be written for our learning.[4]

The fact that our Lord did afterwards ordain a baptism of His own in the name of the Trinity makes the reiterated mention of His own submission to the baptism of John exceedingly noticeable.

[1] P. 149.
[2] Chap·xii. pp. 151—160.
[2] Chap. v. pp. 70—83.
[4] P. 7.

We have next to observe that though our Lord taught
the deepest spirituality of life and heart, yet He preached
all this in connexion with the proclamation of a kingdom.
Now a kingdom is necessarily an outward visible state
of things, and the kingdom which Christ preached was
evidently to be outward and discernible amongst the
things of time and sense, and yet its members were to
have some hidden spiritual relationship to Himself.[1]

If Christ had regarded the system which He was about
to establish as consisting of internal affections, or illumination only, or as merely a system of teaching or education, He would hardly have called it a *kingdom*.

The next Scripture fact which calls for notice is one
which connects Baptism with His kingdom, for Christ
enjoined as the entrance into His kingdom a new birth
of water and of the Spirit.[2]

If this had been the only reference to the ritual application of water as, under God, bringing about a change of
spiritual state, we might have been tempted to explain
away the reference to water, as if it were a figurative
allusion to spiritual cleansing only ; but this is impossible,
for our Lord is represented on two other occasions as
enjoining the rite of Baptism, and enjoining it in words
in which He was evidently giving authority to His Apostles
to set up His kingdom.

He is represented by St. Matthew as saying, "Go ye,
and make disciples of all nations, baptizing them." (Matt.
xxviii. 19.) He is represented by St. Mark as saying,
"Go ye into all the world, and preach the Gospel to
every creature. He that believeth and is baptized shall
be saved." (Mark xvi. 16.) On the day of Pentecost the
doors of the long-promised kingdom were actually thrown

---

[1] Pp. 31, 49, 50.   [2] Chapter iii.

open in the words, " Repent, and be baptized every one of you in the name of Jesus Christ for the remission of sins." So that, comparing those words of our Lord, in which He enjoins a new birth of water and of the Spirit as the entrance into His kingdom, with His injunctions respecting the actual establishment of His kingdom in His last words to His Apostles, and also with the words of St. Peter, in which His kingdom was actually inaugurated, we are driven to the conclusion that our Lord must have alluded to the grace of Baptism when He said, " Except a man be born of water and of the Spirit, he cannot enter into the kingdom of God."

We have now in connexion with this to consider some other Scripture allusions to Baptism, all connecting some great grace from Christ with its due reception.

To St. Paul, on his conversion, it is said, " Arise, and be baptized, and wash away thy sins." (Acts xxii. 16.) Writing to members of Churches which were tempted to fall back into Jewish ceremonial, he reminds them that their Baptism was the sign of their adoption—" Ye are all the children of God by faith in Christ Jesus. For as many of you as have been baptized into Christ have put on Christ."[1]

In two other Epistles he employs remarkable terms to describe the reception of Baptismal union with Christ, in that he speaks of Baptism as that in which the Christian dies, is buried, and is raised up again with Christ (Rom. vi. 1-4, Colos. ii. 11, 12), as if the tomb of the Saviour were always open, and Christians at their entrance into the Church descended into it, and so were to be accounted sacramentally or mystically "dead with Christ."[2]

In another place (Ephes. iv. 4-6) he associates the one

[1] P. 105. [2] Pp. 95—102.

Baptism with the "one Spirit," "one hope," "one Lord," "one faith." [1]

In another place in the same Epistle the Apostle speaks of the Church as sanctified and cleansed with the washing of water by the word. (Ephes. v. 26.) [2]

In another place (1 Corinth. x. 1–10) he likens by implication the saving effects of Baptism to the deliverance effected for the Israelites by their passage through the Red Sea. [3]

In another place (1 Corinth. xii. 13) he speaks of all his converts having been "baptized by one Spirit into one body;" [4] and in another (Titus iii. 5) he asserts that God in His mercy hath saved us "by the bath of new birth." [5]

And lastly, another Apostle is inspired to assert that Baptism sincerely and faithfully received "saves us by the resurrection of Jesus Christ." [6] (1 Peter iii. 21.)

What are we to make of such remarkable assertions as these?

Are they to be treated as if they were exaggerated rhetorical figures contrary to the Spirit of the dispensation, in that they connect salvation in some sense with what is outward and visible? or are they rather to be understood as implying what they certainly seem to imply —that the God who knows our nature and its needs has seen fit to annex some gracious influence from Himself to the due reception of an outward sign? [7]

The most of them were uttered on occasions which forbid all idea of rhetorical exaggeration, and others are so closely associated with what is moral and practical, rather than with what is imaginative and poetical, that it

---

[1] P. 124.   [3] P. 87.   [5] P. 6.
[2] P. 128.   [4] P. 36.   [6] P. 181.
                     [7] Pp. 49—53.

is exceedingly dangerous to treat them as tropes or figures. The very spirituality of the dispensation comes in here to assist us in ascertaining the relations of Baptism to the rest of the Christian system. Christ would hardly give to a mere outward rite such a place in such a system as the Christian ; *that* would be to revert to the dead elements of Judaism— the rites of Judaism being mere types, having no inward and spiritual grace, as far as we know, connected with them.

If Baptism be not normally connected with an inward spiritual grace—that is, if it be a rite only touching the flesh, as the Jewish rites were, and yet if believers in Christ are bound to receive it, then those who have begun in the Spirit, by believing in Christ, would have to be made perfect in the flesh, by submitting to what, on the low view, is a mere substitute for circumcision.[1] Such a thing is impossible in a dispensation of the Spirit.

It is equally impossible to imagine that the Sacraments are types primarily intended to instruct us. If so, they would be out of place in a system replete with direct instruction by preaching and catechizing. Neither of the two sacraments teaches directly, for neither tells its own story ; both of them imperatively require much direct teaching, in the way of explanation, to enable us to understand any one fact connected with them.

So that they cannot possibly be regarded as condescensions to the weakness of our understanding, for few things in the dispensation require more of the spirit of understanding to enable us to realize their true position or import.

What then (to confine ourselves to the first sacrament) is its theory, so to speak? How can we account for its place in the spiritual kingdom of Christ?

Now, to ascertain this, we must remember that the direct and explicit assertions respecting some saving grace being

[1] Page 48.

T

connected with Baptism form but a very small part of the Scripture teaching, which we must take into account if we would hope to have a right view of the matter.

To ascertain the import of circumcision, we have not only to refer to the account of its institution as the sign of God's covenant, but also to the fact that on the strength of their circumcision the children of Israel are addressed by the prophets of God as in His family, and so in some sense His children, and this compared with the heathen.[1]

And so with Baptism. Not only are we taught that God confers therein something requisite to salvation, but the baptized are uniformly treated as if they had received grace, for the reception of which they are ever after held responsible.[2] In addition to this we find that when the members of baptized Churches fall into sin, they are always assumed to fall from grace, and in no one case are they treated as if their baptism had been unaccompanied by its inward grace,—for instance, they are never called upon to be born again, or to get themselves engrafted into Christ as for the first time.

We have now to combine all this, and see whether the scattered notices of the grace of Baptism, which is described in various places as "a new birth," as "forgiveness of sins," as "cleansing," as "being buried with Christ," or a "death to sin in Christ," as "the putting on of Christ," as "the bath of new birth," as "salvation," and as "incorporation into the one body;" we have now, I say, to see whether these various statements can be included under one idea and expressed by one term, and whether this term corresponds with the grace which all the baptized are assumed to have received.

One term representing one idea will undoubtedly com-

[1] Chap. v., particularly pages 71, 72.
[2] Chaps. vi. vii. viii. ix. x. xi. *passim.*

bine all this, and that term is "union with Christ"; *i.e.*
union with Him as the Second Adam by incorporation into
His mystical body.

First of all our Lord describes the spiritual organization
which He was about to establish as the kingdom of God,
and the entrance into it as a new birth "of water and of
the Spirit."

His servant, St. Paul, evidently describing the same
organization, describes it as the body of Christ,—*i.e.* His
Church ; and speaks of his converts as " by one Spirit baptized into one body," and saved by "the bath of new
birth." In speaking of this mystical body, he identifies
it in some mystical holy sense with Christ Himself, Who
is its Head (1 Cor. xii. 12, 13, 27) ; just as Christ had in
the same sense identified Himself with His Church in the
similitude of the "Vine and the branches."

Now if the Church be thus identified with Christ, when
men are brought into it they must receive forgiveness of
past sin, and cleansing from the defilement of their natural
state ; and so Baptism is represented as a "cleansing with
the washing of water by the word," and men are told that
they must be "baptized for the remission of sins," and are
bidden to be "baptized, and wash away their sins." But
how did Christ procure forgiveness for His Church ? Evidently by His Death, and this forgiveness is assured by
His Resurrection ; and so, strictly adhering to and following up the same figure of "union with Christ," the believer
is assumed to be mystically "buried with Christ," and
mystically raised from the dead with Christ in the font,
and this because Baptism is the sacrament of mystical
union with a Saviour Who underwent death and burial,
and rose again, to procure for us remission of sins.

So that the sequence of grace in Baptism is not cleansing
or remission first, and then incorporation into Christ, but

T 2

rather the reverse: by being made members of Christ we are brought into union with One in Whom is all propitiatory virtue, and so, being united to Him, we partake of this propitiation which is in Him, and so we "wash away our sins," or are "cleansed with the washing of water," or are "baptized for the remission of sins."

Being thus brought into union with Christ, we are "born again." A new birth implies not so much a change of heart as a change of family. We are brought into a new family, of which we become members, and are entitled to the present privileges and future prospects of the members of such a family: and looking upon this new or second birth as contrasted with our old or first birth into the family of Adam, it implies that we are born into or made members of a New Man—the Second Adam.

Again, by having been brought into union with Christ we are "in Him," and so it is naturally said that in Baptism we "put Him on." (Gal. iii. 27.) And lastly, being thus federally or mystically incorporated into Him Who is our salvation, we are brought into a state of salvation, and so we read: "Baptism doth now save." (1 Peter iii. 21.) "He that believeth and is baptized shall be saved." (Mark xvi. 16.) "By His mercy He saved us, by the bath of New Birth." (Titus iii. 5.) Such strong assertions as these can only be accounted for on the hypothesis that Baptism is ordained to be the formal, but necessary, means whereby those who believe (or, as in the case of infants, are in the same position in the sight of God as adult believers) are mystically joined with, or incorporated into, One in Whom is salvation, or Who is Himself our salvation.

And so union with Christ, or incorporation into His body, is the root idea of all these Scripture declarations respecting the grace of Baptism, making them consistent with one another and with the general tenor of Scripture.

'And so also union with Christ, or incorporation into His body, is at the root of all the terms setting forth the covenant blessings which the baptized members of the Church are, in the Apostolical Epistles, always assumed to have received.

The characteristic phrase of the writings of St. Paul, in addressing his converts, is "in Christ." To give anything like an adequate idea of the use St. Paul makes of this term for the encouragement, establishment, or warning of his converts, would require us to copy out the greater part of some of his Epistles.

I would, however, notice the following: "We, being many, are one body in Christ." (Rom. xii. 5.) "Know ye not that your bodies are the members of Christ?" (1 Cor. vi. 15.) "As the body is one, and hath many members, and all the members of that one body, being many, are one body : so also is Christ. For by one Spirit are we all baptized into one body. Now ye are the body of Christ, and members in particular." (1 Cor. xii. 12, 13, 27.) "Ye are all one in Christ Jesus." (Gal. iii. 28.) "Head over all things to the Church, which is His body." "In Christ Jesus ye who sometime were afar off are made nigh by the blood of Christ. That He might reconcile both to God in one body by the cross." (Ephes. i. 22, 23 ; ii. 13, 16.) "The mystery of Christ : that the Gentiles should be fellow-heirs, and of the same body." (Ephes. iii. 4, 6.) "We are members of His body, of His flesh, and of His bones." (Ephes. v. 30.) "The Head, from which all the body by joints and bands having nourishment minis- tered, and knit together, increaseth with the increase of God." (Colos. ii. 19.) This inherence in the body of Christ is considered by St. Paul to be the ultimate or crowning grace of the dispensation. All possible spiritual and eternal benefits, and holy relationships to God and one another, are summed up in it (see Ephes. i. ii. iii. ; Colos. i. ii.) ; and yet it is the primary grace : for all the baptized are assumed to have been made partakers of it, and it is brought to bear upon them to preserve them from the commission of the lowest sins, and to establish them in the practice of the most ordinary Christian duties and virtues.

When the most imperfect Christian is warned against falling back into the sins of his heathen state, he is warned on the assumption that he has once been made a member of Christ (1 Cor. vi. 15) ; and considerations drawn from the assumption of his having once entered into this state are brought to bear upon him to make him humble (Rom. xii. 3, 4, 5), peaceable (Colos. iii. 15), forgiving, forbearing, charitable, and sympathising (1 Cor. xii. 12—27), and also to make him a good husband (Ephes. v. 25), and a truthful member of the Christian society (Ephes. iv. 25).

We now come to the question, To what does the state described by the expression "in Christ" correspond? for the very fact of having been in Baptism brought into Christ implies our previously having been "in" some other state antagonistic to our being "in" Christ. We have no difficulty in ascertaining this. The expression "in Christ" is correlative to the expression "in Adam."[1] (See Rom. v. 12—21; 1 Corinth. xv. 21, 22 ; Ephes. iv. 11—32 ; Coloss. iii. 9, 10, 11.) The analogy between Adam and Christ at once prepares us to receive the truth of some mysterious communication of the nature of the Second Adam to those in Him. We sin and are lost because we partake in some real, though mysterious way, of the whole natural and spiritual being of the first Adam,[2] and the expressions describing our union with Christ evidently point to some real, though mysterious, communication of

[1] Chap. ii.   [2] Pages 9—18.

His whole nature to us; for instance, we are said to be "members of His body, of His flesh, and of His bones."

The analogy between the two Adams not only removes all the difficulties out of the way of the Baptismal Regeneration of all infants, but makes some such doctrine (if it be lawful to say so) necessary.[1]

For all our doubts respecting Infant Baptism, as well those respecting the reception of grace by infants in that Baptism, arise from the difficulty of supposing that the entrance into a spiritual state, or a change of spiritual condition, can belong to those who, being in a state of unconsciousness, cannot exercise a lively faith, or understand the nature of what they receive ; but they who urge this objection forget that all men, without exception, enter into a state of spiritual evil whilst they are in a state of perfect unconsciousness, for whilst unable to exercise either faith or unbelief all men are born into the first Adam, and so into a state of sin and death.

Now, if Christ be the Second Adam, it seems only natural that He should, as the Second Adam, be the counterpart to the first Adam in the matter of the communication of grace from Himself to those who are in the state of unconscious infancy, seeing that all such have received evil from the first Adam in a like state of unconscious helplessness.

This seems still more likely when we take into account the fact that He has redeemed them all.

It seems fitting also that to those who are involved in evil by their *first* birth He should communicate His grace by that *second* birth of water and of the Spirit which He has ordained as the entrance into His kingdom.[2]

Especially does this seem fitting when we remember that of children He says, " Of such is the kingdom of God."[3]

[1] Pages 61—66.   [2] Page 65.   [3] Page 57.

Besides this, all His words respecting children, and His demeanour towards them, leads us to infer that He accounts them to be equally as fit for receiving the grace of incorporation into Himself as those who are able (from mature years) to exercise conscious faith, for He declares respecting some who had already exercised some degree of conscious faith, that they must become *as* little children before they can enter into His kingdom.

Now this analogy between the two Adams, coupled with the demeanour of our Lord towards children, must be taken into full account in estimating the force of the reasons which we adduce from Scripture for the practice of Infant Baptism, for even those who receive and practise the doctrine of Infant Baptism are too apt to look upon it as an abnormal thing which God tolerates in this dispensation of faith, or which He has permitted His Church to adopt on her own suggestion, as it were, rather than (as it is) the normal type of all Baptism. For though Infant Baptism, with its inward grace, may appear somewhat exceptional when viewed in connexion with that part of God's dealings by which He requires conscious faith in the adult before He blesses him, yet it is the reverse of exceptional when viewed in connexion with that part of God's dealings whereby He ordains that unconscious children should receive moral and spiritual good or evil from their earthly progenitor. When viewed in this light, Infant Baptismal Regeneration is the natural and fitting counterpart in the kingdom of grace to the transmission of original sin in the kingdom of evil.

The Scripture proofs of the practice of Infant Baptism are all incidental. They fall in with the idea of it as naturally following on the doctrine of the two Adams, and as naturally succeeding circumcision.

They are just such intimations as we might expect of

a practice which was received as a matter of course. The New Testament is not an outward law, giving a rule for everything, fixing the hour of the day for every act of worship, or the year of life for the due reception of every ordinance. Even meetings for the celebration of the Eucharist, the · characteristic act of Christian worship, though we know that such took place weekly, are only mentioned by the way, as it were.

There is not throughout the whole book a formal treatise on any one single point of faith or morals. Didactic instruction is given in the form of familiar letters, all, without exception, written to those who were already well grounded in all Christian doctrine. Throughout each letter it is taken for granted that they to whom it was addressed were acquainted with first principles, and above all with the first grand principle of the Incarnation— that the Eternal Son has come amongst us for our redemption ; that He has come amongst us by assuming our flesh ; and that He did this, not only that He might die for us, but that in His flesh He might become the New Man, so that we should as really and effectually be "in" Him as we are or have been "in" the first Adam.

Such is the great principle. One of the most natural and necessary deductions from it seems to be, that they who have unconsciously received a seed of evil at their first birth into the first Adam should be entitled in a like state of unconsciousness to receive a seed of good by a second birth into the Second Adam.

So that St. Peter proclaims what seems to be in strict accordance with a great principle of Divine truth, as well as what is in strict accordance with the great law of God's dealings, whereby children inherit the moral nature of their parents, when he proclaims that the promises on the strength of which he calls upon his hearers to be baptized are for their *children* as well as for themselves. So that when we find in the earliest records of the Church that whole households were baptized, it is only what we should have expected from all the indications of the mind of God towards little children which we have in the old dispensation, especially in God's ordinance of circumcision, and also from all indications of the mind of His Son towards children which we can gather from the Gospels.[1] So when we find in letters written to the various Apostolic Churches that children are included amongst the baptized members of the mystical body, and addressed as if they were in fullest communion with the Church,[2] it is in strict accordance with the great facts of redemption— that Christ's blood is shed for all, and has purchased all ; that He is the Second Adam of the race, and so, as Jeremy Taylor rightly argues, " It is all the reason of the world that, since the grace of Christ is as large as the prevarication of Adam, all they who have been made guilty by the first Adam should be cleansed by the Second. But as they are guilty by another man's act, so they should be brought to the font to be purified by others ; there being the same proportion of reason that by the act of others they should be relieved, who were in danger of perishing by the act of others."

The above is a sketch of the line of thought in the preceding chapters, the various links of argument being somewhat differently arranged, and expressed, as far as possible, in different words.

The reader will perceive at a glance the unspeakably important bearing of the whole argument on our views of Christianity—

First. As an Educational,

Secondly. As a Supernatural, system.

[1] Chap. iv.   [2] Page 129.

I. The teaching of Baptismal Regeneration is diametrically opposed to that spirit of fanaticism which altogether sets aside the educational aspect of Christianity.

The prevailing form of fanaticism is a caricature, or rather a dangerous perversion, of the true doctrine of conversion. It is that every man, no matter what his previous life, must at some definite moment pass through an internal spiritual revolution, into which he enters in a state of the deepest despondency, and from which he emerges in a state of peace. Before this moment all his life practically counts for nothing, either for or against God. All that we are led to expect from the teaching of Scripture is reversed. Innocence of youth is practically treated as dangerous, making its possessor more liable to the spirit of legality, or Pharisaism; and the greater the wickedness of an ill-spent youth, the more marked and distinguishable the signs of a great change, and so the less danger of self-reliance. Till this change takes place, and can be accurately described and registered, no one can be called for a moment a child of God; his virtue is either mere natural virtue, or else it is hypocrisy; his faith in the Divine mission of the Son of God, or even in His Deity and Atonement, puts him in no better position than if he were a heathen.

Now, the doctrine of the Church is, of course, the opposite of all this. It is that each person baptized in infancy has had an interest in Christ given to him before the dawn of his reason, *i.e.* in the same state of unconsciousness in which a part in the effects of Adam's sin was communicated to him. It is that Christ has actually done for our children what He did for those who were once brought to Him: He has favourably received them; He has embraced them in the arms of His mercy; nay, more, He has made them members of His body. We are not then

to wait till we see in children such workings of grace as
we look for in grown-up sinners before we pronounce
such children members of Christ and children of God.

Our teaching of children is not to be merely with tacit
or implied reference to some future reception of them on
Christ's part, when their feelings are excited ; but it is
rather to be with a view to their abiding in a fold into
which they have already been gathered.   Children are to
be brought up in the nurture and admonition of a Lord
who is already *their* Lord, and is already in covenant
relationship with them.

In the true sense of the word "educate," they are to be
educated in Christ rather than merely instructed in His
doctrine.

Of course Christianity is much more than a merely
educational system.   It is designed for the recovery of
the fallen, for the conversion of sinners, and for the evangelization of the heathen ; but though by no means *merely*
an educational system, yet unquestionably it *is* such a
system.   It contemplates a state of things under which
the Church absorbs nations.   Under such a system the
children of the Church, instead of first hearing of the
claims of Christ at some period of life when all their
mental powers are fully developed, will have those claims
set before them from the earliest dawn of their reason.
They will be brought up as children of the light and of
the day.   They will never know the time in which Christ
was not, with more or less distinctness, set before them as
a Saviour Who had already owned them as His own.

But of course Christianity, or rather the Church, is a
system of restoration for the fallen, for the conversion of
those in error, and for the cleansing of those that are in
sin.   And here, too, the doctrine of the Church on Holy
Baptism, if rightly apprehended, comes in with real

power ; for what more fitting call can possibly be addressed
to the "prodigal" than this, that he *is* a son, and God
is his Father, who descries him afar off, and is waiting to
receive him back again ?

And so none have preached conversion more warmly
and effectively than those who have most freely acknowledged Baptismal Grace.

II. The teaching of the Church on Holy Baptism is
also diametrically opposed to that spirit of rationalism
which refuses to contemplate Christianity as in reality
anything more than a human philosophy, or an educational system, which, if it have not the same origin, at
least has now the same mode of operation, in all respects,
as any other philosophical or educational system : any
supernatural character which it may once have had having
long since passed away, it must now work its work as any
other system of opinions must do, by appealing to the
reason, or imagination, or affections, of those brought
within its influence.

Now the doctrine of Baptismal Grace is unquestionably
opposed to any such limitation of the power of God in the
matter of our salvation, for if we accept it we must, per-
force, believe that each Christian, at the commencement of
his discipleship—at his first entrance into the kingdom
which Christ has established—receives some mysterious
communication from Christ Himself, or is brought into
some supernatural state of union with Him as the Second
Adam.[1]

If we look into the origin of the dispensation, in the
Incarnation of the Eternal Son, it seems intended to be
far more than a mere system of teaching, no matter how
exalted the truth which is the subject-matter of such
teaching.

[1] See pages 217, 218.

The Son of God took our flesh in order that He might
reconcile us to God "in the body of His flesh, through
death." He came also to exalt our nature so exceedingly,
that it is true to say of such as we, that "we are raised up
together, and made to sit together in heavenly places in
Christ Jesus."

It seems most incongruous to speak of our merely
receiving knowledge from Christ under such a form of
words as that "we are members of His body, of His flesh,
and of His bones." (Ephes. v. 30.) If words can possibly
express a supernatural system established upon earth, they
are the words of the Epistles to the Ephesians and Colossians. Throughout these Epistles the spiritual and moral
light which men receive is supposed to be conveyed to
them in a way above nature, and by a direct act of God,
enlightening some, and not others. Men's minds are
supposed to be opened to receive mysteries by a direct
gift of God's Spirit, not given according to any law of the
transmission of knowledge with which we are acquainted.

Very much in the New Testament would lead us to
believe that the present dispensation is a continuous
supernatural system, discernible by faith, and by faith
only.

The Son of God comes amongst us by a supernatural
interference of the most marvellous character. The most
prominent feature of His life, as recorded in the Gospels,
is the exercise of supernatural power.

The mode of the exercise of this power by Him seems
to look to far more than the mere accrediting of His
mission.

It seems written for the purpose of calling out faith in
Him, as at once in His own person the Ever-present
Physician and the Ever-present Remedy. He does His
mighty works in such a way as, at times at least, to fasten

attention upon His bodily presence. His promises respecting His future exercise of power in His Church lead
us to expect nothing less than a perpetual supernatural
presence. "Lo, I am with you alway." "Where two or
three are gathered together in my name, there am I in the
midst of them." "He that eateth my flesh, and drinketh
my blood, dwelleth in me, and I in him."

Such words *may*, in the mouth of a mere human
teacher, be exaggerated modes of expressing commonplace
truths; but in the mouth of One Who is God and man in
One Person, they seem to me to point to mysteries in
harmony with the deeply mysterious nature of Him Who
spake them, and also in harmony with the mysterious
transmission and indwelling of sin in the flesh of that
being whom He came to save. The first promulgators of
Christianity evidently regarded it as altogether "not of
this world," and they as clearly believed that its unearthly
nature and pretensions were in no degree affected by the
fact that the outwardly marvellous powers which accompanied its first development were beginning to be with-
drawn, and its heavenly nature was left more and more to
be discerned by faith only.

Throughout the Epistles of St. Paul "nature" and
"grace" are, in almost every page, opposed to one another;
grace being the "gift" of God, specially given by Him
to enable men to do what by nature they could not do,
and given too by Him in subservience to none of the
natural laws which regulate the transmission of knowledge, or the action of one human mind on another. A
miracle of Divine grace is supposed to have been put forth
in the conversion of each soul, and the growth in holiness
of each soul, and its power to gain the victory over its
spiritual enemies, is invariably ascribed to a continued
exercise of the power of God in that particular soul's

behalf; not of course superseding its endeavours, but acting in accordance with them, and upholding them. Such is the character of the dispensation in the eyes of those whom God commissioned to found it, pervaded by a mode of acting on the part of God strictly analogous in the spiritual world to the sudden healing, by way of miracle, of the bodies of men in the natural world.

Every Scripture writer assumes that this dispensation is to have a sudden and miraculous termination, by the appearance of its Divine Founder in the clouds of heaven, to conduct in His own person a judgment of an astonishingly miraculous character, and to raise up the dead bodies of those who have slept in Him, and transform them in a moment, by an instantaneous act of power, into spiritual bodies, in the likeness of His own glorious body; these spiritual bodies being endued with properties which, compared with those of our present frames, we cannot but account to be supernatural.

All through the period of this dispensation, too, the members of Christ's Church are assumed to have to do with invisible spiritual intelligences, who act upon us for weal or woe according to laws or modes of operation totally unknown to us. We are supposed by almost every inspired writer to be, in some real way, under the guardianship of good angels, " sent forth to minister to them who shall be heirs of salvation ;" and at the same time we are supposed to be engaged in a warfare with other invisible beings, respecting whom we are most expressly warned that they are "not flesh and blood, but principalities, powers, rulers of the darkness of this world, wicked spirits in heavenly places."

Such is the dispensation in which we are now passing the time of our probation. In such a state of things is it not the safest course to call upon men to take heed to beware of unbelief in the matter of the Sacraments of the God-man? The words in which God has revealed to us the doctrine of Baptism demand faith—faith in a very peculiar system of Divine acting; for on the one side the Sacraments are not mere physical acts, and on the other they cannot be regarded as merely intended to increase knowledge. The action of God therein is no doubt mysterious and peculiar; but its peculiarity is adapted to a dispensation which dates its origin from the manifestation of God in the flesh—a dispensation, too, designed for the restoration of a being who unites in himself the two natures of flesh and spirit, and has in some mysterious way received the sin and death in which he is involved through his fleshly connexion with his progenitors; the present design of the dispensation being that our whole body, soul, and spirit, should be preserved blameless till the day of the Lord Jesus—its termination being the appearance of God in our glorified humanity, to raise up in spiritual bodies those who have had His life abiding in them.

APPENDIX A.

As many of my readers may be by no means aware how thoroughly the mode of address noticed between pages 70 and 82 pervades the Old Testament, I think it may be well in the following pages to give some of the more prominent instances, and to refer to others, so that the student may see for himself how very full the Old Testament is of this way of speaking to the whole circumcised race of Abraham.

SECTION 1.

THE WHOLE CIRCUMCISED NATION OF ISRAEL CALLED GOD'S CHILDREN.

Exodus iv. 22, 23. "And thou shalt say unto Pharaoh, Thus saith the Lord, *Israel is my son, even my firstborn:* and I say unto thee, Let *my son* go, that he may serve me: and if thou refuse to let him go, behold, I will slay thy son, even thy firstborn."

Deut. viii. 5. "Thou shalt also consider in thine heart, that, *as a man chasteneth his son, so the Lord thy God chasteneth thee.*"

Deut. xiv. 1. "*Ye are the children of the Lord your God,* ye shall not cut yourselves," &c.

Deut. xxxii. 6, 18, 19. "Do ye thus requite the Lord, O foolish people and unwise? *Is not he thy father that* hath bought thee?" "*Of the Rock that begat thee* thou art unmindful." "And when the Lord saw it, he abhorred them, because *of the provoking of his sons and of his daughters.*"

Ps. lxxxii. 6. "I have said, Ye are gods, and *all of you are children of the Most High. But ye shall die like men.*"

Prov. i. 8. "*My son,* hear the instruction of thy father."

Prov. ii. 1. "*My son,* if thou wilt hear my words."

So also Prov. iii. 1, 11 ; iv. 1, 20 ; v. 1, 20 ; vi. 1, 3, 20 ; vii. 1 ; xxiii. 15, 26 ; xxiv. 21 ; xxvii. 11.

Note here particularly how the Apostle draws attention to this way of speaking in Hebrews xii. 5, as being not hypothetical or figurative, but as implying real covenant relationship.

Isaiah i. 2. "*I have nourished, and brought up children,* and they have rebelled against me."

Isaiah xliii. 3, 6. "For I am the Lord thy God, the Holy One of Israel thy Saviour. I gave Egypt for thy ransom," &c. "I will say to the north, Give up ; and to the south, Keep not back : *bring my sons from far, and my daughters* from the ends of the earth, *even every one that is called by my name.*"

Isaiah xlv. 11, 13. "Thus saith the Lord, the Holy One of Israel, and his Maker, Ask me of things to come *concerning my sons*." "I have raised him (Cyrus) up in righteousness, and I will direct his ways : he shall build my city, and he shall let go *my captives*."

Isaiah lxiii. 16, 17. Doubtless *thou art our father*, though Abraham be ignorant of us, and Israel acknowledge us not : thou, O Lord, art *our father, our redeemer;* thy name is from everlasting. O Lord, why hast thou made us to err from thy ways, and hardened our heart from thy fear? Return for thy servants' sake, *the tribes of thine inheritance.*"

Jerem. iii. 3, 4, 19. "Therefore the showers have been withholden, and there hath been no latter rain ; and thou hadst a whore's forehead, thou refusedst to be ashamed." "Wilt thou not from this time cry unto me, *My father, thou art the guide of my youth?*"

Jerem. xxxi. 8, 9, 20, 21. "Behold, I will bring them from the north country. . . . They shall come with weeping, and with supplications will I lead them : I will cause them to walk by the rivers of waters in a straight way, wherein they shall not stumble, for *I am a father to Israel, and Ephraim is my firstborn.*" "*Is Ephraim my dear son? is he a pleasant child?* for since I spake against him, I do earnestly remember him still." "Set thee up waymarks, make thee high heaps: set thine heart toward the highway, even the way which thou wentest: turn again, O virgin of Israel, turn again to these thy cities."

Ezek. xvi. 20, 21. "Moreover thou hast taken *thy sons and thy daughters*, *whom thou hast borne unto me,* and these hast thou sacrificed unto them to be devoured. . . . *Thou hast slain my children*, and delivered them to cause them to pass through the fire for them."

Ezek. xxiii. 36, 37. "The Lord said moreover unto me : Son of man, wilt thou judge Aholah and Aholibah? yea, declare unto them their abominations · that they have committed adultery, and blood is in their hands, and with their idols have they committed adultery, and have also caused their *sons, whom they bare unto me,* to pass for them *through the fire, to devour them.*"

SECTION 2.

THE WHOLE CIRCUMCISED NATION CALLED "GOD'S PEOPLE :"
"FLOCK :" "SHEEP :" "HOSTS :" "ARMY."

Exod. iii. 7. "And the Lord said, I have surely seen the affliction of *my people* which are in Egypt."

Exod. v. 1. "Thus saith the Lord God of Israel, Let *my people* go, that they may hold a feast unto me in the wilderness."

Exod. vi. 7. "I will take you *to me for a people, and I will be to you a God.*"

Exod. vii. 4. "That I may lay my hand upon Egypt, and bring forth *mine armies,* and *my people the children of Israel,* out of the land of Egypt."

Exod. viii. 23. "And I will put a division between *my* people and thy people."

Exod. xii. 41. "Even the selfsame day it came to pass, *that all the hosts of the Lord* went out from the land of Egypt."

Exod. xxxii. 11. "Lord, why doth thy wrath wax hot against *thy people,* which thou hast brought forth out of the land of Egypt?"

Exod. xxxiii. 13, 16. "Consider that this nation is *thy people.*" "So shall we be separated, I and *thy people*, from all the people that are upon the face of the earth."

So also Exod. viii. 1, 20, 22 ; ix. 1, 13, 17 ; x. 3, 4 ; xv. 16 ; xviii. 1 ; xxxii. 12, 14.

Levit. xxv. 42. "For they are *my servants*, which I brought forth out of the land of Egypt. *They shall not be sold as bondmen.*"

Deut. iv. 20. "But the Lord hath taken you, and brought you forth out of the iron furnace, even out of Egypt, to be *unto him a people of inheritance*, as ye are this day."

Deut. ix. 26. "O Lord God, destroy not *thy people*, and *thine inheritance.*"

Deut. xxi. 8. "Be merciful, O Lord, unto *thy people Israel.*"

Deut xxvi. 15. "Bless *thy people Israel*, and the land which thou hast given us."

Deut. xxxii. 36. "The Lord shall judge *his people*, and repent himself for his servants."

Also Deut. xxvi. 18 ; xxxii. 9, 43 ; Judges v. 11 ; xx. 2 ; Ruth i. 6.

1 Sam. ii. 24, 29. "Ye make *the Lord's people* to transgress." "To make yourselves fat with the chiefest of all the offerings of *Israel my people.*"
1 Sam. ix. 16, 17. "That he may save *my people* out of the hand of the Philistines, for I have looked upon *my people*, because their cry is come unto me."
Behold the man whom I spake to thee of ! this same shall reign over *my people.*"
1 Sam. xvii. 26, 36, 45. "Who is this uncircumcised Philistine that he should defy *the armies of the living God?*" "This uncircumcised Philistine, shall he as one of them, seeing he hath defied *the armies of the living God.*" "I come to thee in the name of the Lord of Hosts, *the God of the armies of Israel*, whom thou hast defied."
For practical application of this text see quotation from Bishop Latimer at the end of this Appendix.
2 Sam. i. 12. "And they mourned, and wept, and fasted until even, for Saul and for Jonathan his son, and *for the people of the Lord.*"

Also 2 Sam. v. 2, 12 ; vi. 21 ; vii. 7, 8, 10, 11, 23, 24 ; x. 12 ; xiv. 13.

1 Kings iii. 8, 9. "And thy servant is in the midst of *thy people, which thou hast chosen*, a great people, that cannot be numbered nor counted for multitude. Give therefore thy servant an understanding heart to judge *thy people*, that I may discern between good and bad : for who is able to judge this *thy so great people?*"

Also 1 Kings vi. 13 ; viii. 16, 34, 36, 38, 41, 43, 44, 50, 51, 56, 59 ; xiv. 7 ; xvi. 2.

2 Kings ix. 6. "And he arose and went into the house; and he poured the oil on his head, and said unto him, Thus saith the Lord God of Israel, I have anointed thee king over *the people of the Lord, even over Israel.*"
2 Kings xx. 5. "Turn again, and tell Hezekiah *the captain of my people.*"
1 Chron. xxviii. 8. "Now therefore in the sight of all Israel, *the congregation of the Lord.*"

Also 1 Chron. xi. 2 ; xvii. 7, 9, 21, 22 ; xxi. 17.

2 Chron. xiv. 13. "And the Ethiopians were overthrown, that they could not recover themselves; for they were destroyed *before* the Lord, and *before his host.*"
2 Chron. xxxvi. 15, 16. "And the Lord God of their fathers sent to them by his messengers, rising up betimes, and sending; because he had compassion on *his people*, and on his dwelling place. But they mocked the messenger of God, and despised his words, and misused his prophets, until the wrath of the Lord arose against *his people*, till there was no remedy."

Also 2 Chron. ii. 11 ; vi. 5, 6, 24, 25, 27, 29, 39 ; vii. 10 ; xx. 7 ; xxxi. 8, 10 ; xxxv. 3.

Also Ezra i. 3 ; Nehemiah i. 10 ; xiii. 1.

Psalm xiv. 7. "When the Lord bringeth back the captivity of *his people*, *Jacob shall rejoice, and Israel shall be glad.*"
Psalm l. 4, 7. "He shall call to the heavens from above, and to the earth, that he may judge *his people.*" "Hear, *O my people*, and I will speak ; O Israel, and I will testify against thee : I am God, even thy God."
Psalm lxxiv. 1, 2. "O God, why hast thou cast us off for ever? why doth thine anger smoke against *the sheep of thy pasture?* Remember *thy congregation*, which thou hast purchased of old."

Psalm lxxviii. 20, 62, 71. "Can he give bread also? can he provide flesh for *his people?*" "He gave *his people* over also *unto the sword.*" "From following the ewes great with young he brought him *to feed Jacob his people.*"

Psalm lxxxi. 8, 11—13. "Hear, *O my people,* and I will testify against thee : *O Israel.*" "But *my people* would not hearken unto my voice . . . so I gave them up unto their own hearts' lusts. . . . O that *my people* had hearkened unto me !'"

Psalm xcv. 7. "For he is our God, and *we are the people of his pasture, and the sheep of his hand. To-day if ye will hear his voice.*"

Psalm cvi. 40. "Therefore was the wrath of the Lord kindled against *his* people, insomuch that he abhorred *his own inheritance.*"

Also Psalm xliv. 12 ; xlvii. 9 ; liii. 6 ; lx. 3 ; lxviii. 7, 35 ; lxxx. 4, 8, 15 ; lxxxv. 1, 2, 6 ; xciv. 5, 7, 14 ; cv. 24, 25, 43 ; cxi. 6 ; cxlviii. 14.

Isaiah i. 3. "Israel doth not know, *my people* doth not consider."

Isaiah ii. 6. "Therefore thou hast forsaken *thy people the house of Jacob,* because they be replenished from the east," &c.

Isaiah v. 13. "Therefore *my people are gone into captivity,* because they have no knowledge."

Isaiah xvi. 4. "Let *mine outcasts* dwell with thee, Moab."

Isaiah xlvii. 5, 6. "Sit thou silent, and get thee into darkness, O daughter of the Chaldeans : for thou shalt no more be called, The lady of kingdoms. I was wroth *with my people,* I have polluted *mine inheritance,* and given them into thine hand : thou didst show them no mercy."

Isaiah lxiii. 11, 14, 17, 18. "Then he remembered the days of old, Moses and *his people,* saying, Where is he that brought them up out of the sea with the shepherd of *his flock?* where is he that put his holy Spirit within him? . .. As a beast goeth down into the valley, the Spirit of the Lord caused him to rest: so didst thou lead *thy people,* to make thyself a glorious name."

Isaiah lxiv. 9. "Be not wroth very sore, O Lord, neither remember iniquity for ever : behold, see, we beseech thee, *we are all thy people.*"

Also Isaiah iii. 12, 14, 16 ; x. 24 ; xi. 11, 16 ; xxxii. 13, 18 ; xlvi. 3, 4 ; lii. 4, 5 ; lviii. 1.

Jerem. ii. 11, 13, 32. "Hath a nation changed their gods, which are yet no gods ? but *my people* have changed *their glory* for that which doth not profit." "For *my people* have committed two evils ; they have forsaken me the fountain of living waters, and hewed them out cisterns, broken cisterns, that can hold no water." "Can a maid forget her ornaments, or a bride her attire ? yet *my people* have forgotten me days without number."

Jerem. v. 26, 31. "Among *my people* are found wicked men : they lay wait," &c. "The prophets prophesy falsely, and the priests bear rule by their means ; and *my people* love to have it so."

Jerem. viii. 7. "Yea, the stork in the heaven knoweth her appointed times ; and the turtle and the crane and the swallow observe the time of their coming : *but my people know not the judgment of the Lord.*"

Jerem. ix. 1, 2, 3. "O that my head were waters, and mine eyes a fountain of tears, that I might weep day and night for the slain of the daughter of *my people !* O that I had in the wilderness a lodging place of wayfaring men ; that I might *leave my people,* and go from them ! for they be all adulterers, an assembly of treacherous men. And they bend their tongues like their bow for lies : but they are not valiant for the truth upon the earth ; for they proceed from evil to evil, *and they know not me, saith the Lord.*"

Jerem. xxiii. 1, 2. "Woe be unto the pastors that destroy and scatter *the sheep of my pasture !* saith the Lord. Therefore thus saith the Lord God of Israel against the pastors that feed *my people :* Ye have scattered *my flock,* and driven them away," &c.

Also Jerem. xi. 15, 16, 17 ; xii. 14 ; xiii. 17 ; xv. 7 ; xviii. 15 ; xxii. 6 ; xxiii. 22, 32 ; xxx. 3, 14 ; xxxi. 7 ; xxxii. 21 ; l. 6.

Ezek. xiii. 10. "Because, even because they have seduced *my people.*"

Ezek. xx. 32. "And that which cometh into your mind shall not be at all, that ye say, We will be as the heathen, as the families of the countries, to serve wood and stone."

Ezek. xxxiv. 6. "*My sheep* wandered through all the mountains, and upon every high hill: yea, *my flock* was scattered upon all the face of the earth."

Also Ezek. xiii. 18, 19, 21; xxi. 12; xxv. 14; xxxvi. 20.

See also Daniel ix. 15; Hosea i. 9, 10; ii. 23; iv. 6, 8, 12; vi. 11; xi. 7.

Joel ii. 17. "Let them say, Spare *thy people,* O Lord, and give not *thine heritage* to reproach."

Also iii. 2, 3, 16; Amos vii. 8, 15; viii. 2; ix. 10, 14; Obadiah 13; Micah ii. 8, 9; iii. 3, 5; vii. 4, 14; Habakkuk iii. 13.

Zeph. ii. 8, 9. "I have heard the reproach of Moab, and the revilings of the children of Ammon, whereby they have reproached my people. . . . . The residue of *my people* shall spoil them, and *the remnant of my people* shall possess them. This shall they have for their pride, because they have reproached and magnified themselves *against the people of the Lord of Hosts.*"

Also Zechariah x. 3.

SECTION 3.

THE WHOLE NATION IN COVENANT WITH GOD.

(*a.*) God the *God of Israel.* "Our God." "Your God," &c.

Genesis xvii. 7, 8, 10. "And I will establish my covenant between me and thee and thy seed after thee in their generations for an everlasting covenant, *to be a God unto thee,* and to thy seed after thee." "*And I will be their God.*" "This is my covenant, which ye shall keep, between me and you and thy seed after thee : *Every man child among you shall be circumcised.*"

Gen. xlix. 24. "The hands of the *mighty God of Jacob* (from thence is the shepherd, the *stone of Israel*)."

Exod. iii. 18. "*The Lord God of the Hebrews* hath met with us: and now let us go, we beseech thee, three days' journey into the wilderness, that we may sacrifice to the Lord *our God.*"

Exod. v. 1, 3. "Thus saith *the Lord God of Israel,* Let my people go." "*The God of the Hebrews* hath met with us.*"

Exod. vi. 7. "*I will be to you a God:* and ye shall know that *I am the Lord your God.*"

Exod. xx. 2, 5, 7, 10. "*I am the Lord thy God,* which have brought thee out of the land of Egypt." "Thou shalt not bow down to them, nor serve them : for *I the Lord thy God* am a jealous God." "Thou shalt not take the name of *the Lord thy God* in vain." "The seventh day is the Sabbath of *the Lord thy God.*"

Also Exod. x. 25, 26; xv. 2.

Levit. xi. 44, 45. "I am *the Lord your God:* ye shall *therefore* sanctify yourselves." "I am the Lord that bringeth you up out of the land of Egypt, *to be your God:* ye shall *therefore* be holy, *for I am holy.*"

Levit. xviii. 4. "Ye shall do my judgments, and keep mine ordinances, to walk therein : *I am the Lord your God.*"

Also Levit. xix. 2, 3, 4; xx. 24, 26; xxii. 32, 33; xxiv. 22; xxv. 36; xxvi. 44, 45.

Numb. xxiii. 21. "*The Lord his God is with him,* and the shout of a king is among them."

Deut. i. 6, 10, 21. "The *Lord our God* spake unto us in Horeb." "The *Lord your God* hath multiplied you." "Behold, *the Lord thy God* hath set the land before thee."

According to Buxtorf's Hebrew Concordance, the expression "Thy God," addressed to the whole nation, occurs in this Book of Deuteronomy alone two hundred and eight times. "Our God" occurs twenty-nine times. "Your God" forty-two times.

Joshua iii. 9. "Come hither, and hear the words of the *Lord your God.*"

Also Josh. ii. 11; x. 42; xxiii. 3, 5; xxiv. 2; Judges v. 3, 5; vi. 8, 10; Ruth ii. 12.

1 Sam. x. 18, 19. "Thus saith *the Lord God of Israel,* I brought up Israel out of Egypt." "*Ye have this day rejected your God.*"
1 Sam. xvii. 45. "I come to thee in the name of the Lord of Hosts, *the God of the armies of Israel.*"

See also 1 Sam. i. 17; vii. 8; 2 Sam. xii. 7.

1 Kings xvii. 14. "Thus saith *the Lord God of Israel,* The barrel of meal shall not waste, neither shall the cruse of oil fail."

See also 2 Kings xvii. 7, 9, 14, 16, 19; 1 Chron. xiii. 2, 3; 2 Chron. xxxv. 3; xxxvi. 13; Ezra iii. 2; ix. 8, 9, 10, 13, 15; Nehemiah ix. 3, 5.

Ps. ix. 5. "Thou therefore, O Lord God of Hosts, *the God of Israel.*"

See also xli. 13; lxviii. 35; lxxviii. 41; lxxxi.; xcv. 7.

Isaiah xxxvii. 16. "And Hezekiah prayed unto the Lord and said, *O Lord of Hosts, God of Israel.*"

See also Isaiah xxi. 17; xlviii. 1, 2.

Jerem. iii. 21. "They have perverted their way, and they have forgotten *the Lord their God.*"
Jerem. li. 5. "For Israel hath not been forsaken, nor Judah, of *his God, of the Lord of Hosts: though their land was filled with sin against the Holy One of Israel.*"

See also Jerem. xvi. 9, 10; xix. 15; xlii. 2, 3, 4, 5, 6, 9, 11, 15.

Ezek. viii. 4. "And, behold, *the glory of the God of Israel was there,* according to the vision that I saw in the plain."

See also Ezekiel xx. 5, 19, 20.

Dan. ix. 9. "To the *Lord our God* belong mercies and forgivenesses, though we have rebelled against him; neither have we obeyed the voice of the Lord *our God.*"

Also verses 14, 15.

See also Hosea v. 4; vii. 10; ix. 1; xiii. 16; xiv. 1; Joel ii. 13, 14; Haggai i. 12, 14.

(*b.*) The Covenant of God with the whole people mentioned in terms taken from the marriage contract.

Jerem. iii. 1, 14, 20. "*Thou hast played the harlot with many lovers: yet return again to me, saith the Lord.*" "Turn again, O backsliding children, saith the Lord; *for I am married unto you.*" "Surely *as a wife treacherously departeth from her husband, so have ye dealt treacherously with me,* O house of Israel, saith the Lord."

Ezek. xvi. 8, 9, 20. "Yea, I sware unto thee, and entered into a covenant with thee, saith the Lord God, *and thou bec mest mine.*" "Then washed I thee with water: yea, I thoroughly washed away thy blood from thee, and I anointed thee with oil." "Moreover thou hast taken thy sons and thy daughters, *whom thou hast borne unto me,* and these hast thou sacrificed unto them to be devoured."

Ezek. xxiii. 5, 37. "And Aholah played the harlot *when she was mine*" "That they have committed adultery, and blood is in their hands, and with their idols have they committed adultery, and have also caused *their sons, whom they bare unto me,* to pass for them through the fire, to devour them."

Hosea ii. 2, 7. "Plead with your mother, plead; *for she is not my wife, neither am I her husband:* let her therefore put away her whoredoms out of her sight, and *her adulteries from* between her breasts; lest I strip her naked." "Then shall she say, I will go and return *to my first husband;* for then was it better with me than now."

(*c*) National and individual sins said to be a *breaking of God's Covenant* entered into between God and the nation or individual.

Deut. iv. 23. "Take heed unto yourselves, lest ye *forget the covenant of the Lord your God.*"

Deut. xxix. 9, 24, 25. "Keep therefore *the words of this covenant,* and do them, that ye may prosper in all that ye do." "Even all nations shall say, Wherefore hath the Lord done thus unto this land? what meaneth the heat of this great anger? Then men shall say, *Because they have forsaken the covenant of the Lord God of their fathers, which he made with them when he brought them forth out of the land of Egypt.*"

Judges ii. 12, 20. "And I said, *I will never break my covenant with you.* And ye shall make no league with the inhabitants of this land." "And the anger of the Lord was hot against Israel, and he said, Because that this people hath *transgressed my covenant* which I commanded their fathers, and have not hearkened unto my voice," &c.

Prov. ii. 17. "Which forsaketh the guide of her youth, and *forgetteth the covenant of her God.*"

SECTION 4.

GOD'S PRESENCE IN THE MIDST OF ISRAEL AND IN THE EARTHLY JERUSALEM.

Numbers xiv. 14. "For they have heard that *thou, Lord, art among this people,* that thou, Lord, art seen face to face, and that *thy cloud standeth over them.*"

Numbers xxiii. 21. "*The Lord his God is with him,* and the shout of a king is *among them.*"

Deut. xii. 5. "But unto the place which the Lord your God shall choose out of all your tribes to put *his name there,* even unto *his habitation* shall ye seek."

2 Sam. vii. 6, 7. "Whereas I have not dwelt in any house since the time that I brought up the children of Israel out of Egypt, even unto this day, but *have walked in a tent* and in a tabernacle. *In all the places wherein I have walked with all the children of Israel* spake I a word," &c.

1 Kings xviii. 36. "Lord God of Abraham, Isaac, and Jacob, let it be known this day that thou art *God in Israel.*"

2 Chron. vi. 41. "Now therefore arise, *O Lord God, into thy resting place, thou* and the ark of thy strength."

Ezra vii. 15. "And to carry the silver and gold, which the king and his counsellors have freely offered unto *the God of Israel, whose habitation is in Jerusalem.*"

Psalm ix. 11. "Sing praises unto the Lord, *which dwelleth in Zion.*"

Psalm xlviii. 1, 2, 8. "*The city of our God.*" "Mount Zion." "*The city of the great King.*" "*The city of the Lord of Hosts.*"

Psalm lix. 13. "God ruleth *in* Jacob unto the ends of the earth."
Psalm lxxiv. 2. "*This mount Zion, wherein thou hast dwelt.*"
Psalm cxiv. 2. "*Judah* was *his sanctuary*, and *Israel his dominion.*"
Psalm cxxxii. 13, 14. "The Lord hath chosen Zion ; *he hath desired it for his habitation.* This is my rest for ever: here *will I dwell ; for I have desired it.*"
Psalm cxxxv. 21. "Blessed be *the Lord out of Zion, which dwelleth at Jerusalem.*"
Isaiah viii. 18. "The Lord of Hosts, *which dwelleth in mount Zion.*"
Jerem. xiv. 8, 9. "O the hope of Israel, the saviour thereof in time of trouble, *why shouldest thou be as a stranger in the land, and as a wayfaring man that turneth aside to tarry for a night?* Why shouldest thou be as a man astonied, as a mighty man that cannot save? yet thou, *O Lord, art in the midst of us,* and we are called by thy name ; *leave us not.*"
Ezekiel xxxv. 2, 10. "Son of man, set thy face against mount Seir, and prophesy against it." "Because thou hast said, These two nations and these two countries shall be mine, and we will possess it ; *whereas the Lord was there.*"

See also Numbers v. 3 ; Leviticus xxvi. 11, 12 ; Ezekiel xliii. 7, 9 ; xlviii. 35 ; Joel iii. 17, 21 ; Micah iv. 2 ; Zephaniah iii. 15, 17 ; Zechariah ii. 10, 11, 12, 13 ; viii. 3.

SECTION 5.

THE WORDS "HOLY," "HOLINESS," "SANCTIFY," "HALLOW," ETC., MEANING "SEPARATION TO GOD'S SERVICE," AS DISTINGUISHED FROM INTERNAL SANCTIFICATION.

Gen. ii. 3. "And God blessed the seventh day, and *sanctified it.*"
Exodus iii. 5. "The place whereon thou standest is *holy* ground."
Exodus xiii. 2. "*Sanctify unto me all the firstborn*, whatsoever openeth the womb among the children of Israel, *both of man and of beast: it is mine.*"
Exodus xix. 10, 14. "And the Lord said unto Moses, Go unto the people, and *sanctify them to-day* and to-morrow, and let them *wash their clothes.*" "And Moses went down from the mount unto the people, and *sanctified the people ;* and they *washed their clothes.*"
Exodus xxii. 31. "Ye shall be holy men unto me: neither shall ye eat any flesh that is torn of beasts in the field."
Exodus xxvi. 33. "The vail shall divide unto you between the *holy place* and *the most holy.*"
Exodus xxviii. 2. "Thou shalt make *holy garments* for Aaron."

Also xxix. 29, 31, 33, 34, 36, 37, 43, 44, 45 ; xxx. 10, 29, 31, 32, 35, 36, 37 ; xxxi. 13 ; Levit. ii. 3 ; vi. 16, 17, 18 ; viii. 10, 11, 12, 15 ; Levit. xix. 24.

Levit. xx. 24, 25, 26. "I am the Lord your God, which *have separated you from other people.* Ye shall therefore put difference between clean beasts and unclean . . . and *ye shall be holy* unto me: for I the Lord am holy, and have *severed you from other people, that ye should be mine.*"
Levit. xxi. 8. "Thou shalt *sanctify him* therefore ; *for he offereth the bread of thy God: he shall be holy unto thee, for I the Lord, which sanctify you, am holy.*"

Also verses 21, 22, 23 ; xxii. 2, 3, 32.
Also Numbers iii. 12, 13 ; vi. 5, 7, 8 ; viii. 17, 18 ; xx. 12, 13.

Numb. xvi. 38. "The censers of these sinners against their own souls, let them make them broad plates for a covering of the altar: for *they offered them before the Lord, therefore they are hallowed.*"

Also 1 Kings ix. 3, 7 ; 2 Chronicles v. 11 ; viii. 11 ; xxiii. 6 ; xxix. 5 ; xxx. 8, 18, 19, 20 ; Ezra ii. 62, 63 ; viii. 28, 29 ; ix. 2 ; Nehemiah vii. 64, 65 ; xi. 1.

Psalm lxxix. 1, 2 ; lxxxv. 8; cxlviii. 14.

Jerem. xi. 15. "What hath my beloved to do in mine house, seeing she hath wrought lewdness with many, and *the holy flesh is passed from thee ?*"

Ezekiel xx. 12 ; xxi. 1, 2 ; xxii. 26 ; xxxviii. 23 ; xlii. 13, 14 ; xliii. 12, 26 ; xliv. 19, 23, 24, 25 ; xlvi. 19, 20 ; xlviii. 12, 14.

Our Blessed Lord very distinctly recognises the relative use of these terms, in that He speaks of "The temple which sanctifieth the gold" "The altar which sanctifieth the gift" (Matt. xxiii. 17, 19). The practical application of this to us, in this dispensation of the Spirit, is indicated in chap. viii., pp. 111—117.

SECTION 6.

THE WHOLE BODY OR NATION OF THE CHILDREN OF ISRAEL REDEEMED, PURCHASED, SAVED.

Deut. xxi. 8. "Be merciful, O Lord, unto *thy people Israel, whom thou hast redeemed*, and lay not innocent blood unto thy people of Israel's charge."

Also Deut. ix. 26 ; xxxii. 6, 9, 15 ; xxxiii. 29.

1 Sam. xxvi. 19. "For they have driven me out this day from abiding in the inheritance of the Lord."

1 Kings viii. 51, 53. "For they be thy people, *and thine inheritance, which thou broughtest forth out of Egypt*, from the midst of the furnace of iron." "For thou didst separate them from among all the people of the earth, *to be thine inheritance.*"

2 Kings xxi. 14. "And I will forsake *the remnant of mine inheritance.*"

Also 1 Chron. xvii. 21.

Psalm lxxvii. 15. "Thou hast with thine arm *redeemed thy people, the sons of Jacob and Joseph.*"

Psalm lxxviii. 35. "And they remembered that God was their rock, *and the high God their redeemer.*"

Psalm cvi. 40. "Therefore was the wrath of the Lord kindled against his people, *insomuch that he abhorred his own inheritance.*"

Psalm cxxxv. 4. "For the Lord hath chosen Jacob unto himself, and *Israel for his peculiar treasure.*"

Isaiah xliii. 1, 3, 14. "But now thus saith the Lord that created thee, O Jacob, and he that formed thee, O Israel, Fear not : *for I have redeemed thee,* I have called thee by thy name ; *thou art mine.*" "For I am the Lord thy God, the Holy One of Israel, thy Saviour : *I gave Egypt for thy ransom, Ethiopia and Seba for thee.*" "Thus saith the Lord, *your Redeemer,* the Holy One of Israel : *For your sake I have sent to Babylon, and have brought down all their nobles, and the Chaldeans, whose cry is in the ships.*"

Also Isaiah xliv. 22; xlvii. 6; xlviii. 17.

Jeremiah x. 16. "The portion of Jacob is not like them : for he is the former of all things, *and Israel is the rod of his inheritance.*"

Jeremiah xii. 7—10. "I have forsaken mine house, *I have left mine heritage ;* I have given the *dearly beloved of my soul* into the hand of her enemies. *Mine heritage is unto me as a lion of the forest ;* it crieth out against me : therefore have

I hated it. *Mine heritage is unto me as a speckled bird*. . . . Many pastors have *destroyed my vineyard*, they have *trodden my portion* under foot, they have made my *pleasant portion a desolate wilderness.*"
Jeremiah l. 11. "Because ye were glad, because ye rejoiced, *O ye destroyers of mine heritage.*"

Also Jeremiah xxxi. 11; Micah iv. 10.

SECTION 7.

THE ELECTION OF THE OLD TESTAMENT CONDITIONAL IN THIS RESPECT, THAT THOSE ELECTED HAD TO CONTINUE IN GOD'S FAVOUR, AND MIGHT LOSE IT. THE NATION WAS ELECTED UNCONDITIONALLY IN THEIR FATHERS, BUT THIS ENTIRELY CONSISTENT WITH EACH GENERATION HAVING TO MAKE ITS CALLING AND ELECTION SURE.

Exodus xix. 4, 5, 6. "Ye have seen what I did unto the Egyptians, and how I bare you on eagles' wings, and *brought you unto myself*. Now therefore, *if ye will obey my voice indeed*, and keep my covenant, *then* ye shall be a peculiar treasure unto me above all people: for all the earth is mine: *and ye shall be unto me a kingdom of priests, and an holy nation.*"

Also Exodus xxxii. 10, 11, 12, 13, 14.

Numbers xiv. 34. "After the number of the days in which ye searched the land, even forty days, each day for a year, ye shall bear your iniquities, even forty years, *and ye shall know my breach of promise.*"
Deuteronomy vii. 12. "Wherefore it shall come to pass, *if ye hearken to these judgments, and keep and do them*, that the Lord thy God *shall keep unto thee* the covenant and the mercy *which he sware unto thy fathers*. And he will love thee and bless thee."

Also Deut. v. 28, 29; vii. 7, 8, 9, 10; x. 15, 16; xxxii. 12, 20, 21, 29.

Judges ii. 1—3. "*I said, I will never break my covenant with you*. And ye shall make no league with the inhabitants of this land; ye shall throw down their altars: *but ye have not obeyed my voice*. . . . *Wherefore I also said, I will not drive them out from before you.*"
1 Samuel ii. 27, 28, 30. "Did I plainly appear unto the house of thy father, when they were in Egypt in Pharaoh's house? *And did I choose him* out of all the tribes of Israel to be my priest, to offer upon mine altar, &c. Wherefore kick ye at my sacrifice, &c." "Wherefore the Lord God of Israel saith, *I said indeed* that thy house and the house of thy father should walk before me *for ever : but now the Lord saith*, Be it far from me ; for them that honour me I will honour, and they that despise me shall be lightly esteemed."
1 Samuel ix. 17. "And when Samuel saw Saul, the Lord said unto him, Behold the man whom I spake to thee of! this same shall reign over my people."

Compared with—

1 Samuel xiii. 13, 14. "And Samuel said unto Saul, Thou hast done foolishly: thou hast not kept the commandment of the Lord thy God, which he commanded thee: for *now would the Lord have established thy kingdom upon Israel for ever. But now thy kingdom shall not continue:* the Lord hath sought him a man after his own heart, and the Lord hath commanded him to be captain over his people, *because thou hast not kept that which the Lord commanded thee.*"

See also 1 Kings ix. 3—7 (quoted above in page 247); xi. 37, 38; xiv. 7—10. Also 2 Kings xxi. 7—15; 1 Chron. xxviii. 5, 6, 7, 8, 9 (quoted above in page 247); 2 Chron. vii. 16—20.

Again, the restoration of Israel to God's favour is said to be a *fresh choosing* or election.

Isaiah xiv. 1. "For the Lord will have mercy on Jacob, and *will yet choose Israel.*"
Zechariah i. 17. "The Lord shall yet comfort Zion, *and shall yet choose Jerusalem.*"
Also ii. 12. "The Lord . . . shall choose Jerusalem again.,"

A moment's consideration will convince the reader how impossible it is, except on such a principle as that of Baptismal Regeneration, to apply to the present baptized body this way of speaking, adopted by all the prophets in addressing the whole circumcised body, and of which I have given such a multitude of instances in the few preceding pages.

On such a principle only can all the baptized be addressed, as we see the prophets invariably addressed all the circumcised, as God's children—people—flock.*

And this is borne out by facts. They who deny Baptismal Regeneration carefully restrict all such terms as " God's people," &c. to true Christians. They who hold it apply these terms to the whole visible body, as the prophets did. The latter can make present use and application of THIS LEADING FEATURE OF OLD TESTAMENT TEACHING ; the former cannot, and do not.

So that, on the theory of those who oppose Church teaching, God has nothing like the hold on the Baptized nominal Christian which he had on the Circumcised Jew. Circumcision, the legal type, had a more sure application to the heart and conscience than Baptism, its evangelical antitype. Can this be ?

* "Circumcision, at that time, was a certain, sure, infallible, and effectual token of God's good will towards them to whom it was given: for, as many as did believe the covenant of God, it did ascertain them of the good will of God towards them, that they should be delivered out of all their troubles and adversities, and that they should be sure of the help of God. An example we have in that good young man Jonathan : he comforted himself with his circumcision, saying to his weapon-bearer, 'Come, let us go to these uncircumcised ;' as though he had said, 'Come, let us go, we have circumcision ; God hath promised to be our God, to aid and help us, and deliver us out of all our troubles and calamities.' . . . . So likewise did David ; when he should fight against Goliath the Philistine, he saith, 'What is this uncircumcised Philistine, that he should revile the host of the living God ?' So they exhorted themselves, and confirmed their faith with this circumcision. So let us ever consider, in what trouble and calamity whatsoever we be, let us remember that we be baptized ; that God hath promised to help us, to deliver us from all our sins and wickedness, to be our God. And again, let us consider our promise which we have made unto Him, namely, that we will forsake sin, the devil, and all his crafts and illusions, and cleave unto God only ; and so, by the remembrance of this, we shall be more ready and earnest to strive and fight against the devil."—LATIMER's *Sermons*, Serm. XXXVII. in volume lettered "Remains," Parker Society, p. 133.

APPENDIX B.

CONTAINING EXTRACTS FROM DIVINES.

LUTHER.

FOLLY OF SUPPOSING BAPTISMAL GRACE CONTRARY TO SALVATION BY FAITH.

"BUT in reference to what our wiseacres, that is, these new spiritualists, are each superciliously feigning, viz. that it is faith by itself which saves, but that works and external rites are of no force or efficacy to the attainment of salvation, I answer, that assuredly *in ourselves* no other thing works out or accomplishes our salvation than faith; on which matter I shall by and by speak more fully.

"But these blind leaders of the blind are determined not to see, that faith must have something which it may believe, *i.e.* on which it may lean, and by the support of which it may stand. So in the present case, faith fastens on the water, and believes that it is a Baptism in which is unmixed happiness and life, not by virtue of the water, as has been sufficiently enforced, but on this account, that Baptism is joined to God's word, and confirmed by His decree, and ennobled by [the invocation of] His name.

"Now, when I believe this, what else do I believe in but in God, even in Him who laid up and implanted His own word in Baptism, and places before our eyes outward things in which we are enabled to perceive a store of things of such surpassing value?"—(*Opera, Wit.* vol. v. p. 637, quoted in Archbishop Lawrence's "Doctrine of the Church of England upon the Efficacy of Baptism Vindicated," p. 29.)

BAPTISM AN ACT OF GOD, WHEREBY, THROUGH THE INSTRUMENTALITY OF MAN, HE BRINGS US INTO UNION WITH THE SECOND ADAM.

"Baptism cannot fail to effect that for which it was appointed, namely, regeneration and spiritual renewal, as St. Paul teaches in the third chapter to Titus. For as we were born into this life from Adam and Eve, so our old man, which was before born in sins to death, must be regenerated to righteousness and eternal life, by the power of the Holy Ghost. To this regeneration and renewal there lacks the application of no other external means than water and words; of the one whereof our eyes take note, our ears of the other.   Yet they have such virtue and energy, that the man who was conceived and born in sin is regenerated in the view of God ; and that he who was before condemned to death, is now made truly God's son.   This glory and virtue of Holy Baptism who can attain and perceive by sense, thought, and human intellect?   You should not, therefore, regard the hand or mouth of the minister who baptizes—who pours over the body a little water, which he has taken in the hollow of his hand, and pronounces some few words (a thing slight and easy in itself, addressing itself only to the eyes and ears, and our blinded reason sees no more to be accomplished by the minister)—but in all this you must behold and consider the work of God, by whose authority and command Baptism is administered, who is its founder and author ; yea, who is himself the Baptist.   And hence has Baptism such virtue and energy (as the Holy Ghost witnesses by St. Paul), that it is the laver of regeneration and of the renewal of the Holy Ghost ; by which laver the impure and condemned nature which we derive from Adam is altered and amended."—(*Homiliæ de Baptismo*, vol. vii. p. 377, quoted in Lawrence, as above.)

Again, from Luther's Commentary on Joel. "Moreover, when we speak of the word of the Gospel, we also include the Sacraments ; for they have the promise of the Holy Ghost annexed, as well as remission of sins.   Thus Peter, when asked what was to be done, replies, 'Repent, and let each be baptized in the name of Jesus Christ,' &c.   And Christ says, 'Unless a man be born again, by water and the Spirit, he cannot enter into the kingdom of God.'   This view is manifest, that the Holy Spirit wills, by means of Baptism, to exert His influence with efficacy on the mind.   So St. Peter also says, 'And ye shall receive the gift of the Holy Ghost.'   And this, too, is the cause why we bring infants also to Baptism, following the examples of the Apostles and the primitive Church.   For because it is certain that the Holy Spirit wills to be efficacious through the water of Baptism, we determine that the action of the Holy Ghost is in the same point of view unimpeded by the want of consciousness [ἀναισθησία] of infants, as we adults do not render the work of the Holy Spirit more perfect by our strength and senses."— Luther on Joel. ii. 28.—(*Opera*, vol. iv. p. 672, Ed. Jenæ, 1558, quoted in Archbishop Lawrence's "Doctrine of the Church of England upon the Efficacy of Baptism," page 88.)

MELANCTHON.

"The command respecting Baptism is of universal application, and belong to the whole Church : 'Except a man be born of water and of the Spirit, he cannot enter into the kingdom of God.' It belongs, therefore, to infants, in order that they may become a part of the Church. And there is no doubt but that there always have existed some significant acts by which infants are offered up to God in the Church. . . . But the Anabaptists make an objection. They deny that Baptism is of any service to infants, since they do not understand ' the word ; ' and (they affirm that) ceremonies, unless the recipient of them have faith, are vain.

" To this I reply, that it is most true that in all adults repentance and faith are required ; but with respect to infants, it is sufficient to hold that the Holy Spirit is given to them in Baptism, who works in them new stirrings of heart, new inclinations towards God, *in accordance with the circumstances of their state and condition* (pro ipsorum modo) : nor do we make this affirmation rashly ; for it is certain that infants are received by God through this ministration ; and that there is also alway given along with remission of sins the Holy Spirit, and no man is pleasing to God unless he be sanctified by the Holy Ghost. As Christ distinctly says, ' Unless a man be born of water and of the Spirit, he cannot enter into the kingdom of God ; ' and again, 1 Corinth. xv., ' Flesh and blood (*i.e.* without the Holy Spirit) cannot inherit the kingdom of God ; ' and Rom. viii., ' As many as are led by the Spirit of God, they are the sons of God.' Since, then, it is certain that infants are a part of the Church, and are pleasing to God, this too is to be relied on, that God is effectually working in them, so that life eternal is begun in them on this side the grave. Let us all religiously and diligently lay to heart these truths, in order that we too, who are more advanced in years, may receive consolation from that comfort and covenant (*i.e.* of Baptism), as I have before urged (see above, page 239). But, above all, let the young beware lest they waste and lest they lose that wondrous glory which Christ publishes respecting infants in his Church—' It is not the will of your Father which is in heaven that one of these little ones should perish.' What glory can be conceived greater than that He should say of them, that they of a certainty please God, and are the objects of His care ?

" And let parents, in this faith respecting Baptism, call upon God for their infants, and commend them to God ; and, as soon as they are able to learn, accustom them to call upon God and His Son for themselves, and by degrees commit to them the sum and substance of the Gospel.

" In the last place, since children compose a great part of the Church, let parents and preceptors be well assured that no small treasure is committed to them and so let them bestow faith and diligence on the instruction and discipline of youth."—(*Loci Theologici. De Baptismo Infantium. Lips.* 1569.) *

CRANMER.

In Cranmer's works on the Lord's Supper, we find from a multitude of places that, so far from considering an exalted view of the Sacrament of Baptism Popish, he, in answer to Gardiner, vindicates its position as a thing that makes us partakers, not only of Christ's Spirit, but of Christ Himself.

"You conclude your book with blasphemous words against both the Sacrament of Baptism and the Lord's Supper, niggardly pinching God's gifts, and diminishing His liberal promises made unto us in them. For where Christ hath promised in both the Sacraments to be assistant with us whole, both in body and spirit (in the one to be our spiritual regeneration and apparel, and in the other to be our spiritual meat and drink), you clip His liberal benefits in such sort, that in the one you make Him to give but only His Spirit, and in the other but only His body."—(*First Book of the Sacrament, Park. Soc.* p. 45.)

"The minister of the Church speaketh unto us God's own words, which we must take as spoken from God's own mouth, because that from His mouth it came, and His word it is, and not the minister's. Likewise, when He ministereth to our sights Christ's holy Sacraments, we must think Christ crucified and presented before our eyes, because the Sacraments so represent Him, and be His Sacraments, and not the priest's ; as in Baptism we must think that, as the priest putteth his hand to the child outwardly, and washeth him with water, so must we think that God putteth to His hand inwardly, and washeth the infant with His Holy Spirit ; and, moreover, that Christ Himself cometh down upon the child, and appareleth him with His own self ; and as at the Lord's holy table the priest distributeth wine and bread to feed the body, so must we think that inwardly by faith we see Christ feeding both body and soul to eternal life."—(*The Fifth Book, Park. Soc.* p. 366.)

"For this cause, Christ ordained Baptism in water, that, as surely as we feel and touch water with our bodies, and be washed with water, so assuredly ought we to believe, when we be baptized, that Christ is verily present with us, and that by Him we be newly born again spiritually, and washed from our sins and grafted in the stock of Christ's own body, and be appareled,

---

* Want of space compels me to omit several extracts from Melancthon, asserting most strongly the remission of original sin to all infants grafted into the Church by Baptism.

clothed, and harnessed with Him, in such wise that, as the devil
hath no power against Christ, so hath he none against us *so long
as we remain grafted in that stock*, and be clothed with that
apparel, and harnessed with that armour."—(*Defence of the True
Doctrine*, &c. pp. 9, 10.)*

RIDLEY.

The works of Ridley published by the Parker Society are
almost entirely on the Romish controversy. Baptism is mentioned but three times. In one of these places it is called " the
fountain of regeneration." (P. 12.) In another, grace is said
to " come by it ; " in a third, " Baptism is ordained in water to
our spiritual regeneration." (Pp. 238, 240.) Beside these places,
regeneration is only mentioned once, and then with evident
reference to the baptismal vow and promise. " Likewise, when
I consider that all that man doth profess in his regeneration—
when he is received into the Holy Catholic Church of Christ,
and is now to be accounted for one of the lively members of
Christ's own body—all that is grounded upon God's Holy Word,
and standeth in the profession of *that faith*, and obedience of
those commandments." (P. 57.)

JEWEL.

" Baptism, therefore, is our regeneration or new birth, whereby
we are born anew in Christ, and are made the sons of God and
heirs of the kingdom of heaven: it is the Sacrament of the
remission of sins, and of that washing which we have in the blood
of Christ. We are all born the children of wrath, and have our
part in the offence of Adam. St. Paul saith, ' By one man sin
entered into the world.' Augustine saith, ' *Non dixit, veniet
super eum, sed manet super eum. Respexit originem, &c.:* ' Christ
said not ' it shall come upon him,' but, ' it abideth on him.' He
had regard to our offspring when He saith, ' the wrath of God
abideth on him ; ' upon which, when the Apostle also looked, he
said, ' And we ourselves also were sometime the children of
wrath.' That which in Adam was imputed to his offence, and not
to be of nature, is now in us, who are come of Adam, become
natural. Therefore, saith the prophet, ' Behold, I was shapen in
iniquity ; and in sin hath my mother conceived me.' So that we
have all cause to cry out and moan with St. Paul : ' I see another

* See also particularly Cranmer's Disputations at Oxford, (Parker Society's
Edition), on the Lord's Supper, p. 411 ; also same vol. pp. 25, 34, 64, 92, 150, 176,
180, 228, 342, 356. If the reader refers to these places he will find each one as
strong and distinct as those I have given above in full.

law in my members rebelling against the law ot my mind, &c.
Hereof speaketh our Saviour : 'That which is born of the flesh
is flesh, and that which is born of the Spirit is spirit.' *And for
this cause, saith He,* ' *Except a man be born of the water and the
Spirit. he cannot enter into the kingdom of God.*'
 " For this cause are infants baptized, because they are born in
sin, and cannot become spiritual but by this new birth of the
water and the Spirit. They are the heirs of the promise : the
covenant of God's favour is made with them."

The above extract forms the commencement of that part of
Jewel's " Treatise of the Sacraments " which relates to Baptism.
(Parker Society's Edition, p. 1104.) The whole treatise is well
worthy of the reader's attentive perusal, not only from its intrinsic
excellence, but because garbled extracts from it have been frequently used, by men who should have known better, in order to
make Jewel speak in utter disparagement of the Sacrament. For
instance, Jewel, with a view to some false doctrine on the subject
(most probably the *opus operatum*), says at the beginning of one
paragraph, "The water wherein we are baptized doth not cleanse
the soul," but " the blood of Jesus Christ His Son doth cleanse us
from all sin." " Not the water, but the blood of Christ, recon-
cileth us to God, strengtheneth our conscience, and worketh our
redemption." Taking this by itself, we should gather that he
held Baptism to be a mere figurative act, to be altogether disso-
ciated from the thing which it typifies ; but what says he in the
beginning of the very next paragraph ? " Such a change is made
in the Sacrament of Baptism. Through the power of God's working, the water is turned into blood. They that be washed in it
receive the remission of sins ; their robes are made clean in the
blood of the Lamb. The water itself is nothing ; but, by the working of God's Spirit, the death and merits of our Lord and Saviour
Christ are *thereby* assured unto us."— (*Jewel on Sacraments,*
p. 1106, volume lettered, " Harding, Thessalonians, Sermons.")

In accordance with the above, Jewel would have Christian education based on baptismal teaching. " Therefore, a father must
teach his child what God is—that He is our Father, that He hath
made us, and doth feed us, and giveth us all things needful both
for soul and body ; that He is our Lord, and therefore we must
serve Him and obey Him, and do nothing whereby He may be
displeased ; that He is our Judge, and shall come to judge the
quick and the dead, and that all men shall come before Him, to
receive according as they have done in the flesh. *He must put his
child in mind of his Baptism,* and teach him that it is a covenant
of God's mercy to us, and of our duty to God ; that it is a mystery
of our salvation ; that our soul is so washed with the blood of

Christ, as the water of Baptism washeth our body. . . . Let us look upon our children as upon the great blessings of God. They are the Lord's vessels, ordained to honour ; *let us keep them clean :* they are Christ's lambs and sheep of His flock ; let us lead them forth into wholesome pasture : they are the seed-plot of Heaven ; let us water them, that God may give the increase : their angels do always behold the face of God ; let us not offend them : *they are the temples and tabernacles of the Holy Ghost; let us not suffer the foul spirit to possess them and dwell within them.*" —(*Jewel on Confirmation,* pp. 1127, 1128.)

HOOKER.

" The grace which is given them with their Baptism does so far forth depend on the very outward Sacrament, that God will have it embraced not only as a sign or token what we receive, but also as an instrument or mean whereby we receive grace, because Baptism is a Sacrament which God hath instituted in His Church, to the end that they which receive the same might thereby be incorporated into Christ, and so through His most precious merit obtain as well that saving grace of imputation which taketh away all former guiltiness, as also that infused divine virtue of the Holy Ghost which giveth to the powers of the soul their first disposition towards future newness of life."—(*Eccles. Polity,* book v. chap. lx. sec. 2.)

"Predestination bringeth not to life without the grace of external vocation, wherein our Baptism is implied. For as we are not naturally men without birth, so neither are we Christian men in the eye of the Church of God but by new birth ; nor, according to the manifest ordinary course of divine dispensation new born, but by that Baptism which both declareth and maketh us Christians. In which respect we justly hold it to be the door of our actual entrance into God's house, the first apparent beginning of life, a seal, PERHAPS, to the grace of election before received, but to our sanctification here a step that hath not any before it."— (Book v. chap. lx. sec. 3.)

Again, speaking with respect to the iteration of Baptism :—

" We serve that Lord which is but one, because no other can be joined with Him ; we embrace that faith which is but one, because it admitteth no innovation ; that Baptism we receive which is but one, because it cannot be received often. For how should we practise iteration of Baptism, and yet teach that we are by Baptism born anew, that by Baptism we are admitted into the heavenly society of saints, that those things be really and effectually done by Baptism which are no more possible to be often done than a man can naturally be often born, or civilly be often adopted into any one's stock or family."—(Book v. chap. lxii. sec. 4.)

"They with whom we contend are no enemies to the Baptism of infants ; it is not their desire that the Church should hazard so many souls by letting them run on till they come to ripeness of understanding, that so they may be converted and then baptized, as infidels heretofore have been ; they bear not toward God so unthankful minds as not to acknowledge it even amongst the greatest of His endless mercies, that by making us His own possession so soon, many advantages which Satan otherwise might take are prevented, and (which should be esteemed a part of no small happiness) the first thing whereof we have occasion to take notice is, how much hath been done already to our great good, though altogether without our knowledge."—(Book v. chap. lxiv. sec. 1.)

"At the time, therefore, when He giveth His heavenly grace, He applieth, by the hands of His ministers, that which betokeneth the same ; not only betokeneth, but being also accompanied for ever with such power as doth truly work, is in that respect termed God's instrument—a true, efficient cause of grace : a cause not in itself, but only by connexion of that which is in itself a cause, namely, God's own strength and power. Sacraments, that is to say, the outward signs in Sacraments, work nothing till they be blessed and sanctified of God. But what is God's heavenly benediction and sanctification, saving only the association of His Spirit ? Shall we say that Sacraments are like magical signs if thus they have their effect ? Is it magic for God to manifest by things sensible what He doth, and to do by His most glorious Spirit really what He manifesteth in His sacraments ? the delivery and administration whereof remaineth in the hands of mortal man, by whom, as by personal instruments, God doth apply signs, and with signs inseparably join His Spirit, and through the power of His Spirit work grace."—(Book vi. chap. vi. sec. 11.)

MEDE.

"'Not by works of righteousness which we have done, but by His mercy He saved us, by the washing of regeneration, and renewing of the Holy Ghost.' (Tit. iii. 5.)

"These words, as it is easy to conceive upon the first hearing, are spoken of Baptism ; of which I intend not by this choice to make any full or accurate tractation, but only to acquaint you (as I am wont) with my thoughts concerning two particulars therein, both of them mentioned in the words of the text. One, from what propriety, analogy, or use of water the washing therewith was instituted for a sign of new birth, according as it is here called, λουτρὸν παλιγγενεσίας, the washing of regeneration. The other, what is the proper countertype, or thing which the water figureth in this Sacrament.

" I will begin with the last first, because the knowledge thereof must be supposed for the explication and more distinct understanding of the other. In every Sacrament, as ye well know, there is the outward symbol or sign, *Res terrena*, and the signation figured and represented thereby, *Res cœlestis.* In this of Baptism, the sign, or *Res terrena*, is washing with water. The question is, What is the signation, the invisible and celestial thing which answers thereunto ? In our catechetical explication of this mystery it was wont to be affirmed of the blood of Christ, namely, that as water washeth away the filth of the body, so the blood of Christ cleanseth us from the guilt and pollution of sin. And there is no question but that the blood of Christ is the fountain of all the grace and good communicated to us in this or in any other Sacrament or mystery of the Gospel. But that this should be the antistoichon, the counterpart or thing figured by the water in Baptism, I believe not ; because the Scripture, which must be our guide and direction in this case, makes it another thing—to wit, the Spirit or Holy Ghost ; this to be that whereby the soul is cleansed and renewed within, as the body with water is without. So saith our Saviour to Nicodemus (John iii. 5), ' Except a man be born of water and of the Spirit, he cannot enter into the kingdom of God.' And the Apostle, in the words I have read, parallels the washing of regeneration and the renewing of the Holy Ghost, where none, I trow, will deny that he speaks of Baptism.

" The same was represented by that vision at our Saviour's Baptism of the Holy Ghost descending upon Him as He came out of the water in the similitude of a dove : for, I suppose, that in that Baptism of His the mystery of all our Baptisms was visibly acted ; and that God says to every one truly baptized, as He said to Him, in a proportionable sense : ' Thou art my son, in whom I am well pleased.' "—(*Discourse* xvii.)

BISHOP HALL.

" His Baptism gives virtue to ours. His last action, or rather passion, was His baptizing with blood ; His first was His baptization with water : both of them wash the world from their sin. Yea, this latter did not only wash the souls of men, but washeth that very water by which we are washed : from thence is that made both clean and holy, and can both cleanse and hallow us. And if the very handkerchief which touched His Apostles had power of cure, how much more that water which the sacred body of Christ touched. . . . There is no less use of Baptism unto ALL, than there is certainty of the need of Baptism.   John baptized without, Christ within.

"No sooner is Christ baptized than He comes forth of the water. The element is of force but during the use ; it turns common when that is past. Neither is the water sooner poured on His head than the heavens are opened and the Holy Ghost descendeth upon that head which was baptized. The heavens are never shut while either of the Sacraments is duly administered and received ; neither do the heavens ever thus open without the descent of the Holy Ghost.—(*Contemplations*, vol. ii. p. 230. Pratt's Edition.)

The following are from his "Paraphrase on Hard Texts" :—

1 Corinth. xii. 13. "'By one Spirit are we all baptized into one body.' By one and the same Spirit of God, working with and by the outward elements, are we baptized into the communion of one and the same Church."

Galatians iii. 27. " For as many of you as have been baptized into Christ have made Christ your own, and are clothed with His graces, His merits."

Ephes. v. 26. "'That He might sanctify and cleanse it with the washing of water by the Word.' That He might sanctify and cleanse it by His Holy Spirit, working in us by His Word and by His Sacrament of Baptism as the means thereof."

Colos. ii. 11. " In whom also ye are spiritually circumcised in your hearts, by that inward circumcision which is made by His Holy Spirit, and not by the hands of men ; in that ye have, by His gracious work in you, put off your sinful corruptions through the virtue of that circumcision, not which Moses, but which Christ, has wrought in you. The effect of which circumcision ye have received, in that ye have received that Baptism which succeeds that other legal Sacrament ; ye are therefore circumcised in that ye are baptized ; and ye are in Baptism buried together with Christ, in respect of the mortification of your sins, represented by lying under the water ; and in the same Baptism ye rise up with Him, in newness of life, represented by your rising up out of the water again, through that faith of yours which is grounded upon the mighty power of God, who hath raised Him from the dead."

Bishop Hall writes to a Lady Honoria Hay respecting the necessity of Baptism, and the state of those who are necessarily deprived of it. In this letter, whilst reprobating the idea that children are lost who die unbaptized, because their baptism has been unavoidably neglected, he yet takes great care not to ground this, his opinion, on any mere formality in the Sacrament which may allow it to be safely dispensed with, but on the mercy of God, the opinion of the ancient Church, and the analogy of circumcision. The letter, so far as it relates to the subject, begins : " Children are the blessings of parents, and Baptism is the blessing of children and parents : wherein there is not only use, but necessity, in respect not so much of the end as of the precept. God hath enjoined it to the comfort of parents and the behoof of children."

USHER.

Archbishop Usher is sometimes adduced as an opponent of Baptismal Regeneration, on the authority of a "Body of Divinity," in the form of a Catechism, falsely ascribed to him.* This work, however, was repudiated by him in a letter to the editor, a Mr. Downham. It runs thus :—

" SIR,—You may be pleased to take notice that the Catechism you write of is none of mine, but transcribed out of Mr. Cartwright's Catechism, and Mr. Cook's, and some other English divines, but drawn together in one method as a kind of commonplace book, where *other men's* judgments and reasons are strongly laid down, though not approved in all places by the collector : besides that the collection, such as it is, being lent abroad to divers, in scattered sheets, hath for a great part of it miscarried ; the one half of it, I suppose well nigh, being no way to be recovered, *so that so imperfect a thing, copied verbatim out of others, and in divers places dissonant from my own judgment, may not by any means be owned by me.* But if it shall seem good to any industrious person to cut off what is weak and superfluous therein, and supply the wants thereof, and cast it into a new mould of his own framing, I shall be very well content that he make what use he pleaseth of any of the materials thereof, and set out the whole in his own name ; and this is the resolution of your most assured, loving friend,   JA. ARMACHANUS."

In his sermons, vol. xiii. of Elrington's Edition (p. 194), there is a Sacramental Sermon, in which he speaks of the bread and

* The extracts purporting to be from Archbishop Usher in Mr. Ryle's Tracts on Regeneration, and in his "Guide to Churchmen," are from this spurious work, and this notwithstanding the public exposure of its false pretensions some few years ago.

wine of the Holy Communion as "the dishes wherein Christ is served unto us ; that by these the greatest gift is given us, and nourishment conveyed for the maintenance of our spiritual life. *The life was given us in Baptism;* but in and by these signs is conveyed spiritual nourishment for the continuance and maintenance of it."

Again (p. 203), "God hath appointed the Sacrament of the Lord's Supper to strengthen and continue that life which we received in Baptism, as by spiritual nourishment. In Baptism our stock of life is given to us ; by the Sacrament of the Holy Eucharist it is confirmed and continued. If a child be born only, and after birth not nourished, there is none but will know what a death such a soul will die. It will quickly perish by famine. So it is here. Unless Christ be pleased to nourish that life which He hath breathed into me in Baptism, and by His ordinance to give me a new supply and addition of grace, I am a dead man, I am gone for ever—upon this ground, that I receive not the never-perishing food that endureth (as Christ, who is Himself that meat, teacheth us) unto everlasting life."

I would not rely upon the above extract as an *authoritative* statement of the Archbishop's opinions, because these sermons were not published by *him*, but by three Puritan ministers—John Crabb, William Ball, and Thomas Lye—who state "they writ them from his mouth, and compared their notes together." I am aware, also, that Dr. Bernard, the Archbishop's chaplain, declares that any volumes of sermons published in his lifetime were disowned by him ; but taking into consideration the persons who made these notes, I think that the immense probability is that he gave utterance to the above sentiments. Three Puritans who were publishing his sermons were not likely to admit such doctrine unless they had actually heard him preach it.

In a sermon, undoubtedly the Archbishop's, in vol. ii. p. 419, we read, "To begin, therefore, with the first part thereof, as the Apostle in the third to the Galatians maketh our being baptized into Christ to be a testimony that we are all one in Christ, so doth he here make our partaking of that one bread to be an evidence that we also are all one bread and one body in Him. And to the same purpose, in the twelfth chapter following, he propoundeth both our Baptism and our drinking of the Lord's cup as seals of the spiritual conjunction of us all into one mystical body. ' For as the body is one,' saith he, ' and hath many members, and all the members of that one body being many are one body, so also is Christ. For by one Spirit are we *all* baptized into one body,' &c. Afterwards he added that we are the body of Christ, and members in particular ; and in another place, also, that we being many are one body in Christ, and every one members one of another." Now the use which he teacheth us to make of this wonderful conjunction, whereby we are made members of Christ and members of one another. is twofold. 1st, That there should be no schism in the body. 2d, That the members should have the same care one of another.

Again, from Catechism in vol. ii. p. 193. " What is Baptism ?— The Sacrament of our admission into the Church, sealing unto us our new birth, by the communion which we have with Christ Jesus."

JEREMY TAYLOR.

Bishop Jeremy Taylor, in two of his works, viz. " The Life of Christ" (Part I. sec. ix. Discourse 6) and " Liberty of Prophesying" (sec. xviii.), has entered very fully and very deeply into the controversy with the Anabaptists. Let the reader observe, that all throughout his argument he takes the highest ground : viz. that Baptism is an incorporation into the Second Adam, and that infants need this, because they are born with the evil nature of the first Adam.

" Adam sinned, and left nakedness to descend upon his posterity, a relative guilt and a remaining misery ; he left enough to kill us, but nothing to make us alive ; he was the head of mankind in order to temporal felicity, but there was another head intended to be the representative of human nature to bring us to eternal ; but the temporal we lost by Adam, and the eternal we could never receive from him, but from Christ only; from Adam we receive our nature such as it is, but grace and truth come by Jesus Christ ; Adam left us an imperfect nature, that tends to sin and death, but he left us nothing else, and therefore to holiness and life we must enter from another principle. So that besides the natural birth of infants, there must be something added by which they must be reckoned in a new account ; they must be born again, they must be reckoned in Christ, they must be adopted to the inheritance, and admitted to the promise, and entitled to the Spirit. Now, that this is done ordinarily in Baptism is not to be denied : for therefore it is called λουτρὸν παλιγγενεσίας, ' the font or laver of regeneration ;' it is the gate of the Church, it is the solemnity of our admission to the covenant evangelical : and if infants cannot go to heaven by the first or natural birth, then they must go by a second and supernatural ; *and since there is no other solemnity or Sacrament, no way of being born again that we know of but by the ways of God's appointing, and He hath appointed Baptism, and all that are born again are born this way,* even men of reason who have or can receive the Spirit being to enter at the door of Baptism :

it follows that infants also must enter here, or we cannot say
that they are entered at all.   And it is highly considerable, that
whereas the Anabaptist does clamorously and loudly call for a
precept for children's Baptism ; this consideration does his work
for him and us.   He that shows the way, needs not bid you walk
in it : and if there be but one door that stands open, and all
must enter some way or other, it were a strange perverseness of
argument to say that none shall pass in at that door unless they
come alone ; and they that are brought, or they that lean on
crutches or the shoulders of others, shall be excluded and un
done for their infelicity, *and shall not receive help, because they
have the greatest need of it.*"—(*Liberty of Prophesying,* p. 567 ;
Eden's Edition.)

Also : " It is all the reason of the world, that since the grace
of Christ is as large as the prevarication of Adam, all they who
are made guilty by the first Adam should be cleansed by the
Second.   But as they are guilty by another man's act, so they
should be brought to the font to be purified by others ; there
being the same proportion of reason that by others' acts they
should be relieved who were in danger of perishing by the act
of others."—(*Liberty of Prophesying,* p. 541.)

" In Baptism we are born again ; and this infants need in the
present circumstances, and for the same great reason that men of
age and reason do.   For our natural birth is either of itself insuf-
ficient, or is made so by the fall of Adam and the consequent
evils, that nature alone, or our first birth, cannot bring us to
heaven, which is a supernatural end, that is, an end above all the
power of our nature, as now it is.   So that if nature cannot
bring us to heaven, grace must, or we can never get thither ; if
the first birth cannot, a second must : but the second birth spoken
of in Scripture is Baptism ; ' a man must be born of water and of
the Spirit.'   And therefore Baptism is λουτρὸν παλιγγενεσίας, ' the
laver of a new birth.'   Either, then, infants cannot go to heaven
any way that we know of, or they must be baptized.   To say
they are to be left to God is an excuse, and no answer ; for when
God hath opened the door, and calls that the ' entrance into
heaven,' we do not leave them to God when we will not carry
them to Him in the way which He hath described, and at the
door which Himself hath opened ; we leave them indeed, but it
is but helpless and destitute : and though God is better than
man, yet that is no warrant to us ; what it will be to the children,
that we cannot warrant or conjecture.

" And if it be objected that to the new birth are required dispositions of our own, which are to be brought by and in them
that have the use of reason : *besides that this is wholly against*

the analogy of a new birth, in which the person to be born is wholly a passive, and hath put into him the principle which in time will produce its proper actions ; it is certain that they that can receive the new birth are capable of it."—(*Life of Christ,* Part I. sec. ix. p. 260.)

" It (Baptism) does not heal the wounds of actual sins, because they (infants) have not committed them ; but it takes off the evil of original sin ; whatsoever is imputed to us by Adam's prevarication, is washed off by the death of the Second Adam, into which we are baptized."—(*Life of Christ,* Part I. sec. ix. p. 261.)

PEARSON.

" It is certain that forgiveness of sins was promised to all who were baptized in the name of Christ ; and it cannot be doubted but all persons who did perform all things necessary to the receiving the ordinance of Baptism, did also receive the benefit of that ordinance, which is *remission of sins.* '*John did baptize in the wilderness, and preach the baptism of repentance for the remission of sins.*' And St. Peter made this the exhortation of his first sermon, '*Repent, and be baptized every one of you in the name of Jesus Christ for the remission of sins.*' In vain doth doubting and fluctuating Socinus endeavour to evacuate the evidence of this Scripture ; attributing the remission either to repentance, without consideration of Baptism, or else to the public profession of faith made in Baptism ; or if anything must be attributed to Baptism itself, it must be nothing but a declaration of such remission. For how will these shifts agree with that which Ananias said unto Saul, without any mention either of repentance or confession, '*Arise and be baptized, and wash away thy sins*'? And that which St. Paul, who was so baptized, hath taught us concerning the Church, that Christ doth *sanctify and cleanse it with the washing of water ?* It is therefore sufficiently certain that Baptism as it was instituted by Christ, after the preadministration of St. John, wheresoever it was received with all qualifications necessary in the person accepting, and conferred with all things necessary to be performed by the person administering, was most infallibly efficacious as to this particular, that is, to the remission of all sins committed before the administration of this sacrament.

". . . He gave His life a sacrifice for sin—He laid it down as a ransom, even His precious blood, as a price by way of compensation and satisfaction to the will and justice of God ; by which propitiation God, who was by our sins offended, became reconciled, and being so, took off our obligation to eternal punishment, which is the guilt of our sins, and appointed in the Church of Christ the sacrament of Baptism for the first remission, and repentance for the constant forgiveness of all following trespasses. And thus I believe THE FORGIVENESS OF SINS."—(*Exposition of Creed ;* Article, " Forgiveness of Sins.")

" Nothing in the whole compass of the Christian religion is more sure than the exceeding great and most certain efficacy of Baptism to spiritual good. There is, no doubt, an outward and visible sign ; but what is signified by it is an invisible grace, and the sign itself was instituted for the very purpose that it should communicate this grace."—(*Minor Theological Works*, Churton's Ed. vol. i. p. 312.)

I owe this latter quotation to Mr. Gibson's valuable collection of testimonies.

BEVERIDGE.

" What He (Christ) means by being ' born of water and of the Spirit' is now made a question : I say now, for it was never made so till of late years ; for many ages together none ever doubted of it, but the whole Christian world took it for granted that our Saviour, by these words, meant only, that except a man be baptized according to His institution, he cannot enter into the kingdom of God, this being the most plain and obvious sense of the words, *forasmuch as there is no other way of being born again of water, as well as of the Spirit, but only in the Sacrament of Baptism. . . .* But that we may be thus born of the Spirit we must be born also of water, which our Saviour here puts in the first place. Not as if there was any such virtue in water, whereby it could regenerate us ; but because this is the rite or ordinance appointed by Christ wherein to regenerate us by His Holy Spirit : our regeneration is wholly the act of the Spirit of Christ. But there must be something done on our parts in order to it, and something that is instituted and ordained by Christ Himself, which in the Old Testament was Circumcision ; in the New, Baptism, or washing with water—the easiest that could be invented, and the most proper to signify His cleansing and regenerating us by His Holy Spirit. And seeing this is instituted by Christ Himself, as we cannot be born of water without the Spirit, so neither can we, in an ordinary way, be born of the Spirit without water, used or applied in obedience and conformity to His institution. Christ hath joined them together, and it is not in our power to part them : he that would be born of the Spirit must be born of water too.

" This is that which the Apostle also teacheth us where he saith that God our Saviour, according to His mercy, saves us by 'the washing of regeneration, and by the renewing of the Holy Ghost:' by the washing with water, as the sign of our regeneration, and by the renewing of the Holy Ghost, as the thing signified; which is the same in effect with our being born 'of water and of the Spirit,' and a clear explication of it."

In some observations in the same sermon on Matthew xxviii. 19, "Go ye and teach all nations, baptizing them," &c., the Bishop has the following :—" Whosoever understands and consults the original words in the text, will plainly see that our Saviour's meaning is, that not only Jews, but all nations, should be made His disciples by being ' Baptized in the name of the Father, and of the Son, and of the Holy Ghost,' and, by consequence, that this is the way whereby to be ' born of water and of the Spirit,' as He speaks in my text. For as baptizing necessarily implies the use of water, so our being made thereby disciples of Christ as necessarily implies our partaking of His Spirit : for all that are baptized, and so made the disciples of Christ, are thereby made the members of His body, and are therefore said to be ' baptized into Christ.' *But they who are in Christ, members of His body, must needs partake of the Spirit that is in Him, their head.* Neither doth the Spirit of Christ only follow upon, but certainly accompanies, the Sacrament of Baptism, when duly administered according to His institution. For, as St. Paul saith, ' By one Spirit we are all baptized into one body.' So that in the very act of Baptism the Spirit unites us unto Christ, and makes us members of His body, and if of His body, then of His Church and kingdom, that being all His body."

At the end of the sermon, the Bishop has some powerful and pertinent observations upon the responsibility connected with all this, in which he addresses all the baptized to whom he was preaching as already partakers of these benefits of Holy Baptism, but also as in danger of falling from them. All unreal hypotheses that they might have been baptized, and yet, owing to a secret decree, have received no benefit therein, is utterly discarded.

" After all we must observe, that although our blessed Saviour here saith, ' that except a man be born of water and of the Spirit, he cannot enter into the kingdom of God ;' yet He doth not say that every one that is so born shall inherit eternal life. It is true, *all* that are baptized, or born of water and the Spirit, are thereby admitted into the Church, or kingdom of God upon earth ; but except they submit to the government and obey the laws established in it, they forfeit all their right and title to the kingdom of heaven. They are brought into a state of salvation ; but unless they continue in it, and live accordingly, they cannot be saved. For, as St. Peter observeth, ' Baptism now

saves us (not the putting away of the filth of the flesh, but the
answer of a good conscience towards God) by the resurrection of
Jesus Christ.' Baptism puts us into the way of heaven ; but
unless we walk in that way, we can never come thither. When
we were baptized, we were born of water and the Spirit, so as to
have the seed of grace sown in our hearts, sufficient to enable us
to bring forth the fruits of the Spirit, to overcome temptations,
to believe aright in God our Saviour, and to obey and serve Him
faithfully all the days of our life. . . . But if we neglect
to perform what we then promised, and so do not *answer the end
of our Baptism*, by keeping our conscience void of offence toward
God and men, *we lose all the benefit of it*, and shall as certainly
perish as if we had never been baptized. . . .
    " And as for you who are already baptized and born of water
and of the Spirit, remember the promise which ye then made, and
perform it. . . . You were then made the members of Christ,
and so interested in all the merits of His death and passion. You
were then taken out of the world, and translated into the Church
of Christ, to be instructed, governed, assisted, protected, sanctified, justified, and saved by Him. You were then made 'the
children of God ; and if children, then heirs, heirs of God, and
joint heirs with Jesus Christ :' and therefore heirs of the kingdom of heaven and eternal life, which you cannot miss of, *unless
you provoke your heavenly Father to disinherit you*, by the neglect
of your duty to Him, and by the breach of the promise which
you made when you were admitted into this happy state, and by
not repenting of it when you may."—(*Sermons*, xxxv. vol. ii. in
" Library of Anglo-Catholic Theology.")

WESLEY.

    " What are the benefits we receive by Baptism ? is the next
point to be considered. And the first of these is, the washing
away the guilt of original sin, by the application of the merits of
Christ's death. That we are all born under the guilt of Adam's
sin, and that all sin deserves eternal misery, was the unanimous
sense of the ancient Church, as it is expressed in the Ninth
Article of our own. And the Scripture plainly asserts that we
were 'shapen in iniquity, and in sin did our mother conceive us ;'
that we were all 'by nature children of wrath, and dead in trespasses and sins ;' that 'in Adam all die ;' that 'by one man's
disobedience all were made sinners ;' that, ' by one man sin
entered into the world, and death by sin, which came upon all
men, because all had sinned.' This plainly includes infants, for

they too die ; therefore they have sinned : but not by actual sin, therefore by original ; else what need have they of the death of Christ ? Yea, 'death reigned from Adam to Moses, even over those who had not sinned' actually, 'according to the similitude of Adam's transgression.' This, which can relate to infants only, is a clear proof that the whole race of mankind are obnoxious both to the guilt and punishment of Adam's transgression. But, 'as by the offence of one judgment came upon all men to condemnation, so by the righteousness of One the free gift came upon all men to justification of life.' *And the virtue of this free gift, the merits of Christ's life and death, are applied to us in Baptism.* 'He gave Himself for the Church, that He might sanctify and cleanse it with the washing of water by the Word' (Eph. v. 25, 26)—namely, in Baptism, *the ordinary instrument of our justification.* Agreeably to this, our Church prays, in the Baptismal Office, that the person to be baptized may be washed and sanctified by the Holy Ghost, and, being delivered from God's wrath, receive remission of sins, and enjoy the everlasting benediction of His heavenly washing ; and declares in the Rubric at the end of the Office, 'It is certain, by God's Word, that children who are baptized, dying before they commit actual sin, are saved.' "—(*Wesley's Treatise on Baptism*, Works, vol. x. p. 190.)

I have given two extracts of the same import from this treatise of Wesley's on page 226. I am well aware that in a sermon on the new birth Wesley disjoins the birth of water from that of the Spirit in the case of adults ; but then, in the same sermon, he as expressly pronounces that they go together in the case of infants. "I do not now speak with regard to infants. It is certain our Church supposes that all who are baptized in their infancy are at the same time born again ; and it is allowed that the whole Office for the Baptism of Infants proceeds upon this supposition. Nor is it an objection of any weight against this, that we cannot comprehend how this work can be wrought in infants. For neither can we comprehend how it is wrought in a person of riper years." *

DR. ARNOLD.

" Conceive of one—the thing is rare, but not impossible—of one who had been so kept from evil, and so happily led forward in good, that ,when arrived at boyhood, his soul had scarcely more

---

* The reader will find a full discussion of Wesley's opinions on Baptismal Regeneration of Infants, as affecting the relations of the Wesleyans to the Church, in my "Doctrinal Revision of the Liturgy," pp. 38—44.

stain upon it than when it was first fully cleansed, and forgiven,
in Baptism ! Conceive him speaking truth, without any effort, on
all occasions ; not greedy, not proud, not violent, not selfish, not
feeling conscious that he was living a life of sin, and therefore
glad to come to God, rather than shrink away from Him !
Conceive how completely to such an one would Christ's words be
fulfilled, ' Seek and ye shall find' !   When would his prayers be
unblessed or unfruitful ?   When would he turn his thoughts to
God without feeling pleasure in so doing ; without a lively consciousness of God's love to him ; without an assured sense of the
reality of things not seen, of redemption and grace and glory ?
Would not the communion with God enjoyed by one so untainted
come up to the full measure of those high promises, ' It shall
come to pass that before they call I will answer, and while they
are yet speaking I will hear' ? " —(Sermons on Christian Life, its
Course, &c., page 126.)*

I desire now, in conclusion, to draw the reader's attention to
the persons from whose writings I have selected the foregoing
extracts, and also to the principle on which I have selected the
extracts themselves.

The persons whose determinations on this subject I have
adduced were all men who appear to have been actuated by the
love, and taught by the Spirit, of God.   They were all (as far as
we can judge from accounts of their lives, and from their writings)
converted men, in the modern and popular sense of the term. They
were also men in whom the word of God dwelt richly ; they
appear to wish to frame their teaching according to it, for they
appeal to it at every turn.   Moreover, the greater part of them
were men of deep learning and extensive theological reading, and
they appear also to have well digested what they read.   They
were also men of the highest qualities of mind.   Some of them
have moulded the faith of nations ; all, or nearly all, have won
the highest place in theological literature.   Not one of them had
the slightest leaning to the corruptions of the Church of Rome.
Some of them spent their whole lives in opposing its pretensions.

They were all, in the present acceptation of the word, " Evangelical," if to be evangelical means to set forth the Saviour as
the sinner's only hope, and the Holy Spirit as the Agent by Whom
alone Christ can be formed in the soul.

* The reader who desires further proof of the opinions of all the leading
Fathers, Reformers, and Anglican divines of all schools in favour of the Church
doctrine of Baptism is referred to a vast mass of testimonies in Mr. Gibson's
valuable collection, entitled, "The Testimony of Sacred Scripture, the Church
of the First Five Centuries, and the Reformed Church of England, to the
Nature and Effects of Holy Baptism." (London : Bell and Daldy.)

If there be any antagonism between Sacramental and Evangelical doctrine, they must have perceived it as clearly as the men who now assume to represent them. All the difficulties that beset Infant Baptismal Regeneration must have presented themselves as strongly to their minds as to those of the leaders of that party amongst us who repudiate sacramental truth. They were also by no means men of one school; on the contrary, there are amongst them men of very opposite habits of thought, and of very different religious training.

Let the reader also notice the principle on which I have made these extracts. The greater part bear directly upon, and assert the Regeneration of Infants in Baptism (for infants are expressly named). In no case is the slightest limitation expressed, as if the elect only received baptismal grace.

Observe also that these extracts are mostly of some length, so that they have some context to guide the reader in judging whether they fairly express the author's full meaning. They are not short sentences or parts of sentences, torn from the context —from places where the writer is occupied with the consideration of some opposite error, and so looks rather to building up a present argument than to the agreement of each particular clause with the rest of Christian truth.

In the last place, the reader will notice, how dishonest it is to quote these writers as not holding the Regeneration of Infants in Baptism, because they sometimes use the word "regenerate" in its loose or popular sense, as meaning real Christian.*

They sometimes use the word (as St. John does) as describing the full effect intended by God to be produced by baptismal grace —the fruitful abiding in Christ, without for a moment meaning to deny, as the above extracts abundantly show, the reception of this grace in Baptism.

* Such writers as Barrow, South, Tillotson, &c. so use it.

APPENDIX C.

In the following pages the reader will find, put side by side, certain statements of St. Augustine on Predestination to Life and on the effects of Baptism on all Infants; and after this, in similar juxtaposition, the opinions of those mediæval divines who expounded Augustine, and adopted his language on both Election and Baptismal Regeneration, without any perceptible deviation from the views of their great master.

This is done for two reasons: first, to show Predestinarians generally how in former ages men gifted with the highest intellect, and undoubtedly spiritual men, expressed themselves in the most unmistakable terms in favour of the Regeneration of all Infants brought to Baptism, and also of the absolute Predestination to Life of those who will eventually be saved.

Secondly, to show how dishonest, as well as futile, are the assertions that our Reformers could not have believed in Baptismal Regeneration, and understood the assertions in their own service absolutely, because we have received from them the Seventeenth Article, as well as the Service for the Baptism of Infants.

If Predestination to life was asserted by Augustine (to whom our Reformers refer in every page of their writings), and also by the Schoolmen, such as Aquinas, Anselm, Bernard,and Peter Lombard, in as strong terms as Calvin himself could use, then what an absurd anachronism to call our Seventeenth Article *Calvinistic*, as if Predestination had never been heard of before the time of John Calvin, and had not been held by a succession of writers, from St. Augustine downwards, with all of whose writings our Reformers were familiar! And if Augustine and this succession of mediæval writers asserted equally absolutely and unreservedly Infant Baptismal Regeneration, then what dishonesty to say that the holding of Predestination to Life by our Reformers was incompatible with their also holding Baptismal Regeneration, when the very divines from whom our Reformers derived what Predestinarian views they had held equally strongly and unreservedly the Regeneration of all baptized Infants!

AUGUSTINE.

PREDESTINATION TO LIFE.

Now this election the Apostle demonstrating to be, not of merits going before in good works, but election of grace, saith thus : "*And at this time a remnant by election of grace is saved,*" &c. This is election of grace ; that is, election in which through the grace of God men are elected : this, I say, is election of grace, which goes before all good merits of men. For if it be to any good merits that it is given, then it is no more gratuitously given, but is paid as a debt, and consequently is not truly called grace ; where "*reward,*" as the same Apostle saith, "is not imputed as grace, but as debt." Whereas if, that it may be true grace, that is, gratuitous, it find nothing in man to which it is due of merit (which thing is well understood by that saying, "Thou wilt save them for nothing," Psalm lvi. 7, Septuagint), then assuredly itself gives the merits, not to merits is given. Consequently it goes before even faith, from which it is that all good works begin. "*For the just,*" as is written, "*shall live by faith.*" But, moreover, grace not only assists the just, but also justifies the ungodly. And therefore when it does aid the just, and seems to be rendered to his merits, not even then does it cease to be grace, because that which it aids it did itself bestow. With a view therefore to this grace, which precedes all good merits of men, not only was Christ put to death by the ungodly, but died for the ungodly. And ere that He died He elected the Apostles, not of course then just, but to be justified : to whom He saith, "*I have chosen you out of the world.*" For to whom He said, "*Ye are not of the world,*" and then, lest they should account themselves never to have been in the world, presently added, "But I have chosen you out of the world ;" assuredly that they should not be of the world was conferred upon them by His own election of them. Wherefore, if it had been through their own righteousness, not through His grace, that they were elected, they would not have been chosen out of the world, because they would already be not of the world if already they were just. And again, if

BAPTISMAL REGENERATION.

He (St. Paul, Rom. vi.) proposed to himself the question, whether one be to continue in sin, in order to obtain abundance of grace. But he answered, "Far be it !" and added, "If we are dead to sin, how shall we live therein ?" (Rom. vi. 2.) Then, in order to show that we are dead to sin : "*What, know ye not,*" says he, "*how that we, whosoever have been baptized in Jesus Christ, have been baptized into His death ?*" If, therefore, we are hence shown to be dead to sin, in that we have been baptized in the death of Christ, assuredly little children also who are baptized in Christ die unto sin, because they are baptized in His death. FOR WITHOUT ANY EXCEPTION IT IS SAID : "So many of us as have been baptized in Christ Jesus, have been baptized into His death." And therefore it is said, that it may be shown that we are dead to sin. But to what sin do little children die by being born again, except to that which, by being born, they have derived? and thus to them also pertains what follows, wherein he says : "*Therefore we have been buried with Him through Baptism unto death, that in like manner as Christ,*" &c.—*Enchiridion* (written after A.D. 420), translated in "Library of the Fathers," vol. xxii. page 117.

This is that very thing which is solemnized among us, the great Sacrament of Baptism, that whosoever pertain to that grace may die unto sin, as He is said to have died unto sin who died unto the flesh, that is, the likeness of sin : and may live by being born again from the laver (as He also by rising again from the grave), of whatever age their bodies be. For from the little child but lately born even to the decrepit old man, as no one is to be prohibited from Baptism, so there is no one who in Baptism dies not unto sin : but little children only to original sin ; elder persons however die unto all those sins also whatsoever by ill-living they had added to that which they derived by birth.—*Enchiridion,* p. 113, vol. xxii. of Oxford Translation.

That poisonous serpent stung the whole mass of mankind in the first

| PREDESTINATION TO LIFE. | BAPTISMAL REGENERATION. |

the reason why they were elected was that they were already just, they had already first chosen the Lord. For who can be righteous but by choosing righteousness? But Christ is the end of the law for righteousness, &c. &c.

But it was not so, as Himself saith to them, "Ye have not chosen me, but I have chosen you." Of which the Apostle John saith, "Not that we loved God, but that He loved us."— *De Patientia*, pp. 555—557, "Library of the Fathers," vol. xxii.

Whoever, therefore, are separated by Divine grace from that original damnation, we doubt not but that there is procured for them the hearing of the Gospel; that when they hear, they believe, and that in that faith which worketh by love they continue unto the end: that if they even go astray they are corrected, and being corrected grow better, or that if they are not corrected by men, they still return into the path they left. All these things in them He worketh whose handiwork they are, and who made them vessels of mercy; He who chose them in His Son before the foundation of the world, according to the election of grace: "and if of grace, then no more of works: otherwise grace is no more grace." These were not called so as not to be chosen, as those of whom we hear, "many are called, but few chosen;" but they are called according to His purpose, and therefore elected according to the election of grace. . . .

They are chosen to reign with Christ; not as Judas was chosen, of whom our Lord said, "I have chosen you twelve, and one of you is a devil," *i.e.* chosen for the work of damnation: but chosen in pity, as He was in judgment; chosen to obtain their kingdom, as He was to spill His own blood.—*De Correptione et Gratiâ*, chap. vii. (translated in *Christian Remembrancer*, January, 1850, No. lxvii. vol. xix. page 6).

Such is the predestination of the saints, the foreknowledge, that is, and preparation of the Divine acts of grace, by which every one is infallibly saved who is saved. But for the rest, where are they but in that mass of perdition

man. No one passes from the first man to the second man except through the Sacrament of Baptism. In children born, and not yet baptized, let Adam be recognised. In children born and baptized, and on this account born again, let Christ be recognised.—Sermon on 1 Tim. i. 15 (Benedictine Edition, vol. vii. p. 834, translated in "Gibson's Testimonies," p. 241).*

If you understand this aright, you would with simplicity and truth acknowledge the grace of Christ towards infants, and not be driven to say things so exceedingly impious and absurd, either that infants ought not to be baptized, or that so great a Sacrament is, in their case so utter a mockery, that they are baptized in a Saviour, and not saved; redeemed by a Deliverer, but not delivered; washed in the laver of regeneration, but not cleansed.—*Against Julian, the Pelagian* (A.D. 421), iii. 11 (Ed. Bened. tom. xiii. p. 690).

We affirm therefore that the Holy Spirit dwells in baptized infants, though they know it not; for after the same manner they know Him not, though He be in them; as they know not their own soul, the reasoning faculty of which, though they cannot yet make use of it, is in them, as a spark, dormant for the present, which will kindle as they grow in years.— *Epistle* (57) *to Dardanus*, quoted in Wall, vol. i. page 278. (Ed. Ben. vol. ii. p. 893, written about 417 A.D.)

If the child live after Baptism, and come to an age capable of obeying God's commandments, then he has that concupiscence to fight against, and with God's help to conquer, IF HE HAVE NOT RECEIVED HIS GRACE IN VAIN, AND IF HE RESOLVE NOT TO BECOME A CASTAWAY.—*On the Guilt and Remission of Sin*, i. 69 (written about 412), Ed. Ben. vol. xiii. 47, 48 (Gibson's "Testimonies," p. 255).

And when once the child has received the grace of Christ, he does not lose it, UNLESS BY HIS OWN UNGODLINESS, IF IN ADVANCING YEARS HE

The references to Augustine's Works are to the Benedictine Edition, published at Venice (Bassano), 1802.

PREDESTINATION TO LIFE.

where the Divine justice most justly leaves them? where the Tyrians are, and the Zidonians are, who would have been able to believe had they seen the miracles of Christ; but who, inasmuch as faith was not destined for them, were denied the *means* of faith as well.—*De Dono Perseverantiæ*, cxiv. (*Christian Remembrancer*, No. lxvii. page 7).

Of two pious men, why final perseverance is given to one and not given to another, is a still more inscrutable part of God's judgments. But thus much we are quite certain of, that one is predestinated and the other not.— *De Dono Perseverantiæ*, ch. viii. ix.

Whence is clearly shown that the grace of beginning and the grace of persevering to the end is not given according to our merits, but is given according to a MOST SECRET, most just, most wise, most beneficent will, inasmuch as whom He predestinated, them He also called, and called with that calling of which it is said, "the gifts and calling of God are without repentance." TO WHICH CALLING NO MAN MUST BE certainly asserted by man to pertain till he has departed this life. — *De Dono Perseverantiæ*, c. xiii. (*Christian Remembrancer*, as above, p. 9).

BAPTISMAL REGENERATION.

TURNS OUT SO BAD. For then he will begin to have sins of his own, which are not to be taken away by regeneration, but remedied by another mode of cure.—*Epistle to Bonifacius*, xcviii. 2, circa A.D. 408, vol. ii. p. 347.

Let not that disturb you, that some people do not bring their infants to Baptism with that faith (or purpose) that they may by spiritual grace be regenerated to eternal life, but because they think they do procure or preserve their bodily health by this remedy. FOR THE CHILDREN DO NOT THEREFORE FAIL OF BEING REGENERATED, BECAUSE THEY ARE NOT BROUGHT BY THE OTHERS WITH THIS INTENTION. — *Epistle to Bonifacius*, quoted in Wall, vol. i. page 263 (Ed. Ben. vol. ii. pages 348, 349).

Therefore the Baptism of Infants is no more than is necessary: that they who by their generation are subject to that condemnation, may by regeneration be freed from it. And as there is not a person in the world who is carnally generated but from Adam, so neither is any spiritually regenerated but by Christ. The carnal generation is liable to that one offence and the condemnation thereof; but the spiritual regeneration takes away not only that for which infants are baptized, but also those many which, by wicked living, men have added to that in which they are generated.—*Epistle to Hilarius*, Wall, page 394 (Ed. Ben. vol. ii. page 711, written about A.D. 414).

Who knows not that if a baptized infant comes to years of discretion and believe not, nor restrain himself from unlawful lusts, WHAT HE RECEIVED AS A LITTLE ONE WILL PROFIT HIM NOTHING?—*De Peccatorum Meritis et Remissione*, ch. 19 (§ 25).

When infants then are conformed to the death of Christ by the Sacrament of Baptism, we must acknowledge that they are freed from the bite of the serpent, if we would not err from the rule of the Christian faith.—*De Peccatorum Meritis et Remissione*, ii. ch. 27 (§ 43); *Christian Remembrancer*, No. xciii. page 237.

Those that have been born of sinful flesh escape from the condemnation which is the due of the old man by the

BAPTISMAL REGENERATION.

Sacrament of Spiritual Regeneration and Renewal. For on account of the questions which have been raised, or yet may be raised, on this subject, we ought especially to observe and remember this, that the *remission of all sin is alone* effected fully and perfectly in Baptism : yet that the quality of the man himself is not wholly changed at once ; but that by a newness, increasing from day to day *in those who make good progress*, the spiritual firstfruits change into themselves what was old and carnal, till the whole is so renewed that even the animal infirmity of the body comes to spiritual firmness and incorruption. — *De Peccatorum Meritis et Remissione*, lib. ii. ch. 27 (§ 44.)

" Let the reader mark the following places :—
Would ye know the Holy Ghost, that He is God ? Be baptized, and ye will be His temple.—*De Symbolo*, "Library of the Fathers," vol. xxii. page 574.
The very sin which He remits first, He remits not but to the baptized. When? When they are baptized. The sins which are afterwards remitted upon prayer, upon penance, to whom He remits, it is to the baptized that he remitteth. For how can they say "Our Father," who are not yet born sons ? The Catechumens, as long as they be such, have upon them all their sins.—Page 575.
Nicodemus did understand aright the birth of flesh ; so understand thou too the birth of the Spirit, as Nicodemus understood the birth of the flesh. What did Nicodemus understand? Can man enter anew into his mother's womb and be born? So whosoever shall bid thee be spiritually born a second time, answer thou in the words of Nicodemus, "*Can a man enter a second time into his mother's womb, and be born?* Already I am born of Adam ; Adam cannot gender me a second time : already I am born of Christ : Christ cannot gender me a second time. As of the womb there can be no repetition, so neither of Baptism."
—On John iii. 5, in "Homilies on St. John's Gospel," Oxford Trans. page 171.
Nothing more execrable or detestable can be said or thought, than that when the form of Baptism is imparted to infants it is unreal or fallacious, in that remission of sins is spoken of and appears to be given, and yet is not at all effected.—*De Peccatorum Meritis et Remissione*, lib. i. ch. 34, sec. 62, vol. xiii. page 43.

BERNARD.

PREDESTINATION TO LIFE.

Showed him the kingdom of God. The kingdom of God is granted, is promised, is shown, is received. It is granted in predestination, is promised in vocation, is shown in justification, is received in glorification. Whence the invitation, "Come, ye blessed of my Father, receive the kingdom of God." For thus saith the Apostle, "Whom He predestinated, them He also called ; and whom He called, them

BAPTISMAL REGENERATION.

What is the grace then wherewith by Baptism we are invested ? Assuredly the purging away of our sins. . . .
We soon can be washed, but for our healing there is need of much care and pains. We are washed then in Baptism because the handwriting of our condemnation is then taken out of the way, and this grace is conferred upon us, that now henceforth concupiscence

PREDESTINATION TO LIFE.

He also justified; and whom He justified, them He also glorified." In predestination is grace, in vocation is power, in justification is joy, in glorification is glory.—St. Bernard's *Works*, Paris Edition, 1640, p. 392; *Christian Remembrancer*, No. lxvii. page 10.

Now consider with me, that in this great work of our salvation are three things of which God claims for Himself the authorship, and which He does prior to all assistance and concurrence, viz. predestination, vocation, inspiration. Predestination precedes not only the rise of the Church, but the foundation of the world. Predestination is before time, vocation with time, inspiration in time.

According to Predestination, the time never was when the Church of the elect was not with God; nay, and if the unbeliever wonders, he shall wonder still more—was not acceptable —was not beloved. But why should I use my own language upon a mystery which the delator of the heavenly councils has unfolded straight from the Divine mind? St. Paul has not shrunk from disclosing this secret respecting the Divine goodness. "He hath blessed us with all spiritual blessings in heavenly places in Christ, according as He hath chosen us in Him before the foundation of the world, that we should be holy and without blame before Him in love, having predestinated us," &c.—*Works*, page 804, *Christian Remembrancer*, as above, page 11.

BAPTISMAL REGENERATION.

should not injure us at all if we withhold our consent, and so, as it were, the corrupted humour of the inveterate ulcer is removed, whilst condemnation is taken away, and the sentence of death which before proceeded from it.—*From Sermon "in Cœna Domini."*

For with Him there is no stinted, but plenteous redemption. For what proportion does the number (*i.e.* of infants) bear to the greatness of the price of their redemption? They then who would empty Him of His goodness rather wrong themselves. For what if the infant cannot speak for himself on whose behalf the voice of his Brother's blood, AND SUCH A BROTHER, crieth to God from the earth.

The Church, his mother, stands by and cries on his account no less (earnestly). What then does the infant do? Does he not seem to thee to pant eagerly after a certain fashion for the fountains of salvation, to call aloud to God, and in his childish cries to exclaim, "O Lord, I am oppressed, intreat for me . . . .?" So then all these cry aloud on his behalf—the blood of his Brother, the faith of his mother, the very destitution of the miserable, and the misery of his destitution, and they cry to the Father, and the Father too cannot deny Himself, for He is the FATHER.—*Sermones in Cantica.* Vol. 183 of Migne's "Patrologia," pp. 1098, 1099.

AQUINAS.

PREDESTINATION TO LIFE.

God wished to represent His goodness in the human race, but He represents it multiformly. As respects some, those viz. whom He predestinates, He represents it *per modum misericordiæ*, by sparing them; as respects others, those viz. whom He reprobates, He represents it *per modum justitiæ*, by punishing them. This is the reason why God elects some and reprobates others. It is the reason which the Apostle assigns in the Epistle to the Romans, when he says, "God, willing to show His wrath (*i.e.* the

BAPTISMAL REGENERATION.

Question—Has Baptism an equal effect in all? I answer that we must affirm that the effect of Baptism is twofold; one *per se*, the other *per accidens*. The effect of Baptism *per se* is that for the producing of which Baptism was instituted, *i.e.* to regenerate men to spiritual life, and this effect it produces equally in all who are equally disposed to Baptism (or who receive the Sacrament with like dispositions of mind). Hence because all children receive Baptism with like dispositions, since they are baptized

vengeance of His justice) and to make His power known, endured (*i.e.* permitted) with much long-suffering the vessels of wrath fitted to destruction, that He might make known the riches of His glory on the vessels of mercy, which He had afore prepared unto glory." And again, "In a great house there are not only vessels of gold and silver, but also of wood and earth, and some to honour and some to dishonour." But why God hath elected some and reprobated others there is no account to be given, except the Divine will, as St. Augustine saith, "Why He draweth this man, and draweth not that, desire not to explain, if thou desirest not to err. . . . Nor can any charge of injustice be brought against God on this account, because He provides unequally for beings who are to begin with equal. This would, indeed, be contrary to justice, if that which Predestination conveyed to a man were given him because it was owing to him. But this is not the case. That which Predestination conveys is the result of free grace; and in matters of free grace a person can give more or less, exactly as he likes, without infringing any rule of justice.— *Summa Theologica*, pars 1, q. 23, a. 5. Translated in *Christian Remembrancer*, No. lxvii. page 15.

Art. 5. Whether the foreknowledge of desert is the cause of Predestination. It might appear that the knowledge of desert was the cause of Predestination; because, after mentioning other points, it might be argued that Predestination is an act of the Divine Will; and that we cannot suppose the Divine Will to act without reason; and no other reason can be given for it to act upon but this foreknowledge of desert in the individuals predestinated. But the contrary is asserted by St. Paul, Epistle to Titus iii. 5, "Not by works of righteousness which we have done, but according to His mercy He saved us." As He hath saved us, so hath He predestinated us to be saved. *Therefore He hath not predestinated us to be saved* on account of any works of righteousness foreseen to be done by us.— Ibid. p. 1, q. 23, a. 7. Translated in *Christian Remembrancer*, as above, p. 16.

not in their own faith, but in the faith of the Church, *all receive an equal effect in Baptism.*

Adults, on the contrary, since they approach to Baptism through their own faith, are not equally disposed when they receive it, for some approach to Baptism with greater, some with less, devotion, and so some receive more, some less, of the grace of renewal, as from the same fire he who approaches nearest to it receives the most heat, although the fire, so far as itself is concerned, pours its heat equally on all.— *Summa Theologica*, pars tertia (page 661 of vol. iv. of his works, in Migne's "Patrologia").

Children contract original sin from the transgression of Adam, which thing is manifest from this, that they are subject to that mortality which passed upon all men through the sin of the first Adam, as the Apostle says in the same place. Whence much more can children receive grace through Christ that they may reign in eternal life. But the Lord Himself says, "Except one be born of water and of the Spirit, he cannot enter," &c. Whence it has become necessary that children should be baptized, that as through Adam they incurred damnation by being born, so through Christ they might obtain salvation by being born again.— *Summa Theologica*, pars tertia, quæst. lxviii. vol. iv. p. 646, in Migne.

The above extracts will serve to show that if our Reformers were influenced by the opinions of Augustine, so as to derive from him the Augustinian theory of Election, they would find in their oracle on this subject equally clear enunciations of the Baptismal Regeneration of all infants brought to the font.

The absurdity of supposing that our Reformers were in the least degree influenced by the name or writings of Calvin is amply refuted by the works of the Reformation period, published by the Parker Society.

A very full and complete index to the fifty-three volumes closes the series.

In this index the references to the name and works of Calvin occupy two pages and a half, whereas the references to Augustine occupy thirty-eight pages. Of these two pages and a half of references to Calvin, above one page and a half (i.e. considerably above half) are from the writings of Whitgift, who by no stretch of language can be called one of our Reformers, as he was an undergraduate at Cambridge at the death of Edward the Sixth, and only ordained in 1560. Of these references in Whitgift's works, nearly all are references to Calvin's opinions on the Church and its Ministry as bearing on the Puritan controversy.

Of the remainder of the references to Calvin, four-fifths are from Elizabethan divines, or from Bullinger, who never set foot in England in his life.

Cranmer only mentions Calvin once, and that in a somewhat formal and supercilious letter to him, inviting him to a general conference of the Reformers, English and Foreign.

Ridley never once alludes to him. Latimer but once, as having written well against the Interim. His Predestinarian views are only alluded to twice : once by Philpott, as being in accordance with the ancient doctors of the Church ; once by an obscure individual, named Traheron, who only figures in the Zurich Letters as a correspondent of Bullinger.

Calvin was absolutely unknown as a Predestinarian to the leaders of the English Reformation, and no marvel, for he advanced nothing new. He only stated harshly what Thomas Aquinas and the Romish Schoolmen had stated long before him. He wrote well on this, as he did on every subject, because he had a clear head, with a cold, spiteful, unloving heart.

The only difference between him and the Predestinarians who preceded him was, that he held Predestinarianism in *antagonism*, whilst Augustine and his successors held it in *subordination*, to other great doctrines of the faith.

The reader may ask, How is it that Augustine expresses himself so absolutely and unreservedly in favour of two doctrines which we are now told cannot be held together?

I answer, that he himself tells us how he does so by his quotations from Scripture. When his subject leads him to speak of Predestination, he quotes the passages usually brought forward in favour of it, and deduces from them Predestinarian doctrine. When his subject leads him to take up, or defend, the doctrine of Baptismal Regeneration, he quotes the texts which assert Baptismal Grace, or the analogy between the two Adams, and equally unreservedly deduces from them the doctrine they contain or imply.

For instance, in the first of the extracts which I have given (that from the Enchiridion) Augustine especially notices the universality of the Apostolic assertion, "*So many of us as were baptized,*" &c.

Then, with respect to Augustine's reconciliation of these statements in his own mind, it appears to me that he took no pains to do so. I believe that if formally called upon to do so, he would have repudiated the attempt, as irreverently trenching upon the deep things of God.

One thing, however, is perfectly clear, which is, that he did not use for this purpose the hypothetical assumption, as men now use it to set aside the statements of the Bible and the Prayer-Book.

Those who now make use of the hypothetical theory confine its application entirely to the time of the administration of Baptism. They say that our Service is constructed on the idea that you are charitably to assume or suppose that the baptized child is regenerate ; but, as soon as ever the reasoning faculties of the child develop, then you are at once to drop all idea of hypothesis or charitable assumption, and you are to judge whether it has received God's grace by its bringing forth the fruits of grace.

Augustine, on the contrary, lays down most distinctly, that if the child turns out ungodly you are to suppose, or to assume, that it has fallen from grace. In other words, you are to suppose that the child has lost grace, rather than that God has withheld it. Any after-fall into sin is to be laid to the fault of the child, not to any deficiency in the grace of its Baptism. You are not to constitute yourself a judge as to whether it *has* received grace by its present continuance in grace, or rather appearance of continuance in grace.

The secret of the child's or of the man's election to eternal life can never be certainly known till the great day, and till that day no amount of apparent godliness can give any man any warrant whatsoever for pronouncing on his own or his brother's eternal state. Such is Augustine's view.

It is quite clear that he asserted most dogmatically that all infants are regenerate in Baptism. It is equally clear that he held that an after-life of sin in the baptized is to be accounted for, not on the supposition that God withheld grace, but that the person baptized has lost it.

It is equally clear he held that a man may fall from grace, or at least from a thing which by no judgment of the man himself or of his fellow-men can in this life be distinguished from it.

INDEX.

334 INDEX.

THE END.

LONDON: R. CLAY SON, AND TAYLOR, PRINTERS.

Printed in the United States
105973LV00006B/74/A

9 780548 736371